Identity-Cons
in Student Af

MW01195364

This guide offers current and future student affairs practitioners a new conceptual framework for identity-conscious and intersectional supervision. Presenting an original and transformative model to address day-to-day challenges, this book gives practitioners a strategic approach to engage in self-work, identity exploration, relationship building, consciousness raising, trust development, and organizational change, ultimately helping them become more adept at supervising people from a range of backgrounds and experiences. Chapters include theoretical underpinnings, practical tips, case studies, and discussion questions to explore strategies in real-life contexts. *Identity-Conscious Supervision in Student Affairs* is a key tool for student affairs practitioners to effectively change systems of dominance and inequity on their campuses.

Robert Brown is Director of Social Justice Education at Northwestern University, USA.

Shruti Desai is Chief of Staff at the Gephardt Institute for Civic and Community Engagement at Washington University in St. Louis, USA.

Craig Elliott is Assistant Vice President of Enrollment and Student Services and Assistant Professor at Samuel Merritt University, USA.

Identity-Conscious Supervision in Student Affairs

Building Relationships and Transforming Systems

Robert Brown, Shruti Desai, and Craig Elliott

Routledge
Taylor & Francis Group

NEW YORK AND LONDON

First published 2020
by Routledge
52 Vanderbilt Avenue, New York, NY 10017

and by Routledge
2 Park Square, Milton Park, Abingdon, Oxon, OX14 4RN

Routledge is an imprint of the Taylor & Francis Group, an informa business

Library of Congress Cataloging-in-Publication Data
A catalog record for this book has been requested

ISBN: 978-1-138-36556-8 (hbk)
ISBN: 978-1-138-36559-9 (pbk)
ISBN: 978-0-429-43066-4 (ebk)

Typeset in Sabon
by Apex CoVantage, LLC

We dedicate this book to our loving families.

We also dedicate this book to all those courageously leading organizations and individuals toward identity-consciousness.

Contents

CONTENTS

Foreword

"Don't behave like an angry Black woman."
"Are all the gay people applying to work here?"
"You are a good one, but it takes a strong whip to keep you in line."
"You might want to be a little less colorful."
"The organization is not quite ready for a transwoman in that position."
"How is a blind person going to be the Director of Multicultural Affairs?"

These statements and many others make the case for the necessity of this book. I have had nearly 40 years of experience within the context of higher education. Supervision has been a consistent dynamic during that time. From the time I was supervised as an undergraduate student to my first experience as a supervisor during graduate school, and through current day where I work with President's cabinets, boards of regents and trustees, human relations directors and more, supervision is an everyday dynamic I engage with in organizations. The authors have taken on a topic that is, without question, one of the biggest challenges in preparing the workforce for the 21st century.

Demographic diversity is on everyone's screen. You can't open a job posting or visit any campus where the discussion of diversity and inclusion is not in the top five priorities. That being said, the challenge to meet the needs and support the development of ever-growing diverse populations is also ever present. As stated, in the context of student affairs and higher education, there is an expectation that one will develop the capacity to be good supervisors through observation, practice, and maybe a class or two in graduate school. Most of these opportunities do not offer the focus and intentionality needed to address the dynamics that are present as we engage the changing and expanding demographic diversity of college and university campuses across the country.

I spend over 250 days a year on college campuses around the country. I get to witness and see the impact of well-intentioned supervisors who have not been prepared with an identity-conscious approach to supervision struggle and, in many cases, do harm to themselves and those they supervise. This dynamic often results in a high degree of turnover, low morale and performance, and increased emotional labor for minoritized employees. The authors have thoroughly and thoughtfully offered insights, tools, and practices that will help address these concerns.

Each chapter delivers on key components to the supervisory relationship. The book starts off reminding us that "Relationships Matter." This first chapter sets the tone for the book not simply being a cognitive experience. Much of the work that has been done on supervision has focused on mechanics or setting clear expectations, measurable outcomes, deadlines, and open feedback. While all of these things are important and discussed in the book, they often fall short of engaging the emotional intelligence needed to address these topics and others through an identity-conscious lens. The next generation of supervisors are going to need to be as emotionally intelligent as they are cognitively intelligent. It will simply not be enough to have read all of the latest diversity material; there will be a need to actively engage how that material impacts supervisory relationships.

In Chapters 2–5, the authors invite the readers on the journey to do the self-work needed to build capacity for greater effectiveness in supervising with an identity-conscious lens. These chapters embody the essence of why this book is needed. It is critical that supervisors not only be able to name their identities but also explore how those identities impact their relationships and supervision. Through this exploration the discovery of internalized dominance and oppression, unconscious attitudes and assumptions, and potential microaggressions will emerge. These chapters are great professional development topics, and I recommend that they be included in the community of a supervisory team or a classroom setting. Chapters 6–8 are some of my favorite parts of the book because they position the work done in Chapters 2–5 as not just "fluff" or "touchy feely." I often hear these words associated with doing "self-work." The authors remind us that identity-consciousness is a skill set that is needed in order to engage effectively across difference.

Finally, the last chapters bring it home with an understanding that one must build the supervisory skill set to sustain identity-consciousness in order to spark institutional change. The model that is being offered in this book reminds us that the we are often engaged in a culture change process. Supervision does not happen in a vacuum. It happens in the context of a department, a division, and a campus. One must build capacity to engage beyond interpersonal relationships to examine the institutional and cultural dynamics that impact the supervisory relationship. Conflict and courage are key dynamics involved in culture change. As one builds identity-consciousness to work at the interpersonal level in supervisory relationships it will be imperative that they are also understanding the larger contexts that are at play. Failing to address both of these major contributing factors will result in slow to no movement and ongoing disappointment.

I see this book as a welcome contribution to the literature on supervision, diversity, equity, and inclusion. I respect the work that it is building upon and trust that it will spark further and deeper engagement as we continue to prepare the next generation of leaders in higher education.

Rev. Dr. Jamie Washington

Preface

This book has been a labor of love for many years. It began as a conversation between colleagues, mostly out of frustration, about how our identities, and our whole selves, were not acknowledged or discussed in the context of supervision. While mentorship models have made some progress in holding identities with professional growth, it fails to address a number of the structural elements that perpetuate oppression. This was our experience for sure, and we also heard it shared by colleagues in our training and consulting work at other institutions.

These conversations led to conference presentations, which sparked more opportunities for training and conversation. Eventually, all the listening and storytelling helped form a model for Identity-Conscious Supervision.

The historical model for supervision in student affairs and higher education negates room for identity at an organizational and supervisory level. We found our supervisors were not sure how identity fit into the "work" conversation or flat out refused to discuss it. Similarly, our supervisees were hesitant to bring identity into conversations with us because of power dynamics and a fear of how these conversations would be used.

The environment in higher education is changing and has been for many years. Student demographics are changing, which is surfacing evolving needs, as professionals attend and navigate higher education. Further, shifting demographics of new and mid-level professionals necessitate a simultaneous shift in supervision practices. Methods of supervision without identities at the center for both the supervisor and supervisee impact persistence of the staff, limit promotion opportunities, and increase burn-out. All of which negatively impact our ability to serve students at our institutions and retain strong professionals in the field.

As supervisors we must do our own work around our dominant and privileged identities and heal within our marginalized identities to have the capacity to effectively guide and coach the professionals with whom we work. Our internal development and growth allow us to help hold the pain that our supervisees may experience around their marginalized identities. Supervisors must spend time building relationships and working with supervisees to help navigate the identity politics present in our institutions so we can navigate and manage systems of power. As supervisors, we must also focus on systems change as we supervise. This focus creates an opportunity to effectively change systems of dominance and inequity on our campuses. Learning how to influence change is essential to our work. Identity-Conscious Supervision will take collective courage, vulnerability, and humility.

INTENDED AUDIENCE

The primary audience is current student affairs professionals in supervisory roles or those seeking supervisory roles. The secondary audience is prospective student affairs professionals or those in graduate preparation programs.

HOW TO USE THE BOOK

This book has been designed around our model for Identity-Conscious Supervision. Our goal has been that this book would serve as a tool for our day-to-day growth and development, as well as the challenges, regarding our supervision practices. The chapters are organized around each component to give the reader a theoretical understanding, with practical suggestions for use in practice. We provide a number of examples from our experiences, along with our thoughts on how the model can be helpful. Each chapter concludes with a case study, written by fellow practitioners in the field, to give the reader an opportunity to explore that element of the model in a real-life context. We follow each case study with some reflection questions to further prompt the readers' learning. These case studies can serve as a professional development tool for individual, staff, and team development. Intentionally, we want this model and book to guide the development of current supervisors and the training model for new professionals.

We recognize that some supervisors will be strong in some areas and need development in others, and the design of the book also allows supervisors to access the areas most relevant for their development. The book ends with a cumulative chapter with application of the model and ongoing development.

FINAL THOUGHTS

The process of developing this model and writing the book offered us many opportunities to reflect on supervision, how we have been trained, how we continue to replicate systems of oppression within our supervision practice, and how we want to transform our professional practice toward equity and justice. We hope that your engagement with the model and this book, as well as your reflective practice on your own supervision, will do the same for you.

Note: Names and details have been obscured in all of the examples used from the authors' our own experiences.

Acknowledgements

As we began thinking about the (dis)connection between our identities and supervision a few years ago, we never imagined that we would have the privilege of contributing our ideas through this project. We would not have arrived at this point without the love and support of so many contributors, colleagues, mentors, and family. We'd like to start with a big thank you to our families who have invested in us, loved us and have given us immense support during this journey.

Ashley, Evie, Nicole, Jackson, and Tom, you fill our hearts and souls, laugh with us and at us, and remind us to keep striving for our better selves. We love you. Much love also to our parents and siblings: Perry, Stephanie, Crystal, and Darius; Mukti, Praful, Smruti, and Shreya; Craig, Susan, Margaret, and Linda. Thank you for your patience and encouragement as this book captured our time, energy, and focus. To our ancestors, we thank you for your sacrifices to bring us to this day and your continued care and influence in helping us achieve our wildest dreams.

There are so many additional contributors, who offered their brilliance and perspective in shaping this book. We are forever grateful to Rev. Dr. Jamie Washington, our mentor and friend, who wrote the foreword of this book. Your grace, wisdom, and love continue to inspire and motivate us to engage this work more deeply. We would especially like to thank Pamela Graglia for bringing our concepts to life visually with your creativity and our case study authors for adding their voices and diverse perspectives to our book. All of you enriched this book with your gifts.

This is book is the result of many years of professional experience supervising and being supervised. We would be remiss not to acknowledge our past and current supervisors and supervisees who we have learned from and with throughout our careers. We hope this book serves as a testament of your support, guidance, and many conversations we were able to explore together.

To our mentors, colleagues, and friends, Mamta Accapadi, Dr. Jillian Martin, and the Social Justice Training Institute faculty: Jamie Washington, Kathy Obear, Vernon Wall, Maura Cullen, becky martinez, Tanya Williams, Carmen Rivera, Sam Offer, Alejandro Covarubias, and Beth Yohe. Your vision for a just world continues to inspire us, and we are deeply grateful for your investments of time, talent, and energy with us in our social justice journeys.

Finally, we would like to acknowledge and express gratitude to the editorial staff at Taylor & Francis/Routledge, for their ongoing support and encouragement to write this book. Most notably, Heather Jarrow, who approached us at NASPA to highlight the need for this book in our field. Thank you for your support, investment, and guidance. We are grateful for your advice and patience.

Tables and Figures

Chapter One

Introduction

I (Shruti) was a newer professional and was reporting to a Person of Color. This was the first time I had an opportunity to be supervised by a Person of Color and was so excited about it. After a few months of being in the role, I noticed organizational dynamics that perpetuated dominant norms such as promotion of white individuals, perpetuation of professional norms such as articulation and dress, and policies that disenfranchised Students of Color and international students. It caused me to feel silenced and small. I wanted to get guidance from my supervisor and discuss strategy on how to navigate the institution and department as a Person of Color while living my values with integrity. At my next supervisory meeting, after we addressed our task lists, I brought up that I had an additional item. I asked him, "As a seasoned professional, how do you navigate your career and this institution as a Person of Color?" He directly and flatly responded with, "We don't talk about it." I was bewildered and disappointed. I entered the field hoping to impact students and shift systems toward equity and justice but was told I could not do that and function within my wholeness. I began to question if I entered the right field. I talked to mentors and colleagues who helped ground me and affirmed that I was in the right field and would be able to make an impact, but they were not able to give me any hope that I could work in higher education in my full self and work for liberation. I wanted to change that.

Throughout our (Robert, Shruti, and Craig) careers, we have had many experiences with supervision. Throughout our careers, we have had supervisors, and about half of our careers, we have been supervising others. Some of these supervision experiences have been positive, and some of them have been negative. Most, though, have been just okay—perhaps helpful for the practical work but not for our growth, development, or ability to thrive. We include ourselves as supervisors in that assessment.

When we were a part of a positive supervisory relationship, it was due to a deep mutual investment that made us feel seen acknowledging how

1

our identities intersected with our professional experience allowing us to produce excellent work in our roles. These experiences seemed happenstance rather than a thoughtful experience, relying more so on the chemistry between the people involved than an intentionally designed approach that could lead to compelling experiences.

As we began to evolve our supervisory practice around creating a deliberate infrastructure to amplify the possibilities of a positive and whole experience, it became clear to us that directly and authentically addressing our identities as part of the supervisory process was essential. And so we set about to map this element of the supervisory process.

That process, outlined in this book, is the culmination of years of reflection, research, practice, and more reflection. We hope that this model and process helps construct and develop your practice.

WHY IS THIS BOOK NECESSARY?

Supervision is universal in the field of student affairs. Staff members from an entry-level academic advisor to the vice president of student affairs all have someone to whom they report. Moreover, many student affairs professionals also have the responsibility to supervise others. Supervisors play an essential role in setting the tone and creating inclusive workspaces that value individuals and embrace diversity (Stock-Ward & Javorek, 2003). Unfortunately, most student affairs professionals receive no instruction on how to supervise, instead learning primarily from their supervisors who likely did not have any formal training (Holmes, 2014). Supervision is challenging and complex, and the literature indicates that student affairs professionals are not doing it well (Winston & Creamer, 1997).

Institutions use various management mechanisms to maintain conformity within the culture and punish actions of employees who act in contrast to the culture. The ripple of this dynamic, more than the impact on an individual, is that it becomes an additional barrier for People of Color, women, gender nonconforming, differently abled, and LGBTQIA professionals to navigate through the field for advancement.

Functionally, the training and development regarding supervision are left to the job site to develop, which, often, is absent. The bulk of the experience is "trial by fire," on the job, and in a "just-in-time" manner. Any professional development in this area often focuses on skill building in functional areas and ignores the lived experiences of the professionals involved, their identities, and their experiences of bias and hostility in the workplace that prevent learning and growth. This path of limited training and identity-neutral practices reflected our experiences when we started supervising too. All three of us lacked the development and skills necessary to supervise effectively and holistically. We received little guidance—we had to figure it out for ourselves and made many mistakes. Ambiguity around our roles as supervisors also affected our capacity to implement the more significant charge of the organization. We did not have a clear sense of our role within the organization, which made it hard to develop our responsibilities and prioritize professional relationships. While we had varying degrees of awareness about our identities, we rarely intentionally engaged them in the supervisory context and had little understanding of how systems of oppression manifested within our role or organization.

The combination of a lack of training on supervision, limited self-work or teamwork around dominant and subordinated patterns at a group and individual level, and inadequate awareness of how systems of oppression operate perpetuated privileged social norms impacted our practice. These dominant norms and the reinforcement of them in practice by supervisors and supervisees leads to attrition and burnout for staff from marginalized backgrounds. (Marshall, Gardner, Hughes, & Lowery, 2016). This revolving door of minoritized staff members demands more time and money from the institution; in addition, sacrificing an opportunity for excellence as homogenous thinking creates an echo chamber and replicates the status quo. This cycle is harmful and needs an interruption.

DEFINING THE PROBLEM

Supervision does not rest solely in the hands of the supervisor; the supervisee also has agency and can have a significant impact on the relationship (Winston & Creamer, 2002). Synergistic supervision is one of the more prominent models within student affairs, characterized by joint-effort, two-way communication, and a focus on competence and goals (Winston & Creamer, 1998; Tull, 2006). However, due to the hierarchical power differences within the supervisory relationship, the supervisor carries more responsibility to cultivate a positive and productive relationship. Supervision is a challenging task and becomes even more so when done within the harmful context of inequitable and oppressive campus and workplace environments.

Effectively defining supervision often results in a vague set of traits due to the broad range of knowledge and skills it requires. In 2015, ACPA and NASPA identified and published ten core competencies for student affairs professionals. These competencies include: 1) personal and ethical foundations; 2) values, philosophy, and history; 3) assessment, evaluation, and research; 4) law, policy, and governance; 5) organizational and human resources; 6) leadership; 7) social justice and inclusion; 8) student learning and development; 9) technology; and 10) advising and supporting (ACPA & NASPA, 2015). Although supervision is officially categorized and described more fully under the competency of organizational and human resources, successful supervision encompasses many of these competencies. For instance, skills within the advising and supporting competency are necessary for supervisors as they coach supervisees to identify and reach goals (Tull, 2006; Winston & Creamer, 1997).

Supervisors need to develop and apply their competency within the social justice and inclusion area, particularly when supervising across difference. Doing so could increase supervisors' understanding of how privilege and oppression affect individuals and increase their capacity to support minoritized staff. Effectively understanding and implementing social justice and inclusion competency can contribute to the development of more just organizations and processes (Perillo, 2011). Failure to develop these skills can lead to an erosion of trust and diminished opinion about our leaders and leadership.

It is vital to provide that training and professional development for all supervisors focused on identity exploration and supervision, particularly across difference. Supervisors need training on the importance of having clear—and communicated—expectations, providing direct and ongoing feedback to supervisees, and understanding how to support their self-work while recognizing the influence of their unique experiences and identity. Training opportunities focused on dialogue, implicit bias, and socialization serve as useful tools for developing competencies and the capacity to engage effectively across difference.

As Harro (2000) observed, we are all socialized to privilege dominant group norms. In light of that reality, we all have internalized dominance and oppression that requires us to be competent about the full scope of our engagement within systems and with others. Literature notes that supervision goes well beyond the practice of managing the day-to-day work of employees; instead, it is a comprehensive process of onboarding, professional development, and feedback, and evaluation (Hirt & Strayhorn, 2011). Hirt and Strayhorn (2011) explain the importance of supervision, citing that effective staffing practices can minimize attrition in the field. They say, "Done right, supervision leads to individual accomplishment, organizational achievement, and professional advancement" (Hirt & Strayhorn, 2011, p. 405). We believe supervision can have this impact and must also incorporate dialogue about identities.

VALUE OF SUPERVISION

A comprehensive discussion of supervision, beyond a checklist of ensuring tasks completion and progressing the mission, does not often occur in student affairs. Our own messaging around supervision starts very early on in our lives, even before employment, with adult family members (parents, guardians, grandparents, older siblings, etc.) serving as supervisors of sorts. Teachers, advisors, and spiritual leaders also served in this capacity until we started our first jobs as teenagers. The supervisors we had generally guided us on the skills needed for the job we had and enforced the rules of the organization, and not much more. These early work settings did not recognize our identities. As we began our full-time careers in higher education, supervisors and advisors came along with our employment. Identity exploration took place in the context of our functional roles, but not in the context of who we were and what we needed to thrive and succeed at our institution.

The value around supervision and styles of management has a direct impact on the daily lives of student affairs professionals. Mid- and senior-level professionals ranked the necessity of skills regarding supervision low but the importance of competent supervision high (Nichols & Baumgartner, 2016). This statistic is dumbfounding. It indicates that leaders at our institution value excellent supervision but not the necessity in skill to ensure that it happens. An innate ability to supervise is one of the biggest myths of supervision. Supervisors (and organizations) that hold onto this myth could mean disaster for new and mid-level professionals, especially those from marginalized identities.

We believe that skills in supervision grow and develop regardless of positional status. There is always something new to learn when supervising. New professionals indicated being the least prepared for supervision and expressed a need for additional training (Nichols & Baumgartner, 2016). If new professionals state they need additional training, then why do mid and senior-level individuals not value this training? Supervision is like any other skill; sharpening and training must occur for excellence. Likely, mid and senior-level professionals learned how to supervise by a job duty as opposed to meaningful training. Additionally, the strength and effectiveness of the profession rest on a better model—one that includes intentional mentorship, ongoing development, identity development, and built to support professionals of all identities.

Some behaviors of a good supervisor include noticing and paying attention to supervisees, trust, and rapport building (Nichols & Baumgartner, 2016). Trust and rapport building do not happen absent from a relationship. A relationship is not enough. A structured and individualized supervision strategy must take place (Stock-Ward & Javorek, 2003). Intentionality goes hand in hand with supervision. A supervision blueprint that empowered and supported one staff member will not always do the same for another staff member. Supervision must be flexible and based on the supervisee (Stock-Ward & Javorek, 2003). Some qualities of supervision remain best practices.

Supervisees frequently appreciate communication of unwritten rules (Saunders, Hirt, & Tull, 2009). Verbalizing unwritten rules enables supervisees to navigate environments successfully and builds a sense of trust between the supervisor and supervisee. Supervision is relational, but it must also be intentional to achieve success. Supervision is often task-focused, and a supervisor often has organizational responsibilities. The focus on mutuality, continuing the relationship, and humility of the supervisor to center the supervisee serve as critical components in successful supervision (Winston & Creamer, 1997). However, this practice, disconnected from social identity, reinforces systems of dominance that support white supremacist and patriarchal attitudes and behaviors. Our model builds upon these practices of supervision, applying an identity-conscious lens.

CHALLENGES WITH SUPERVISION

The messaging we receive about supervision is often limited to, "do not play favorites" or "treat everyone the same." These concepts build on the notion that everyone needs the same thing (equality) or identity-neutral supervision. There needs to be a shift in supervision to an equity-focused practice and a foundation built from the understanding that individuals have unique needs based on identities such as race, gender, religion, socio-economic class, ability, religion, sexual orientation, appearance, and citizenship. Also, essential concepts for employee success, such as belonging, trust, and equitable treatment in the workplace, are different for individuals from various backgrounds.

Many leadership books discuss leadership and supervision strategies but often neglect to acknowledge or address race, gender, sexual orientation, ability, nationality, etc., and thereby reinforce white, male, heteronormative ideologies and ways of being. The lack of conversation around the intersection of leadership, supervision, identity, and oppression creates opportunities for dominance to be "baked into" the culture of an organization. We need to construct a supervision practice that provides holistic and intentionally identity-conscious approaches so we can build competencies around it, assess it, and institutionalize it. We believe that normalizing identity-conscious practices is the best way to create environments where professionals of all identities can thrive and sustainably counter systems of oppression.

Shifting demographics of new and mid-level professionals necessitate a simultaneous shift in supervision practices. Methods of supervision without identities at the center both for the supervisor and supervisee impact persistence, promotion, and burnout. Supervisors must unpack and relearn around dominant and privileged identities. This work creates the capacity to challenge and support supervisees as they navigate the dynamics of identity in a professional context. Further, supervisors must spend time building relationships and working with supervisees to navigate identity politics and to manage systems of power. Shifting to a model of identity-conscious supervision takes courage, vulnerability, and humility.

Data from the Vice President for Student Affairs (VPSA) census indicates top positions are held mostly by members of dominant groups. For example, 73% of VPSAs are white, and 47% are women (NASPA, 2014). New and mid-level professionals often hold several minoritized identities setting up a cultural mismatch. This misalignment leads itself to identity-neutral supervision if senior leadership does not interrogate and reevaluate their privilege. Further, the population of students entering college holds more subordinated identities than ever. Research indicates that when mentors share identities with students, students are more likely to successfully graduate (National Center for Education Statistics, 2013). This same correlation can likely apply to new and mid-level professionals: mentorship within identity groups helps reduce attrition in the field. Attrition rates for new professionals, particularly of color, are high. People often leave the field of student affairs due to supervision (Buchanan, 2012). Professionals from marginalized identities face burnout and microaggressions. Mitigation of trauma, such as racial battle fatigue and sexism, requires that there be a place to make meaning of these events. Processing can happen in peer teams or a supervisory relationship, but it must happen to improve the quality of life and retention of individuals in the margins.

IDENTITY AND SUPERVISION

A supervisor influences job satisfaction (Buchanan, 2012). There are a variety of working definitions for supervision inside and outside of student affairs, but none of them align supervision best practices with the competencies on equity and inclusion. Supervision builds on a power structure. When that inherent power structure intersects with identity, addressing and neutralizing the power falls to the supervisor.

Looking at previous research on supervision, the most thriving supervisors create individualized methods of supervision (Tull, 2006). Individualization allows good supervisors to take aspects such as race, class, ability, gender identity, religion, nationality, gender, and sexual orientation into consideration. An identity-neutral approach to supervision only perpetuates systemic bias individuals with marginalized identities already face. Supervision can serve as a peaceful harbor instead of another arena of microaggressions. Baxter-Magolda and Magolda (2011) call the field of student affairs to put social justice at the heart of student affairs practice. Putting this call into action could turn the field into an environment where minoritized professionals thrive instead of surviving, or worse yet, exiting.

As supervision has a direct impact on our daily work, so do our identities. We need to pay attention to the influence of supervision and our identities in daily work, or in other words, practice critical consciousness. Critical consciousness must occur to shift patterns in supervisory relationships and organizations. Critical consciousness consists of the following: 1) working toward building an understanding of our social identities and the role of these identities in continuing oppressive norms and 2) learning of historical and modern-day examples and events perpetuating systematic oppression (Quaye et al., 2018). Developing awareness of one's social identities and the conditions of the more extensive system (society, institution, etc.) that generate and perpetuate oppressive undercurrents between social identity groups is a requirement of critical consciousness. (hooks, 2010; Zúñiga, Nagda, Chesler, & Cytron-Walker, 2007). An identity-conscious approach enhances the effectiveness of professionals from dominant and marginalized identities. It also creates environments of knowing professionals in their wholeness where systems of oppression can be engaged and interrupted. The intersection of critical consciousness and supervisory practices is the premise and purpose of this book.

Until the culture shifts to expect an identity-conscious approach in supervision with training and development for all supervisors, the burden for the identity-conscious practice will rest on those intentional practitioners who value the need. Until this institutionalization happens, most supervisors will continue to be left off the hook from using an identity-conscious approach. When that happens, people look to People of Color and people with other marginalized identities to educate them. There are countless stories of professionals feeling like they are expected to counsel their supervisor's identity-conscious development, or there is a significant impact by their supervisor's inability to support them in their full selves. Both of these factors create job dissatisfaction and high attrition.

GOALS AND HOPES

As we set out to write this book, we started with our approaches to practice in higher education. In that conversation, we discussed our experiences of supervising and our experiences of being supervised. While the people and locations varied, as well as some of the professional experiences, it quickly became clear that we shared similar goals as we envisioned what an identity-conscious supervision practice entails.

Do No Harm

Most individuals in student affairs have at least one horror story of a bad supervisor. Compelling supervision takes time, energy, humility, and shared trust. It also takes thoughtfulness and building of self-awareness and a strong sense of self. Planning often shows up around student development, strategy, programming, and other everyday student affairs tasks, but the same standard does not exist effort around supervision. Supervision affects job retention, student satisfaction, budget, team morale, and program delivery. It is an essential feature of our work, yet it is unclear what student affairs defines as excellent supervision. Even when a supervisor is okay, an identity-neutral approach can cause harm.

There is a high rate of attrition among faculty and professionals of color. Higher education has yet to reconcile with its history of white, male, heteronormativity (Stewart, 2017). The levels of promotion and demographic makeup of individuals in Senior Student Affairs positions highlight preferences given to dominant identity groups (ACPA/NASPA, 2015). White supremacy culture persists, and it can be particularly damaging to Professionals of Color. Elliott et al. (2013) indicated that almost 50% of faculty and staff of color had experienced offensive or demeaning actions because of race.

Further, there is often an intense sense of fear of retaliation or backlash for challenging the culture toward a more justice-focused one (Elliott et al., 2013). In the current climate, institutions tout diversity and inclusion, yet hiring and promotion practices paint a different picture. Professionals from marginalized backgrounds, making it to the upper echelon of administration in student affairs, continue to be sparse, particularly if an individual holds two or more marginalized identities (NASPA, 2014).

We want to create a structure that promotes a "do no harm" culture. Identity-conscious supervision and management brings marginalized identities to the forefront and allows for processing of microaggressions and other forms of harm. This practice helps build resilience. Resilience is defined as "achievement when such achievement is rare for those facing similar circumstances or within a similar socio-cultural context" (Gayles, 2005, p. 250). Our vision for identity-conscious supervision practices creates opportunities for individual conversations regarding identities. This dialogue can lead to transform the traditional supervision model, and the ripple effects of this transformative model can lead to an institutional change toward liberation. We want professionals of all identities to be able to work and exist in their wholeness within institutions that are designed to support them flourishing in their roles.

Transform Higher Education's Culture

Higher education continues to perpetuate norms of dominant groups and colonization. Identity-neutral practices no longer work. Despite all the rhetoric, mission statements, programming, training, and good intentions, the culture at colleges and universities in the United States has not changed to be more inclusive or socially just. Language and one-time efforts do not create environmental and systemic change. Saying the right thing and spending one hour talking about diversity does not move the climate or sustainably change relationships. The design and structure of higher education institutions occurred with success for wealthy white men. Those same structures and processes do not always ensure that minoritized identities succeed, and intentional use of these structures and processes prevents success.

As graduate programs have grown to educate, train, and develop professionals in higher education, we see classes within the curriculum begin to address inclusion and equity. However, often, these classes are "one-off" and rarely core to the curriculum (Quaye & Harper, 2007). Competency for equity and inclusion in the field stops at individual knowledge and awareness, often failing to include institutional or systematic awareness and intervention. The ACPA/NASPA competencies have further to go in addressing group dynamics, systematic awareness, and historical awareness. ACPA's *Strategic Imperative for Racial Justice and Decolonization* (Quaye et al., 2018) has recently prioritized the need for historical analysis, systematic awareness, intervention, and the centering of identities to conduct effective practice. The imperative is a start to reframing student affairs and catalyzes shifting our institutions.

Further, if we assume a generational identity-consciousness stemming from graduate program curricular change for new professionals (zero to five years), there is no professional development model for seasoned higher educational professionals (ten years or more) already in the field. There is also not curricula for the senior student affairs officers (often 20 years or more) who have the positional power to make some of these systematic shifts. To shift higher education, we must increase training and awareness at every level on both an individual and systems level. Identity-conscious supervision offers a framework to start this process in our organizations and teams.

Beverly Daniel Tatum (2008) reminds us, "A shifting paradigm generates anxiety—even psychological threat—for those who feel the basic assumptions of society changing in ways they can no longer predict." (p. 17). This quote indicates a culture change threatens those who have built it and/or those benefitting from it. Even those who want systems change are benefitting from it at some level, and so the change process is complicated and scary for us as well. Our model presents a structure for culture change that simultaneously showcases strategies for employees to demonstrate their value to the organization.

TERMS

Yehuda Berg stated:

> Words are singularly the most powerful force available to humanity. We can choose to use this force constructively with words of encouragement or destructively using words of despair. Words have energy and power with the ability to help, to heal, to hinder, to hurt to harm, to humiliate, and to humble.
>
> (Berg, cited in Abalu, 2019)

Language is nuanced, fluid, and imperfect. As identities disaggregate and are reimagined and redefined, terms evolve and adapt to allow for more inclusive language that allows for the various intricacies of labeled identities.

Terms related to identity are also personal. In the South Asian community, some individuals prefer their ethnic identities (Indian, Pakistani, Sri Lankan, etc.), others prefer South Asian, and others prefer Desi. The entirety of this text could not encapsulate the importance of language. For the sake of this text, we follow the wisdom of *Teachings for Diversity and Social Justice*, where we will capitalize and not hyphenate ethnicities from geographic regions (e.g., African American, Native American) (Adams & Bell, 2016). We utilize the gender-inclusive pronoun, "they," to reflect individuals identifying their pronoun as "they" or when we do not know their pronoun.

The conversation regarding language and preferences is essential. We hope that this conversation occurs as a portion of your supervision dynamic. A good standard of practice is to mimic the language the individual uses. If they use African American, then use African American. If they use Latinx, then use Latinx. As a supervisor, we must create opportunities to develop a shared understanding of terms such as privileged and marginalized, racism, and prejudices, as well as the identity labels your team utilizes. This critical step creates relationships where individuals feel a sense of belonging.

We must also name both how we identify and how others identify us in each of these categories. In most cases, how we identify and how others identify us is the same, but sometimes they are different. People with multiracial identities are often "mis-raced" and treated based upon that identification, regardless of whether it is correct or not. Gender identity can be hidden to others, and treatment often happens based upon the perception of others. In the United States, Latinx people and people of the Muslim faith are often treated as "foreigners" regardless of their actual citizenship.

11

Supervisor, Manager, and Mentor

Since this is a book about supervision and management, it is essential to distinguish these terms. Supervision occurs within a direct reporting structure in which one individual has organizational power over another individual by the completion of evaluations, hiring and firing, and power given to the individual through a title (Tull & Kuk, 2012). It is important to note that there is a built-in power dynamic. Winston and Creamer (1997) conceptualize supervision as an ongoing process that includes mutuality, being goal-oriented, and promoting a supervisee's growth. This approach to supervision influences the supervisory approach to this book. We emphasize that supervision is a relationship.

Management is often unilateral regarding relationships and task completion, with an individual directing, conducting, and managing as opposed to valuing relationships and mutuality. Vilkinas (2002) defines management as a focus on task completion within a system. There is a focus on goals and achievement of those goals within the larger machine. Often a supervisor must also hold the responsibilities of a manager and mentor.

A mentor has informal authority. An organization does not give a mentor power, and a power dynamic is not always present. In a mentoring relationship, both parties must agree on the structure and role of a relationship (Babette & Beehr, 2003). A mentor focuses on individual development versus organization development. A mentor is not always a supervisor. This is another essential conversation to have in a supervisory relationship. The goals and hopes of everyone in the relationship can vary based on past experiences and identities. This can serve as a foundational conversation to identity-conscious supervision.

Practitioner and professional are defined slightly differently. Practitioner means someone in the field doing student affairs work or an administrator (Kupo, 2014). This can range from individuals with titles of coordinator to senior student affairs officers. Professionals are those who work in higher education who share a standard knowledge of practice or learning and share a commitment to a code of competence and ethics (Cruess, Johnston, & Cruess, 2004). Professionals include faculty and governing board staff and can include practitioners. This text utilizes both terms when referring to individuals in the field of higher education.

Power and Privilege

Following the norms outlined in *Teachings for Diversity and Social Justice* (Adams & Bell, 2016), this text supports the use of terms such as "privileged" and "dominant" for groups with power and "marginalized" and "subordinated" for those groups who have had power withheld from them. Further, we honor individuals at the intersection (Crenshaw, 1990), knowing that systems of oppression have caused many individuals to be understood in dualistic identity groups as opposed to more complex intersections.

We define groups with power not necessarily by quantity, although representation is important, but by who is making systematic decisions, historical context, and representation. For example, scanning the CEOs of Fortune 500 companies or the identities of congressional members demonstrates that many of those individuals still hold dominant identities such as white, Christian, upper-middleclass, straight, cisgender, and able. (DiAngelo, as cited in Goodwin, 2019). Dominant and privileged organizations have greater access to power and resources (Obear, 2014). These resources can include a vast network, access to education, or generational wealth. Privileged groups make the rules and define what is normal, right, and the truth. For example, the national dialogue regarding "traditional family values" and LGB families, presents a false binary, but it continues to perpetuate what is "normal." The practice where individuals with "ethnic names" did not receive an interview at a higher rate than "traditional" names demonstrates an assumption of intelligence and competence to members from the dominant group (Obear, 2014).

Privileged group members are often unaware of their privilege and are more comfortable with members of the subordinated group who share similar behaviors and values (Obear, 2014). This dynamic often shows up in codeswitching. For example, in the book *Whistling Vivaldi: How Stereotypes Affect Us and What We Can*, Steele (2011) discusses his experience of walking down the street as a Black man. He would notice people crossing the street or clenching their purses. Steele goes on to say when he started whistling classical music (Vivaldi) people started smiling at him and felt more relaxed. The association of classical music to upper-class norms and whiteness disarms dominant stereotypes about Black men. This makes privileged groups more comfortable. Finally, individuals in dominant groups often hold on to dominant cultural beliefs without examination and focus on historical progress. This book will address our individual responsibility with individual- and systems-level power further.

Subordinated groups also navigate group patterns such as a desire to "fit in" and do not have access to power. The notion of codeswitching presents itself in this way. Someone who grew up working-class may speak one way to their friends in working-class environments but differently in their "professional" work environment to pass or cover with the dominant group. This often brings conflict between who they are and who they feel they need to be to be "accepted." In the example from *Whistling Vivaldi,* the author did not want to be perceived as a stereotype, so he learned a method to counteract the narrative many created about him. Although he already knew his values and worth internally, the author had to shift behavior to be "accepted." Individuals in subordinated groups often know more about dominant groups than dominant group members know about them (Obear, 2014). Individuals in marginalized groups often struggle to speak up, find their voice, and challenge. This dynamic can show up in a team dynamic or supervision meeting. Finally, marginalized groups often look ahead and focus on how much work needs to be done (Obear, 2014).

The patterns of difference between dominant and subordinated groups impact teams, group dynamics, individual relationships, and the work environment. Therefore, engaging in conversation about these patterns is critical. Table 1.1 indicates which identities are associated with dominant and subordinated groups. It is important to note that the binary nature of dominant and subordinated groups is imperfect and the list of terms within the chart is not exhaustive.

Table 1.1 Examples of Multiple Manifestations and Oppressor and Oppressed Groups

Dominant Groups		Subordinated Groups
30s to early 50s	**Age**	Younger than 30; Older than 50
White	**Race**	Person of Color; people who identify as Biracial/ Multiracial
Male	**Sex**	Female; Intersex
Supporting the Gender Binary System ~ either masculine OR feminine	**Gender Identity and Gender Expression**	Trans; Nonbinary; Genderqueer; Transgender; Agender; Two Spirit, etc.
Heterosexual	**Sexual Orientation**	Gay; Lesbian; Bisexual; Queer; Questioning, etc.
Upper class; Upper-middleclass; Middleclass	**Class**	Working class; Poor; Living in poverty, etc.
Graduate or College degree; Private schooling	**Educational Level**	High school degree; Public schooling

Dominant Groups		Subordinated Groups
Protestant; Catholic	**Religion/ Spirituality**	Muslim, Jewish, Agnostic, Buddhist, Atheist, Hindu, Spiritual, Mormon, Jehovah's Witness, etc.
U.S. born	**National Origin**	"Foreign born"; born in a country other than the U.S.
"Able bodied"	**Ability**	People with a physical, mental, emotional, and/ or learning disability; people living with AIDS/ HIV+, etc.
"American"; Western European heritage	**Ethnicity/ Culture**	Puerto Rican; Navajo; Mexican; Nigerian; Chinese; Iranian; Russian; African, etc.
Fit society's image of attractive, beautiful, handsome, athletic, etc.	**Size/Appearance**	Perceived by others as too fat, tall, short, unattractive, not athletic, etc.
Light skin; European/ Caucasian features	**Skin Color; Physical Characteristics**	Darker skin; African, Asian, Aboriginal features, etc.
Proficient in the "Queen's English"; use "Proper" English	**Use of English**	Not proficient use of English; has an "accent"
Legally married in a heterosexual relationship	**Marital Status**	Single; divorced; widowed; in a same-sex partnership; in an unmarried heterosexual partnership, etc.
Parents of children within a two-parent heterosexual marriage	**Parental Status**	Single parent; do not have children; LGBTQ parents, etc.
Suburban; valued region of the U.S.	**Geographic Region**	Rural; urban . . . less valued region of the U.S.
More years on campus	**Years of experience**	New; little experience on campus

Source: Teachings for Diversity and Social Justice, 2nd ed. (2007)

Our group identities include race, gender identity and expression, socioeconomic class, sexual orientation, level of education, ability, religion, age, and nationality (Figure 2.1), and each of these identities has individual as well as collective meaning and positionality within the system. We have more group identities that have saliency for us as individuals or within a particular context, such as role within the organization (administrator, staff, faculty, etc.) or classification/grade of position we hold, but these eight are the most prominent within higher education. The book focuses primarily on these eight categories. We may identify with some identities more strongly than others. Knowing how we identify in each of these categories begins the process of consciousness building.

HOW TO USE THIS BOOK

This book will advocate for an original approach by presenting nine core strategies of identity-conscious supervision practice, including both traditional and innovative approaches. Figure 1.1 shows how these strategies work together as well as how they function at different levels. Each of these core strategies will also offer a case study that illustrates the application and use of the model.

At the core of identity-conscious supervision is the relationship with yourself and others. Supervisors must function from a strong sense of self and build trust and vulnerability into supervisory relationships. This work occurs at an individual level and impacts a supervisory relationship.

Fostering identity exploration, engaging with conflict, and balancing expectations with identity occurs at a supervision level. These three components (fostering identity exploration, engaging with conflict, and balancing expectations) occur in relationship with a supervisor and supervisee and require dyadic skill-building and support of the three components.

The next set of components: influencing institutional change and sustaining identity-consciousness occur at an organizational level. Institutional change and identity-consciousness rely on the components from the individual and supervision level, meaning they are all interdependent. As many examples in the book demonstrate, a supervisor cannot influence institutional change without a strong relationship with self or engaging with conflict. Finally, managing power, creating a strong sense of self, and acting with courage occur at each level within a fluid process. Identity-conscious supervision has the power to shift culture but requires commitment and courage to sustain over time.

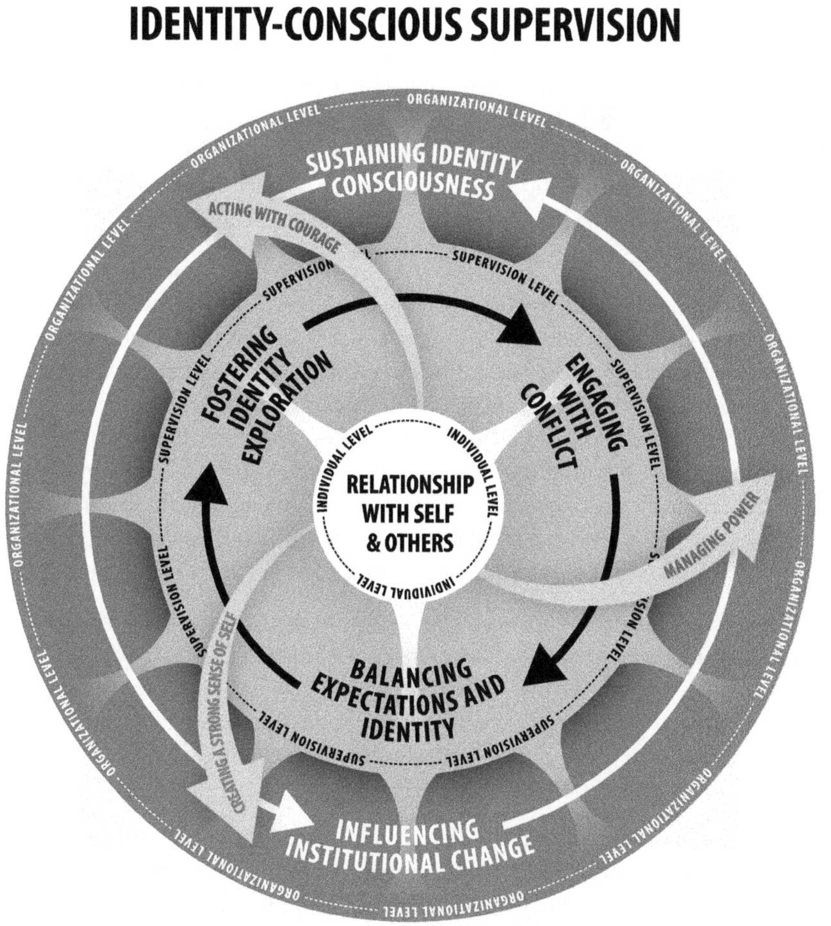

IDENTITY-CONSCIOUS SUPERVISION

Figure 1.1 Identity-Conscious Supervision Model

In the following section we define each component of the model:

Relationships With Self and Others—At the center of our work are relationships, including the relationship we have with ourselves. These relationships matter in our supervision, and strong relationships allow us to create space where we can engage in challenging and stressful dynamics and work in partnership. We connect on how systems of oppression show up in our work and actions (and/or how we continue to invest in systems of oppression). We must trust each other to develop authentic relationships.

Creating a Strong Sense of Self—Supervisors hold a prominent position in role modeling equitable and inclusive behaviors and practices. To engage effectively across difference, managers must engage in their self-work and education (Bailey & Hamilton, 2015). Supervisors must take responsibility for their learning to identify roots of their own biases, discomfort, and fear when supervising across difference (Bailey & Hamilton, 2015). Supervisors develop self-authorship, self-awareness, and cultural humility through reflection and communities of practice.

Managing Power—Supervisory relationships come with power: power to shape one's daily experience, access to resources, connection to opportunities to "be at the table," promotional opportunities, and pay raises. We cannot build a trusting relationship if we do not acknowledge the inherent power dynamic in the relationship as well as the social identities at play in the relationship. Failure to integrate concerns of power, privilege, and oppression into content and dialogue undermines the effectiveness of inclusion efforts and serves to *reinforce* oppressive systems (Walls, Roll, Sprague, & Griffin, 2010). This text aims to provide opportunities for neutralizing power.

Acting with Courage—It takes courage to confront an institutional culture, and it takes courage to acknowledge and address how we continue to invest in systems of oppression. Supervisors must practice vulnerability and empathy to participate with courage. Courage also creates opportunities for resilience and clarity of values, both of which lead to stronger organizations and supervisory relationships.

Fostering Identity Exploration—As we build and develop our supervisory relationships, we must incorporate conversations about the role and impact of identity in our work early in the relationship-building process. Articulating job duties is a critical conversation in initial supervisory conversations. These expectations should pair with a dialogue on the role of identity in our work and career history. Creating a blended dialogue on job responsibilities and the role of identities creates the insight that allows for holistic supervision.

Balancing Expectations and Identity—Distributing a job description and organizational chart helps employees understand their role within the department and broader institution. A supervisor must prioritize discussions that set shared expectations for accomplishing a job (Career Press, 1993). Metrics of success can refocus individuals in their direct roles and responsibilities when burnout or systemic bias occurs. The impact of emotional labor and racial battle fatigue complicate and distract from the ability of minoritized supervisees to accomplish direct job responsibilities (Erickson & Ritter, 2001). The Critical Authentic Leadership can serve as one model for identity-conscious supervision practice to address these challenges.

Engaging with Conflict—Change and challenge bring conflict. As supervisors engage in more just and equitable supervisory practices, conflict is bound to emerge both with individual supervisees and in the process of team development. To engage effectively across difference, managers must embrace conflict as a normative practice (Keehner, 2007). Supervisors must take responsibility for their work in engendering trust, particularly across difference where trust is often lacking.

Sustaining Identity-Consciousness—Increasing awareness of our own biases and the dynamics of oppression is helpful, but awareness alone is not enough. Supervisors must be in a continual process of moving from knowledge and awareness to application. It is through this process that practitioners can shift their consciousness from the individual and group level to the systems level, which can prompt institutional and structural change (Pope et al., 2019). Supervisors can utilize an identity-conscious lens to explore the impact of institutional culture by increasing their ability to support supervisees as they bump against institutional structures that further oppression.

Influencing Institutional Change—Intent to change the organizational culture toward justice needs to be an organizational and personal goal for supervisors committed to social change cloaked in justice and equity. Organizational culture shows up in the patterns of shared values, beliefs, assumptions, and symbols (Bailey & Hamilton, 2015). Supervisors must learn how to develop patience in pushing for broad organizational changes while still utilizing their agency to shift the culture within their spheres of influence. Managers utilizing organizing principles as a strategy to develop coalitions move culture change initiatives strategically forward.

We advise that you read the chapter before jumping into the case study that follows. You can read this book sequentially or each chapter as you need it. We do advise returning to this book, as our journey and experience in diversity and inclusion is never complete, nor is our journey and experience in supervision.

CONCLUSION

Our intention, as you read this book, is that you feel empowered to do your self-work on your dominant identities and advocate for healing in your marginalized identities. We hope that you reflect on how you can weave an identity-conscious supervision approach into your supervision practice. We also hope that you observe how systems of oppression and dominance show up in your organization and through supervision and find ways to work against those systems. The supervisory relationship is challenging, but it also brings about real change in your organizations and teams. The work is hard, and it will require policy, culture, and political changes to make this new model a reality. Identity-conscious supervision and management serves a catalyst for increased retention for professionals of marginalized identities in our field, a change in the student affairs leadership pipeline, and increased job satisfaction. It is time to start being creative and intentional in how we move from identity-neutral approaches to identity-conscious supervision and management.

REFERENCES

Abalu, P. (2019, May 21). We need a new language to discuss diversity and inclusion. *Fast Company*. Retrieved from www.fastcompany.com/90349870/we-need-a-new-language-to-discuss-diversity-and-inclusion

Adams, M., & Bell, L. A. (Eds.). (2016). *Teaching for diversity and social justice* (2nd ed.). New York, NY: Routledge.

American College Personnel Association & National Association of Student Personnel Administrators. (2015). *ACPA/NASPA professional competency areas for student affairs educators*. Washington, DC: Author.

Babette, R., & Beehr, T. (2003). Formal mentoring versus supervisor and coworker relationships: Differences in perceptions and impact. *Journal of Organizational Behavior*, 24(3), 271–293.

Bailey, K. W., & Hamilton, J. (2015). Supervisory style. In M. J. Amey & L. M. Reesor (Eds.), *Beginning your journey: A guide for new professionals in student affairs* (4th ed., pp. 67–94). Washington, DC: NASPA.

Buchanan, J. (2012). *Factors that influence attrition of new professionals in student affairs* (Ph.D. dissertation). Widener University.

Crenshaw, K. (1990). Mapping the margins: Intersectionality, identity politics, and violence against women of color. *Stanford Law Review*, 43, 1241–1299.

Cruess, S. R., Johnston, S., & Cruess, R. L. (2004). "Profession": A working definition for medical educators. *Teaching and Learning in Medicine*, 16(1), 74–76.

Daniel Tatum, B. (2008). *Can We Talk about Race?: And Other Conversations in an Era of School Resegregation (Race, Education, and Democracy)*. Boston, MA: Beacon Press.

Elliott, C. M., Stransky, O., Negron, R., Bowlby, M., Lickiss, J., Dutt, D., . . . Barbosa, P. (2013). Institutional barriers to diversity change work in higher education. *Sage Open*, 3(2), doi:10.1177/2158244013489686

Goodwin (2019, August 6). "White fragility" author offers candid insights on race relations. *Goodwin Insights*. Retrieved from www.goodwinlaw.com/publications/2019/08/08_06-white-fragility-author-offers-candid

Gayles, J. (2005). Playing the game and paying the price: Academic resilience among three high achieving African-American males. *Anthropology & Education Quarterly*, 26, 250–264.

Harro, B. (2000). The cycle of liberation and socialization. In M. Adams, W. J. Blumenfeld, C. R. Castañeda, H. W. Hackman, M. L. Peters, & X. Zúñiga (Eds.), *Readings for diversity and social justice* (2nd ed., pp. 52–58). New York, NY: Routledge.

Hirt, J. B., & Strayhorn, T. L. (2011). Staffing and supervision. In J. H. Schuh, S. R. Jones, & S. R. Harper (Eds.), *Student services: A handbook for the profession* (5th ed., pp. 372–384). San Francisco, CA: Jossey-Bass.

Holmes, A. C. (2014). *Experiences of supervision skill development among new professionals in student affairs* (Unpublished doctoral dissertation). Iowa State University, Ames.

hooks, b. (2010). *Teaching critical thinking: Practical wisdom.* New York, NY: Routledge.

Keehner, J. (2007). Effective supervision: The many roles, responsibilities, and opportunities. In R. L. Ackerman (Ed.), *The mid-level manager in student affairs* (pp. 103–126). Washington, DC: National Association of Student Personnel Administrators.

Kupo, V. L. (2014). Becoming a scholar-practitioner in student affairs. *New Directions for Student Services, 147*(3).

Magolda, P. M. & Baxter Magolda, M. B. (Eds.) (2011). *Contested issues in student affairs: Diverse perspectives and respectful dialogue.* Sterling, VA: Stylus.

Marshall, S. M., Gardner, M. M., Hughes, C., & Lowery, U. (2016). Attrition from student affairs: Perspectives from those who exited the profession. *Journal of Student Affairs Research and Practice, 53*(2), 146–159.

National Association of Student Personnel Administrators (NASPA). (2014). *The chief student affairs officer-2014.* Washington, DC: National Association of Student Personnel Administrators.

National Center for Education Statistics. (2013). *Table 318.30.* Retrieved from http://nces.ed.gov/programs/digest/d13/tables/dt13_318.30.asp

National Center for Education Statistics. (n.d.). Retrieved November 12, 2015, from www.socsci.uci.edu/~castellj/ss70c/webpres/Minority IdentityModel2014

Nichols, K. N., & Baumgartner, L. M. (2016). Midlevel managers' supervisory learning journeys. *College Student Affairs Journal, 34*(2), 61–74.

Obear, K. (2014). Privileged group dynamics: Common patterns of whites. *Dismantling Internalized Dominance.* Workshop handout available by request from kathy@drkathyobear.com

Perillo, P. A. (2011). Scholar practitioners model inclusive, learning-oriented supervision. In P. M. Magolda & M. B. Baxter Magolda (Eds.), *Contested issues in student affairs: Diverse perspectives and respectful dialogue* (pp. 427–432). Sterling, VA: Stylus.

Pope, R. L., Reynolds, A. L., Mueller, J. A. (2019). *Multicultural competence in student affairs: Advancing social justice and inclusion.* San Francisco: Jossey-Bass.

Quaye, S. J., Guido, F. M., Aho, R. E., Lange, A. C., Jacob, M. B., Squire, D., . . . Stewart, D-L. (2018). *A bold vision forward: A framework for the strategic imperative for racial justice and decolonization.* Washington, DC: ACPA-College Student Educators International.

Quaye, S. J., & Harper, S. R. (2007). Faculty accountability for culturally inclusive pedagogy and curricula. *Liberal Education, 93*(3), 32–39.

Saunders, S. A., Hirt, J. B., & Tull, A. (2009). *Becoming socialized in student affairs administration: A guide for new professionals and their supervisors* (1st ed.). Sterling, VA: Stylus Publishing.

Steele, C. M. (2011). *Whistling Vivaldi: How stereotypes affect us and what we can do.* New York, NY: WW Norton & Company.

Stewart, D. L. (March 30, 2017). Language of Appeasement. *Inside Higher Ed.* https://www.insidehighered.com/views/2017/03/30/colleges-need-language-shift-not-one-you-think-essay

Stock-Ward, S. R., & Javorek, M. E. (2003). Applying theory to practice: Supervision in student affairs. *NASPA Journal, 40*(3), 77–92.

Tull, A. (2006). Synergistic supervision, job satisfaction, and intention to turnover of new professionals in student affairs. *Journal of College Student Development, 47*(4), 465–480.

Tull, A. & Kuk, L. (2012). Conclusion. In A. Tull & L. Kuk (Eds.). (2012). *New Realities in the Management of Student Affairs: Emerging Specialist Roles and Structures for Changing Times.* Sterling, VA: Stylus Publishing, (pp. 206–214).

Vilkinas, T. (2002). The PhD process: The supervisor as manager. *Education & Training, 44*(2), 129–137.

Walls, N. E., Roll, S., Sprague, L., & Griffin, R. (2010). Teaching about privilege: A model combining intergroup dialogue and single identity caucusing. *Understanding and Dismantling Privilege, 1*(1), 1–32.

Winston, R. B., & Creamer, D. G. (1997). *Improving staffing practices in student affairs.* San Francisco, CA: Jossey-Bass.

Winston, R. B. & Creamer, D. G. (1998). *Staff supervision and professional development: An integrated approach.* New Directions for Students Services, *84,* 29–42.

Winston, R. B. & Creamer, D. G. (2002). Supervision: Relationships that support learning. In D. L. Cooper, S. A. Saunders, R. B. Winston, Jr., J. B. Hirt, D. G. Creamer, & S. M. Janosik (Eds.), *Learning through supervised practice in student affairs* (pp. 65–96). New York, NY: Routledge.

Zúñiga, X., Nagda, B., Chesler, M., & Cytron-Walker, A. (2007). Educational goals of intergroup dialogues. In *Intergroup dialogue in higher education: Meaningful learning about social justice* (pp. 9–18). ASHE-ERIC report series. San Francisco, CA: Jossey-Bass.

Part I

Action at the Individual Level

Chapter Two

Developing Relationships With Self and Others

One of my (Craig) strongest memories of supervision came four years into my professional career. I had a position in housing at a small, private, liberal arts institution in California. The institution I was at was, like most institutions of higher education at that time, still led by white, cisgender men. Most importantly, the ethos of the "good, old boys" was not only palpable, it was "how things got done." My supervisor, Nora, was the director of housing, and she identified as Latina cisgender woman. She also was upper-class, married, and her highest level of education was a high school diploma. Nora was one of two directors of color in the division of student affairs, and the only Latina at the director level in the entire college.

When Nora hired me, I was a younger professional, and this was my first mid-level management position. I was enthusiastic, well-intended, and wanting to make an immediate impact and difference. But I also had a limited understanding of my own identities, let alone how the systems of oppression operated. At first, Nora and I worked well together and got along well. At some point, however, things changed. I do not remember the details of what happened or how this pattern came to be, but our relationship devolved.

One day, Nora asked me to come into her office. Although the meeting started off like any other, I quickly realized that I had misunderstood the purpose of the meeting. I suspect it was supposed to have been an accountability conversation. But that is not how it came out. Nora scolded me, insulted me, and berated me. I was shocked, caught off guard, betrayed, and humiliated. While today we might call that verbal abuse, we didn't have language or understanding for it then; it was also part of the "good, old boys" practice at the college. From that time forward, I knew that anytime Nora asked me to come to her office, I was going to have one of those experiences. I spent a lot of energy and time trying to avoid having those meetings, so much so that I stopped focusing on the needs of the students and certainly stopped trying to make a difference. I wanted to fly under the radar.

That experience deeply affected me in profoundly negative ways at the intrapersonal and interpersonal levels. While I vowed never to do that to one of the people I supervised, the memory and feelings of those experiences haunted me. To this day, when someone asks me to come into their office, those feelings of fear and belittlement come right back. For a long time, I was angry with Nora. With much distance, professional and personal growth, and therapy, I am no longer hooked by those painful experiences with Nora.

Over the years, I have also been able to develop some compassion for Nora. I don't know what it was like to navigate working at an institution deeply rooted in systems of maleness, whiteness, and sexism as a Latina cisgender woman. I don't know what it was like for her to have a high school diploma working at an institution that only valued college degrees. I assume she had to assimilate to survive, and I imagine how difficult and painful that was for her. And I appreciate that my identity as a white, cisgender man fit into the institutional norm that likely caused her pain. I don't excuse her behavior, but I understand the systems of oppression she was navigating and the defense mechanisms she had to have developed as a result.

With the understanding that our most difficult and painful experiences are the best teachers, I have learned a lot from my time with Nora. Each of the authors have had similar painful experiences with supervisors, all of which inform how we have approached our supervision practice, our research, and the writing of this book. In all of our experiences, we have learned that *people in pain perpetuate and replicate pain: hurt people end up hurting people.* We have learned that we replicate systems of oppression even when we are trying to do good work. We have learned that systems of oppression hurt us all, and we don't have models for healing at the systems level or transcending this system of oppression. We have also learned that very few of us know how to build and sustain loving relationships, especially in the workplace, outside of the dominant model. We know now that we can't practice supervision from an identity-conscious perspective without first developing strong, transformed relationships with our self and with others.

SHIFTING THE MODEL

The conventional, dominant model of working in the United States teaches that we, the employees, serve for the needs of the organization, and that our job as supervisors is to make the people we supervise accountable for their outcomes toward those needs. In this model, caring for people certainly is important, but it is a distant second to the quality and the timeliness of the employee's work product or outcomes. This model views employees as part of the machine, whose only role is to get something done.

We understand many of the ways we have been socialized personally and professionally. Upon reflection and conversation with each other, we authors also know that we operated out of this socialization for a long time. We suspect that we have even caused harm through how we supervised. We understand that we didn't know enough about ourselves at the time to question that socialization. In hindsight, we recognize we were not very good supervisors, and we certainly weren't working with an identity-conscious supervision practice.

Identity-conscious supervision practice centers the people as primary, not the work product. This practice allows for the wholeness of who we are as people, including all of our group identities, to be visible and known. Our abilities to do quality work and serve the mission of the organization is one important part of our wholeness in the work context, but it is not the central aspect. Our roles as supervisors is to know who our team members are in as much fullness as we can (or they wish to reveal), inspire them to work at their full potential, challenge them to deepen their understandings of their identities, connect their work to the larger mission, and provide the support and encouragement they need to do this. Last, our roles as supervisors are to celebrate the contributions and impact of the team.

In other words, at its core, supervision is about relationships with other people. Developing strong relationships provides the foundation for an identity-conscious approach to supervision. Strong relationships are how you build trust, so that you have an anchor to explore how identities are in play and challenge each other to grow in awareness. Strong relationships also allow you to collectively work for social justice in each and every moment, which is essential to shifting the system.

THE SUPERVISION RELATIONSHIP

For many professionals the supervisory role is the most rewarding facet of their professional career (Bailey & Hamilton, 2015). The rewarding feeling, however, relies on the value of relationships that develop throughout the course of a professional's role. In valued connections, not only can you share some small part in the growth and professional trajectory of other professionals, but you also might build relationships that would last a lifetime. These valued connections take time, energy, and effort to cultivate.

Bolman and Deal remind us that "we need managers who love their work, their organization, and the people whose lives they affect" (2013, p. viii). We envision workplaces where the employees matter as much as the work we all do, and we advocate for the shift in focus at our institutions. These kinds of relationships require investment to make happen. They require intentional cultivation, nurturing, thoughtfulness, and heart-focused care. We can't shortcut this process either. While there may be an immediate connection (a spark) that forecasts a positive, strong relationship, we can't realize that potential without the investment. Additionally, strong, trusting relationships are an essential component for identity-conscious practice. We have learned from experience that an identity-conscious practice will not happen automatically, and that we are not sure how to trust each other. An identity-conscious approach asks us to be vulnerable and share our stories as well as the areas where we are still learning or stuck. Strong relationships allow us to walk into that vulnerable space together. This is a radical reconfiguring of the role of supervision through the centering of love.

An identity-conscious supervision approach helps us build these stronger working relationships all across the organization. In many organizations, the individuals and culture of an organization are in conflict with each other. Individuals may love their colleagues or supervisor, but the larger culture may be toxic or harmful. Other times, professionals may love the culture and mission, but their supervisor and colleagues might make the day-to-day working environment unbearable. There is an opportunity for both the individual and the organization to complement one another. A strong identity-conscious supervision practice can help you navigate the complexities of the supervisor/supervisee relationship, where you learn how to value both the individual and the organization.

Further, it is easy to only think of the relationships within your immediate team and to focus on building strong relationships there. But all of the people you will work with on your campus matter. And they may fall into one of more categories depending on your professional work:

- Partners—faculty, staff, and other administrators that you work with across departments or roles. These are people who are invested into your efforts and understand how you are invested in and align with theirs.
- People you interact with on a daily basis—these are colleagues in your immediate surroundings or people with whom your work brings you into regular contact. They are likely part of your immediate team or

department, but they can also be people in other departments that are co-located with yours.

- People you rarely interact with—these are often the majority of employees at a college or university. Most of the time they are in departments with which your role does not interact (i.e., adjunct faculty, employees on another campus). While their work may tangibly relate to yours, there is little overlap or connection.
- People that are essential to your work success that aren't visible to you—these are colleagues in custodial, facilities, payroll, cooks, finance, or those working on the night shift. You notice the outcome of their work (or rather it is clear when they misstep) rather than the people who perform that job.
- Mentorships—professionals, who may or may not be colleagues, with whom you both have agreed to focus on intentional growth and development. Mentorships can be with a supervisor, but most often they are with colleagues at other institutions. Mentorships are unique because of their focus on the growth of the mentee.
- Supervisor—a direct boss who oversees your work and possibly that of others if you are part of a team. They are responsible for the institutional outcomes in a particular area, your goals/deliverables, and, ideally, your support the growth.
- Supervisee—the professionals you oversee, and you are responsible for their set of deliverables or goals within an organization.

While all of these relationships matter for your ongoing and overall success at the university, it is the last two that are the focus of this book.

DEVELOPING A RELATIONSHIP WITH SELF

Our identities are both central to our leadership practice (Accapadi, 2018) and inform how we interact and work with each other. Phrased another way, knowing who we are interpersonally and who we are in relationship to our group identities is central to how we show up as a leader. Our identity-consciousness frames how we connect with our supervisors and supervisees, and how we navigate the dynamics across identities as well. Knowing all of this helps us identify and address how systems of oppression operate at our institutions. We can't engage identity-conscious supervision until we are willing to engage our own identities and practice living and leading from a more equitable and just frame.

The conventional notion in institutions of higher education, especially for those of us in our dominant identities, is that our identities are invisible or "left at the door" of the workplace. Building a strong relationship with ourselves requires us to understand all of our identities, the manifestation of behaviors that reinforce systems of oppression, and our relationship and investment to those behaviors. When we understand the identity-behavior-investment connection, then we begin to have a deeper understanding of ourselves.

We need to have a deep awareness of our identities at the individual level and the group level. Most of us hold a mix of dominant and marginalized identities, but we often have a stronger connection to some of our identities than others. Our lack of understanding of, or our discomfort with, those identities leads us to not acknowledge our access to privilege and power, miss how dynamics of dominance show up in our thinking, knowing, relationships, and behaviors, and/or understand the real impact that those identities have on our relationships.

For example, as I (Craig) continue to understand my privilege around ability, I realize that I am very comfortable taking the stairs—it has often been designed as the most direct and efficient route. As long as I am comfortable, I will never consider that people of other abilities might also want a direct and efficient route, nor will I begin to explore how navigation on campus can be universally designed so that it maximizes direct and efficient access.

Most importantly, we need to be clear about how our supervision behaviors are informed by systems of oppression (as discussed in Chapter 1). Supervisors who embrace these dominant behavioral norms show up in competition, assertiveness, and arrogance, which leads to marginalization, "less-than" treatment, and some forms of abuse. When these behaviors come out of our dominant identities (particularly in race, gender, and class), we show up in arrogance and rightness, and create a vertical hostility with our supervisees that perpetuates the system of oppression; when these behaviors come out of our marginalized identities (because we have assimilated to the dominant norms or we are colluding in oppression), we also show up in arrogance and rightness, and we create a horizonal hostility within our marginalized groups that perpetuates the system of oppression. And, "when we don't give ourselves permission to be free, we rarely tolerate that freedom in others" (Brown, 2010, p. 123).

As we grow in our awareness and take responsibility for the power and privilege that comes with both how we identify and how we are identified, we can then better understand how our actions are either reinforcing or resisting systems of oppression. This deepened level of awareness leads us to behave in new ways that interrupt systems of oppression and also builds capacity for creating and sustaining authentic relationships, both in-group and across difference.

Because this relationship is so central to our identity-conscious supervision practice, Chapter 3 further explores the process of developing a strong relationship with self.

DEVELOPING A RELATIONSHIP WITH OTHERS

Deepening our awareness around our identities and strengthening our relationship with ourselves will influence our relationships with others as well. Because our identities are central to our leadership practice (Accapadi, 2018), we want to foster building strong identity-conscious relationships with others as well. We highlight that this process of relationship building is cyclical—as we have new understandings about ourselves, those understandings influence our relationships with those around us, and vice versa.

Murphy and Kram (2014) offer us a structure to understand the process of developing strong professional relationships. They identified three essential elements that lead to mutual learning and growth: "relationships based in trust, effective communication, and commitment to the partnership" (p. 7). All three are important to an identity-conscious supervision practice, and we know trust is central. Trust creates the conditions for authenticity and vulnerability in an identity-conscious supervision process. It also is the most difficult to attain and sustain and the only element that requires the mutual investment by all people involved.

Trust

We have to start the relationship-building process with a focus on trust before we can start the process of developing authentic rapport with one another. Trusting another can be scary for us, especially if we've had experiences where people haven't been trustworthy. This authentic rapport with others through an identity-conscious lens is essential to transforming supervision practice and influencing systems change (discussed in Chapter 10). Davis and Harrison (2013) articulate that trust is a key first step in the process of dismantling systems of oppression, and when people feel trust, they will be vulnerable, even if it scares them (Bridges, 2009). Strong, honest, and healthy partnerships allow us to create the space where we can start to explore how systems of oppression, and potentially systems of justice, are showing up and playing out in our work, relationships, and interactions.

Authentic relationships require trust and vulnerability. We can't get trust without being vulnerable; and we cannot be vulnerable without trust (Smith & Berg, 1997). Navigating both simultaneously is essential. People need to know they matter, and it is through love, trust, and a sense of justice that mattering happens.

Most institutional cultures, however, focus on the work rather than on the relationships. On some level, institutions need to "get work done," and it is easier to measure products than it is the quality of the relationships and the culture. But we have lost sight of how the quality of work improves when organizational leaders invest time and resources in the development of trust. Hurley (2006) reports that low-trust environments breed stress, tension, and a lack of productivity, and high-trust environments nurture fun, support, and productivity in the workplace. Trust allows us to the have confidence in one another to share our identities, and high trust environments create conditions for employees to thrive and excel. Additionally, students are better served, employees are happier, and both will likely stay longer.

The mutuality of trust, however, requires a significant investment by each member of the relationship, and that investment must both be inwardly felt by all involved and outwardly expressed. Both the feeling and the expression need to remain consistent throughout the course of the relationship. Paradoxically, trust can be one of the strongest elements in a relationship but also the most fragile. Trust in another (or yourself) can carry you through the most difficult of experiences, but as soon as it stops being felt or expressed, trust evaporates.

Trust leads to deeper connections and authentic relationships. A deeper connection allows the partners to be authentic within their relationship, and as authenticity is expressed, trust is deepened. Relationships built on deepened trust is the foundation of identity-conscious supervision. The ability to show up authentically by individuals in the margins is often not valued and a trusting relationship with an identity-conscious focus creates space for the entirety of an individual in professional environments. This cycle, once momentum has been generated, will keep reinforcing the growth and development of trust and authenticity.

Barriers to Trust

In our current system, the structure of a supervisor and supervisee relationship creates a barrier to developing trust because of the power differential. There is a potential for misuse of power, and many of us have had these kinds of experiences, and unless we intentionally address it, the role of supervisors is to serve the needs and interests of the dominant culture because of how the institutional norming takes place. Until we can create another model of organizing people, getting the work done, while also developing people, we work through the existing system. As Scott (2017) shares, "hierarchy is an inescapable part of life. The best way to lower the barriers that hierarchy puts between us is to admit that it exists and to think of ways to make sure everyone feels they are on equal footing at a human level despite the structure" (Scott, 2017, p. 168). There is power in naming challenges and then creating strategy to overcome them.

How we show up as a supervisor or a supervisee in our identities matters, and it can provide a foundation where we can engage challenging and stressful organizational dynamics. Choosing not to acknowledge your identities is a choice, and it has impact. Hierarchy, and the power differential, has been used historically to force conformity and to reinforce dominant ideals. For those with dominant identities, acknowledging these dominant identities allows us to behave in ways that challenge social norming and how we may perpetuate it. For those with marginalized identities, acknowledging them allows us to behave in ways that challenge social norming and how we may be colluding with it. Additionally, while there has been a strong movement away from authoritarian styles of leadership, managing, and supervision, the persistent notion in most institutions is that "I'm the boss and I need you to do what I say," especially when conflict arises.

Communication and Partnership

Effective communication is a skill that an individual can learn and practice on a regular basis, and one can be communicating well even if the other partner isn't. But effective communication requires all participants to be communicating well. There are many models of effective communication, and while they are beyond the scope of this book, we note how central the skill of communication to identity-conscious supervision practice. We highlight that there is no one way to communicate—there are different styles, different cultural norms, and varying institutional expectations. Recognizing differences is essential to our identity-conscious practice. In a supervisory context, we communicate about the tasks of our roles at the institution (the responsibilities, performance standards, and resources needed to accomplish them), and we may even communicate about the strategic and mission-driven efforts of the institution and how our work connects to them. When we also communicate about our identities and how they impact who we are as part of our identity-conscious supervision practice, we create links between our professional practice and our identity-consciousness. We also begin the foundation of partnerships with our supervisors, supervisees, and colleagues.

We want to ensure that these partnerships reflect equitable structures. Eisler (2002) offers a model for partnerships built on equity. Her partnership model contrasts with the dominator model currently in practice in the United States and many other societies. In dominant systems, a few people are in the upper levels of the hierarchy, while most people are at the lower levels. The systems are designed to facilitate and support this power allocation. This is the traditional supervisor and supervisee relationship. In partnership systems, however, relationships are cocreated with respect and care to the community. This transformative model is built on respect and caring, and power is used to empower, not control or marginalize. The central focus of the partnership model is the people, and power is allocated across the relationships equitably. The partnership model allows for identity-conscious supervision to take hold as a practice.

In a supervision context, relationships built from a partnership lead to high quality connections. High quality connections are "when parties feel engaged, energized, and appreciated as a result of their interactions" (Murphy & Kram, 2014, p. 19). High quality relationships also come by a person being seen as a full person, including all of our contributions and gifts, and for who we are. Identities are also a part of who we are and play a role in trust development.

SUPERVISION DYNAMICS

One of the key responsibilities as a supervisor is to accomplish the key objectives, outcomes, deliverables, and goals for our area, and we are responsible for leading a team to accomplish them. Our "job as the boss is to set and uphold the quality bar" (Scott, 2017, p. 65), and while we can have some influence on the culture of the workplace, the work still needs to get done. Edmondson (2012) writes, "What is needed are dynamic, flexible teams that combine employees' strengths, experience, and knowledge to achieve organizational goals" (p. 42). We agree, and when we have the chance to create our own team, or restructure an area, this is possible. When we inherit a team, as we most often do, developing these kinds of dynamic, flexible teams that honor identity-conscious practice while working in partnership with each other is more complicated and takes greater effort.

Providing clear direction, establishing engagement toward a set of community standards or principles, and regular and timely feedback all help to build a strong motivated team that functions for the support of the institution. Our role modeling our identity-conscious practice creates space for employees to engage their identities in practice as well. When we, as supervisors, can serve as coach and partner with our supervisees, the practice feels effortless.

When we need to work with a supervisee who isn't meeting their job functions or performance expectations, it is more difficult. The hardest part of supervision is "telling people clearly and directly when their work wasn't good enough" (Scott, 2017, p. x). Indirect feedback creates lack of clarity and confusion, and this can happen because of an institution's culture or because of a discomfort with speaking across difference. Our identity-conscious supervision practice asks us to approach these difficult conversations acknowledging identities and system dynamics but also with a partnership and investment focus. Timely feedback helps our supervisees understand problematic behaviors and have time to make adjustments. When we communicate this way, rather than keeping silent, we show investment in them as valued people in the organization.

Sometimes, however, our invested, caring feedback leads to the relationship becoming contentious. It shouldn't be, and it doesn't have to be, but realistically, it often is. If we consider socioeconomic class identities and how money functions in our society, it complicates these kinds of conversations. The motivations of the employee and the organization may be very different—the organization wants work done in a particular way, and the employee wants to be well paid to do it. While we might wish that all employees are behind the mission of the organization and know how their daily work contributes to the success of that mission-driven work, we know that life realities are such that some employees experience the job as a means to an end, and the vital paycheck received for the work allows the employee to meet other, more important needs. There is nothing wrong with this and these employees often meaningfully contribute to a strong and successful organization. But it does mean that the process for influencing performance is different. Being able to hold performance and identity-consciousness at the same time is essential to providing this quality feedback.

Scott (2017) concurs with the idea of investment: "You strengthen your relationship by learning the best ways to get, give, and encourage guidance; by putting the right people in the right roles on your team; and by achieving results collectively that you couldn't dream of individually" (p. 8). Our identity-conscious supervision practice requires us to understand who the team members are as individuals in their wholeness, so that we can learn what motivates them and help coach them into the right roles on the team. We strengthen relationships by modeling identity-conscious practices within tour working context. It is essential that we give people the guidance they need to succeed in their jobs (Scott, 2017). Leading, and supervising, with the right blend of identity-consciousness, encouragement, support, inspiration, and accountability is important, and tough. We supervisors need to invest time and energy to build these strong relationships, provide the inspiration and guidance, and celebrate performance and contributions.

LOVE AND VULNERABILITY

Love and vulnerability are essential to building relationships, and we consider it the radical foundation of relationship building in identity-conscious supervision practice. Both bell hooks and Cornel West expressed that love is a radical act: "justice is what love looks like in public" (West, 2011), and "love as the practice of freedom" (hooks, 2006, p. 243). Connecting love and justice within the supervisory relationship is a radical approach and central to this book's idea that a transformed higher education and profession of student affairs starts with a group of professionals infusing a loving and justice-oriented approach into every aspect of their work. Love is also at the center of our identity-conscious supervision model because it is central to having a strong relationship with self and with others. Love is also central to liberation. We view the practice of love as a professional competency.

Central to the cultivation of love, we need to engage and practice our vulnerability. Brown (2010) asks us to join what she calls a "wholehearted revolution" (p. 126). When we have an honest assessment of ourselves, our places of strength and our places of imperfection, we can show up authentically in our relationships with others. Too often, the model of workplace relationships we are shown, and that we tacitly accept, are built upon distant (or lack of) emotion, show-no-weakness, all-about-the-outcome relationship. As shared earlier, this relationship model is rooted in white supremacy, privileged class norms, and patriarchy, and it serves nothing further than perpetuating the status quo of oppression. No one wants to work under these conditions, and yet the field continues to perpetuate them. Vulnerability as supervisors allows us an opportunity to transcend these oppressive structures through our engagement and partnership.

Some of the other benefits of strong relationships infused with love and justice is that they allow us to weather all kinds of challenges in the supervisor/supervisee role, including changes in performance, evaluations, difficult conversations, and interpersonal dynamics. Balancing love and justice create opportunities to build trust. Each of these elements, essential to the role, can cause stress and anxiety, and create tension in the relationship. "Good relationships allow us to cope with the stress and thrive during times of change" (Murphy & Kram, 2014, p. 19). A solid relationship also gives us something to rely upon when there is conflict. There have been more than enough times when we, the authors, have been thankful for our strong relationship as we navigated conflicts or used courage to say what needed to have been said.

Visibility, dignity, and vulnerability are also essential to strong relationships. Strong relationships in an identity-conscious supervision practice allow us to more fully know the people we work with and honor them. These strong relationships help us collectively engage in how systems of oppression are showing up in our work and actions and take action to interrupt these systems. Strong relationships allow us space to explore how we continue to invest in systems of oppression.

There are some logistical challenges to building relationships infused with love and justice. Longevity within the workplace has shortened dramatically and we aren't rooted to one institution anymore. Generational shifts and other professional trends show high job mobility, globalization, technology, and a high pace of change (Murphy & Kram, 2014). For many of our campuses, the rate of change is significant, and when you couple that with high turnover in positions, it can become a barrier to investing the time, energy, and resources into developing relationships. All of this also can exacerbate the problem of transiency, which further exacerbates the challenge in investing in the people. We suspect that an increase in investment will result in a decrease of transiency.

WORK JUSTICE AT THE MICROLEVEL

As discussed earlier, supervisors hold some dominance within the institutional system. We have evaluative power, access to those in power, the ability to define work activities, the ability to approve time off, and access to resources.

One of the important microlevel actions that we can take is to personalize the work relationships with supervisor and supervisee. Relationships in a work setting are often seen in depersonalized ways, where the employee is viewed as part of the machine rather than a whole person. We see this in the growing mistreatment of adjuncts and graduate assistants, in the continued devaluing of administrative assistant level work and in the invisibility of custodial teams. Getting to know the people who work at institutions and directly connecting their work to the mission of the university matters at the microlevel. Engaging staff in this way includes honoring and celebrating their work regularly as well. We envision this process critical to building and sustaining relationships centered in justice and love.

Our intention to see supervisees as whole people is what creates the conditions for authentic relationships rooted in social justice. "Only when you care about the whole person with your whole self can you build a relationship" (Scott, 2017, p. 13). Relationships with anything less are merely transactional and won't lead to the transformative partnerships necessary to support systems level change. "A foundational principle for change agents is the recognition that relationships with other people are very important (Drechsler & Jones, 2009, p. 412).

Modern working conditions at institutions of higher education don't currently encourage this attitude, and as such, it may feel like we are "swimming upstream." Corporate management practices are "bound by rules, processes, hierarchical structures, and fear" (Edmondson, 2012, p. 18). Further, fear continues to dominate the university workplace (Elliott et al., 2013) because of unjust, disparate, and oppressive treatment, which "has long been used as a tool for maintaining control" (Edmondson, 2012, p. 132). These practices are often one of the first things that employees learn when starting jobs at an institution. It is counter to principles of love and justice, and a barrier to social justice and systems change.

It is important for us to work justice at the micro level in our roles as supervisors. Often, we see justice efforts at the macro level such as policy needs, programmatic needs, and staffing. However, we might miss opportunities for social justice work in the everyday interactions, decisions, and judgments. Supervision is delicately attuned to the impact of social justice work at this level because of its direct impact on the relationships with team members, and supervisors and supervisees. It is leading with, not leading over.

Lee Ann Bell (2016) presents a set of practices that is helpful for daily leadership practice for social justice, particularly developing a critical consciousness (as addressed earlier and in Chapter 9), analyzing power (discussed in Chapter 4), and building coalitions. These important competencies lay a foundation for justice-centered leadership.

Infusing justice into our roles as supervisors is more nuanced requiring more analysis of power within the role and can be more complicated to practice. Knowing how our identity is present within a given interaction, how relationships affect a goals conversation, or even how principles of equity lead within a budget conversation matters in shaping the outcomes.

CONCLUSION

Relationships are central to identity-conscious practice and supervision. It is important to build trust in our relationships to allow for vulnerability in acknowledging and engaging our identities in our work. We want to create, develop, and sustain spaces of mattering for our employees so that they can thrive in their work environments. Moreover, we want our relationships to reflect and work toward liberation—systems change work (as discussed in Chapter 10) also starts with strong relationships. After self-work (discussed here and in Chapter 1), building strong supervisory relationships is the most time-intensive aspect of an identity-conscious practice. We will not be effective using other skills until we invest our time and effort to build strong relationships.

It has taken us many years to unlearn the programming of dominant models of workplace relationships and learn a new model centered in justice, love, and liberation. We are still in practice, and still, at times, stumble in our efforts to remain consciously oriented toward justice. Our relationships can reflect oppression or liberation, often along a continuum, and it is up to us to choose. Our intentional practice to deepen awareness of ourselves, of others, build trust, and work toward love and justice is central to an identity-conscious practice, and central to changing systems of oppression.

Case Study
Michelle L. Boettcher and Reyes J. Luna

James (he, him, his; Japanese-American, cisgender, gay man) has completed onboarding and training in a new job. His supervisor, Catrina (she, her, hers; White, cisgender, heterosexual woman), has been with the department for eight years. They have started to set expectations. Catrina shared that her most successful working relationships involve significant connections. She is hoping to connect with James and hopes to be a resource for him.

James shared that he is looking for what he needs from a supervisor. In his first job after graduate school he liked his supervisor as a person but was misled about the work he would be doing. Instead of working with students he provided administrative support. In his next position he felt micromanaged and unsupported. While James does not share this, he also was harassed because of his sexual orientation and has a pending lawsuit against his previous institution.

Catrina has a history of being an excellent supervisor. James's new colleagues told him how lucky he is to have her as a supervisor. They said she cares and invests in her team. His new team is diverse in terms of race, ethnicity, gender, and physical ability. They assure James that Catrina "gets it" when it comes to social justice, equity, diversity, and inclusion. They say she is great with students, and her department has a strong reputation.

Catrina shares that she hopes that over time James will talk about his career experiences and professional goals and dreams. She says she has dedicated time to understanding the many privileges she holds. Her supervision philosophy focuses on developing her team holistically. By getting to know them as individuals, she can have a better idea of their aspirations and can identify opportunities they might be interested in.

Catrina shares that she has been married for 12 years and her husband works in IT at the university. They have three boys and are active in the children's school. Her oldest son just became an Eagle Scout and the other two are both involved in scouting, too. Finally, she shares that she is very involved in her church, where she teaches Sunday school and she and her husband host a weekly Bible study. She also enjoys hiking, camping, and genealogy.

James is not sure if he can be open about his personal life given what Catrina shared. In his previous workplace, there were several colleagues who attended the same church. While they invited James to attend, one colleague in particular said it might not always be comfortable because of "your gay thing." The same colleague said, "Ours isn't that kind of church. But we can help you with your issues if you want to come with us." While this was a peer, their supervisor attended the same church and was present when the comment was made and said nothing to James about it.

Catrina senses James' hesitation to share but does not push him to disclose too much. While affirming of all people,

Catrina knows that sometimes, because of her church involvement, people make assumptions about her. She fears she may have gotten off on the wrong foot with James.

After a few weeks, Catrina asks James what his ideal workplace would look like and what his ideal supervisor would do. "We both have things to learn, James. I want to learn about what you want in your experience here." She asks him to come prepared to share the following week.

In advance of the meeting, James e-mails Catrina and thanks her for the activity. He shares that he learned a lot and includes a bulleted list of "key aspects of my aspirational workplace:"

- Clear communication of expectations and timelines
- Sense of humor
- Authenticity and care
- Trust and rapport
- Assumptions of goodwill
- Opportunity to bring my whole self into the workplace
- Autonomy
- Supervision informed by experience, institutional knowledge, and a desire to help me develop

KEY QUESTIONS

1. What assumptions might James and Catrina be making about each other and how could untangle these assumptions to help build a relationship?
2. What self-work should James and Catrina engage in to deeper their understanding of their dominant and marginalized identities?
3. What other activities could Catrina and James engage in to foster trust and rapport? How might these individual conversations inform the types of staff development that Catrina might offer her entire team?

REFERENCES

Accapadi, M. M. (2018). A journey of reconciliation and healing. In A. K. Gonzalez, D. M. Ching, L. S. White, & R. D. Kelly (Eds.), *Transformational encounters: Shaping diverse college and university leaders* (pp. 115–130). Washington, DC: NASPA.

Bailey, K. W., & Hamilton, J. (2015). Supervisory style. In M. J. Amey & L. M. Reesor (Eds.), *Beginning your journey: A guide for new professionals in student affairs* (4th ed., pp. 67–94). Washington, DC: NASPA.

Bell, L. A. (2016). Theoretical foundations for social justice education. In M. Adams, L. A. Bell, D. J. Goodman, & K. Y. Joshi (Eds.), *Teaching for diversity and social justice*. New York, NY: Routledge.

Bolman, L. G., & Deal, T. E. (2013). *Reframing organizations: Artistry, choice, and leadership* (5th ed.). San Francisco, CA: Jossey-Bass.

Bridges, W. (2009). *Managing transitions: Making the most of change* (3rd ed.). Philadelphia, PA: Da Capo Press.

Brown, B. (2010). *The gifts of imperfection*. Center City, MN: Hazelden.

Davis, T., & Harrison, L. M. (2013). *Advancing social justice: Tools, pedagogies, and strategies to transform your campus*. San Francisco, CA: Jossey-Bass.

Drechsler, M. J., & Jones, W. A. (2009). Becoming a change agent. In S. R. Komives, W. Wagner, & Associates (Eds.), *Leadership for a better world: Understanding the social change model of leadership development* (2nd ed., pp. 397–446). San Francisco, CA: Jossey-Bass.

Edmondson, A. C. (2012). *Teaming: How organizations learn, innovate, and compete in the knowledge economy*. San Francisco, CA: Jossey-Bass.

Eisler, R. (2002). *The power of partnership: Seven relationships that will change your life*. Novato, CA: New World Library.

Elliott II, C. M., Stransky, O., Negron, R., Bowlby, M., Lickiss, J., Dutt, D., . . . Barbosa, P. (2013). Institutional barriers to diversity change work in higher education. *Sage Open*, *3*(2), 1–9. doi:10.1177/2158244013489686

hooks, b. (2006). *Outlaw culture: Resisting representations*. New York, NY: Routledge.

Hurley, R. F. (2006, September). The decision to trust. *Harvard Business Review*. Retrieved from https://hbr.org/2006/09/the-decision-to-trust

Murphy, W., & Kram, K. E. (2014). *Strategic relationships at work: Creating your circle of mentors, sponsors, and peers for success in business and life*. New York, NY: McGraw Hill.

Scott, K. (2017). *Radical candor: How to be a kick-ass boss without losing your humanity.* New York, NY: St. Martin's Press.

Smith, K. K., & Berg, D. N. (1997). *Paradoxes of group life: Understanding conflict, paralysis, and movement in group dynamics.* San Francisco, CA: Jossey-Bass.

West, C. (2011, April 17). *Cornel west: Justice is what love looks like in public* [Video file]. Retrieved from www.youtube.com/watch?v=nGqP7S_WO6o&feature=youtu.be

Chapter Three

Creating a Strong Sense of Self

Throughout our lives, we receive societal messages that impact how we make meaning of the world around us. For example, at a fundamental level, the physical space we navigate creates privilege around ability or the schools we attend, and their composition of students, teachers, and administrators create meaning around authority. Some of these messages cause trauma and deep-rooted pain, while others bring hope affirmation, and healing. Making sense of these messages happens in the community through relationships and, at times, a trained professional. An identity-conscious supervisory lens can also create an opportunity to make meaning of intentional and unintentional socialization. When supervisors take time to heal and unpack the sense they have made from the barrage of indicators and signs in daily life, we can manage and supervise from a place of wholeness. We can also learn to self-reflect when feedback or decisions leave us feeling unsettled as opposed to just reacting based on discomfort.

The work of developing a strong sense of self is challenging and critical to identity-conscious supervision. When supervisors do the work necessary to create a strong sense of self, we demonstrate a commitment to values, courage, and a narrative that values the individual more than the institution or department. When supervisors do not do the work necessary to function from worthiness, we often perpetuate oppressive dynamics and pass on our pain. I (Shruti) was supervising six mid- and entry-level professionals. Many of these individuals identified as white. I often challenged and pushed them to think about the impact of their whiteness. Their whiteness would often show up in citing policy as more important than people, fragility and silence around racist dynamics, and an inability to demonstrate resilience when pushing for change.

Honest, identity-based conversations provided value for our department and increased trust within the team. During one of my supervisory meetings, a white woman, Clara, pushed back. She asked me why I did not talk about being a woman or being queer. At that moment, I realized the pain I had as a Person of Color was limiting my perspective and affecting my relationships. My pain was so steep that it created a singular narrative around who I was and what would create value in my life. I wanted to hold the white individuals on the team responsible for healing my pain around race. I also had pain in my other marginalized identities. The hurt and trauma of my racial identity masked everything else. At this point, I apologized for the pain I had passed on and collusion in which I participated. I was not challenging sexism or homophobia, and that silence perpetuated oppression. This conversation shifted our relationship and my life, but it was challenging, iterative, painful, and slow.

Identity-conscious supervision does not just include relationships with others. It also includes having a strong relationship with the self. Developing this relationship is like any other relationship. It can be painful, and healing takes time and is unending. When self-healing occurs, it feels like a new place of value and belonging. By engaging in a process to develop self-authorship and self-awareness, we can adopt cultural humility in our identity-conscious supervisory practice. This chapter will address steps to create a strong sense of self, including the process of self-authorship, reflection, developing cultural humility, and creating a community of practice.

SELF-AUTHORSHIP

Many graduate preparation programs discuss self-authorship in the realm of students, but the actual journey of self-authorship does not begin for most individuals until after the mid to late twenties (Kegan, 1994). This means that many new and even mid-level professionals are in a stage of self-authorship. These steps and dimensions interact with how one makes meaning as well as a supervisory relationship. Kegan (1994) indicates three dimensions of self-authorship: cognitive, interpersonal, and intrapersonal. Cognitive is the nature of knowledge or who is the holder of knowledge, and how one obtains it. In other words, why do I believe what I know and who do I trust to learn from? Interpersonal is the dependency and importance of relationships. For example, does an individual appease the group to fit in or disrupt to prioritize self-integrity. Intrapersonal is an individual's belief system. These three dimensions are not separate from social identity because of the relationship between individual trust and socialization.

Another way to view this is through meaning-making. I (Shruti) had a faculty member in graduate school who would always tell us in our student development theory course, "You are your meaning-making structure." At the time, I did not understand that my identities and environment impact how I make meaning, now I know that my thoughts, along with the system I live in influence how I make meaning. Kegan (1994) goes on to write that individuals who have obtained self-authorship can meet their own daily needs, self-initiate, create a vision for life, take responsibility for their actions, and develop diversified interdependent relationships. The emphasis on diverse relationships is an essential component of identity-conscious supervision. If we only supervise people precisely like us, there is no need for identity-conscious supervision. It is often easier to supervise people from identical backgrounds than across differences. Supervising individuals with the same values and beliefs means we do not have to reflect as supervisors or challenge our thinking. Individuals who demonstrate self-authorship can hold complex belief systems that also allow for authentic relationships with diverse individuals as well as an understanding of their identities (Kegan, 1994). The capacity to have a healthy relationship with self and others is a crucial component to identity-conscious supervision and makes a significant impact on building trust.

The three dimensions of self-authorship (cognitive, interpersonal, and intrapersonal) also have three stages: external formula, crossroads, and self-authorship. Stage one is an external formula (Kegan, 1994). A formula and external relationships create this stage. In the cognitive dimension, individuals in the external formula believe that only individuals in authority know (Magolda, 2008). Table 3.1 provides a more significant explanation for each stage and dimensions.

Three Stages and Dimensions of Self-Authorship

These three stages (external formula, crossroads, and self-authorship) show up in the cognitive, interpersonal, and intrapersonal dimensions.

Components of the Final Stage of Self-Authorship

Trusting an Internal Foundation

The final stage, self-authorship, takes time to achieve and also includes three components: trusting an internal foundation, building an internal foundation, and securing internal commitments (Magolda, 2008). In the first component, trusting an internal foundation means paying attention to the inner dialogue and controlling how to respond. In identity-conscious supervision, this ability to monitor response is critical. When a supervisor can take a breath and regulate versus being triggered and reacting out

Table 3.1 Three Elements of Self-Authorship

Components and Stages of Self-Authorship

Dimensions	Stage 1: External Variables	Stage 2: Crossroads	Stage 3: Self-Authorship
Cognitive	Views knowledge as certain and relies on authority for right and wrong	Understands the need to take ownership of ideas and beliefs	Knowledge is based on context and must incorporate diverse perspectives
Interpersonal	Identity is based on validation from relationships, base decisions on gaining approval	Develops understanding that relationships can only meet certain needs and other needs must be met by self	Capacity to practice empathy and build authentic relationships with diverse individuals
Intrapersonal	Lack of awareness of individual needs and social identities	Dissonance between internal values and external values prompting self-evaluation	Strong sense of self used as the paradigm to view decision making

Source: (adapted from Magolda, M. B. B. (2008). Three elements of self-authorship. *Journal of College Student Development*, 49(4), 269–284.)

of pain, it impacts the deepening of the relationship (Obear, 2007). The stimulus and trigger response is cyclical, and self-work must be done to interrupt it. Brown (2018) addresses this critical dynamic:

> We work our shit out on other people, and we can never get enough of what it is we are after because we're not addressing the real problem. In general, it's fair to say that we're working our stuff out on people all day long. But when you add the leadership power differential, it gets dangerous.
>
> (p. 112)

In the example with Clara, I (Shruti) wanted her to help work through my pain from white supremacy, but instead, I caused harm from other identity spaces. It took me processing my trauma to learn how to interrupt my brain's reaction. The message I believed was that most white people cause harm. The processing of my trauma allowed a delayed response that helped me to breathe, scan the situation, and then make a decision about safety. I had to retrain my flight or fight response. This untangling of crossed wires takes time.

Building an Internal Foundation

The second component is building an internal foundation (Magolda, 2008). Building an internal foundation means integrating social identity, relationships, and beliefs into a set of commitments to act on (Magolda, 2008). This construction requires clarifying dissonance between old knowledge and new knowledge as well as relationships that function autonomously. This speaks to the component in the model of identity-conscious supervision regarding a sustained change. It cannot be a one-time act but a committed set of values to act upon on an individual and organizational level. Building an internal foundation will require revisiting values, understanding yourself, and determining action repeatedly.

Securing Internal Commitments

The last trait of self-authorship is securing internal commitments, and this means living through individual convictions (Magolda, 2008). For example, as a woman, I (Shruti) have received feedback from supervisees that I am too direct and not friendly in my e-mails. I had a colleague who, as a man, communicated the same way but never received this feedback. Since I had worked on myself, I decided to not incorporate this feedback and the norms of a woman's communication style and continue my directness. Internal commitments can look like still finding value in the identity despite not fitting the stereotype due to a clear set of values and priorities as demonstrated in the example of valuing clear communication higher than a gender stereotype. Self-authorship involves developing a strong sense of self to show up authentically in relationships with worthiness and value.

Identity and Self-Authorship

Magolda (2008) goes on to discuss what self-authorship looks like in dominant and minoritized identities. Dominant identities in self-authorship can hold multiple cultural frameworks to construct an anti-oppressive view that allows for culturally different interdependent relationships. As Audre Lorde (2012) famously said, "I am not free while any woman is unfree, even when her shackles are very different from my own" (p. 127). There must be a commitment to identity-consciousness as an individual for freedom from oppression to occur. Commitment also creates a strong sense of self and clarity around values. When there is a commitment, the capacity to stay focused and engaged creates the sustained practice of developing self-authorship.

The magnitude for holding multiple cultural frameworks will ebb and flow, and it allows for interrogating reactions with open-mindedness and curiosity (Lopez, 2008). Stories and narratives are created based on socialization and experiences. Holding up the mirror creates space for questioning these narratives and interrupting problematic stereotypes and systems. In supervisory relationships, when space and mutuality exist to have challenging conversations that welcome feedback, it shifts the power dynamic.

For minoritized identities, self-authorship means dismantling oppressive messaging to create a positive relationship with one's social identity for authentic, mutually beneficial relationships (Magolda, 2008). Dismantling internalized messages can be painful work and often requires support and an engaged community. As an identity-conscious supervisor, it is essential to remember this need for minoritized supervisees. Professional development is not always related to skill building on direct job responsibilities; spending time and building connections at conferences such as the National Conference on Race and Ethnicity (NCORE), Creating Change, or the Social Justice Training Institute (SJTI) provide opportunities for learning and healing. In return, these experiences help professionals become more grounded and increase their capacity for working in identity-conscious ways. Progress toward self-authorship also shows up in supervisor relationships, and a strong sense of self brings vulnerability, holding multiple perspectives, and integrity to identity-conscious supervision. A strong sense of self also builds self-awareness, cultural humility, and stronger relationships.

SELF-AWARENESS

Supervisors cannot practice self-awareness without reflection. Self-reflection and self-awareness incorporate learning about ourselves as cultural beings and how our identities influence our communication (Lopez, 2008). As described in Chapter 7, self-awareness is defined as demonstrated understanding of how one makes meaning of the world and how that meaning-making process impacts one's subjective view over time (Luthans & Avolio, 2003). Social identities influence how we receive and

49

process information communicated to us. For example, in working-class families, there is often direct communication (martinez & Ardoin, 2019). But in an employment context, directness is less valued and does not usually equate to "professionalism" (martinez & Ardoin, 2019). Paying attention to socialization around communication helps identify and name potential missteps in identity-conscious supervision. As mentioned in developing self-authorship, all individuals are cultural beings and understanding that can create healing and interrupt bias. Self-awareness, "necessitates 'deep cultural self-empathy'" (Sodowsky, Kuo-Jackson, & Loya, 1997, p. 12). Doing self-work involves understanding gut responses, which leads to self-awareness and self-authorship.

Another component of self-awareness is interrogating reactions with open-mindedness and curiosity (Lopez, 2008). Often we judge or evaluate responses as bad or good. Usually, this immediate evaluation shuts down the opportunity for interest. Instead, try wondering why a reaction occurred and what it meant for all parties involved which will allow for fuller self-awareness. Alternatively, in the model of self-authorship, this is called working in the stage of crossroads. Stories are created based on socialization. Brown (2018) writes, "We do not judge in areas where we feel a strong sense of self-worth and grounded confidence, so the more of that we build, the more we let go of judgment" (p. 146). For example, when I talk with a differently abled staff member, I have a tendency to second-guess everything I did and the pain I caused. I have not had to explore this aspect of my identity; therefore, I do not feel a strong sense of self when it comes to an understanding of my privilege around ability. I take those feelings and try to learn as much as I can to help dismantle my internalized dominance. This curiosity also helps supervisors understand their impact on others.

The final components of self-awareness are making it a habit and building, assessing, and connecting (Lopez, 2008). The current language around being "culturally competent" or "woke" implies there is an end stage. Lopez (2008) argues that self-awareness must become a habit. Systems of oppression are pervasive and require the creation of new knowledge, skills, and awareness to continue to dismantle those systems and practice identity-conscious supervision. It must be a habit. The other component involves building, assessing, and connecting. To build a system that allows for persistent naming and work around dismantling internalized messages means consistently reflecting on an individual and systemic level. Second, to assess and connect creates opportunities for continued work that is relevant and measurable. Self-awareness as a department leads to reflection on an organizational level, which will improve job satisfaction and employee retention. Self-authorship and self-awareness lead to empathy, another critical component of identity-conscious supervision.

Often empathy includes a definition such as putting oneself in another person's shoes. That is partially true. Brown's (2018) description offers more nuance:

> One of the signature mistakes with empathy is that we believe we can take our lenses off and look through the lenses of someone else's lenses. We can't. Our lenses are soldered to who we are. What we can do, however, is honor people's perspectives as truth even when they're different from yours. That's a challenge if you were raised in a majority culture-white, straight, male, middle-class, Christian-and you were likely taught that your perspective is *the* correct perspective and everyone else needs to adjust their lens. *Or,* more accurately, you weren't taught anything about perspective-taking, and the default – *My* truth *is* the *truth* – is reinforced by every system and situation you encounter.
>
> (Brown, 2018, p. 143)

When supervisors have not engaged in their work to build cultural humility and self-awareness, they cannot practice empathy or pay attention to the impact of socialization on a single narrative of who is valuable.

In addition to empathy, managing our ego is also essential to our self-work. The work of creating self-awareness can elicit feelings of shame and defensiveness. The Privileged Identity Model (explained in Chapter 5) discusses defensiveness in depth (Watt, 2007). Being able to identify defensive reactions that arise in others and ourselves is an essential skill for reconstructing environments to become more inclusive (Stewart, 2012). We tend to become most defensive when engaging and responding to dominance and privilege. Watt (2007) introduced the privileged identity exploration model as a tool that individuals can use to identify defenses that arise as observed in self or others when introduced to a dissonance-provoking stimulus (DPS). Cultural humility and a strong sense of self diffuse the DPS and move from crossroads to self-authorship.

Self-awareness and cultural humility intersect with the supervisory relationship and require vulnerability, self-work, trust, and accountability. In Soheilian, Inman, Klinger, Isenberg, and Kulp (2014), the researchers found indicators of a culturally healthy supervisor relationship included sharing personal cultural struggles, authenticity and self-awareness, and openness to discussing cultural and racial factors. Building a relationship while practicing self-awareness elicits an array of emotions from confidence to self-doubt, yet in the end, it creates a healthier supervisor relationship. This requires owning that all of us have learning edges and participating in growth is worth the time and effort.

Learning edges, or an area where more education is needed, often show up in our dominance and can be frustrating for individuals who hold a minoritized identity in the same category. For example, when talking with a former supervisor about English not being my (Shruti) first language, he responded with empathy and then disclosed how he had not thought about how hard it must be to navigate the world in two languages. My lived experience had shown me this challenge, and I knew it for others. This authentic conversation had to occur for learning to happen. My supervisor had to continue his work. Soheilian et al. (2014) stated that supervisor self-awareness, genuine interest, *sharing of self,* and support contribute to a supervisory relationship that is culturally relevant. There has to be a vulnerability to share those learning edges in a supervisory dyad, and that requires self-work.

Self-awareness allows for a different supervisory relationship, where the identity-conscious relationship becomes possible. Self-awareness first creates humility to understand that all of us can learn more. It also creates a willingness to ask questions when we don't understand. When a supervisor role models this, it allows a supervisee to do the same. Otherwise, supervision becomes transactional where supervisors share their multicultural knowledge from a distance as opposed to sharing from their own lives. Self-authorship calls for integration and internalization of self-awareness. Self-awareness alone is not enough; an individual must make meaning and decisions from that information. When supervisors share personally instead of focusing on knowledge and skills, it allows for a more significant shift in behavior and relationship (Tyler & Guth, 1999). This shift in actions and relationships leads to a stronger sense of self.

When supervisors have done self-work on their identity, it allows for an elevated supervisory relationship. A healthy supervisory relationship means supervisors navigate through their guilt or pain and put aside their own needs for the sake of their team. Bhat and Davis (2007) discovered that supervisors who had a stronger sense of self around their racial identity had a stronger emotional bond and cohesiveness in their supervisory relationship. When the relationship between a supervisor and supervisee is secure, and individuals with minoritized identities feel valued; it creates a sense of belonging for all members on the team. When people feel like they belong, they stay longer and want to invest in the organization. When minoritized supervisees do not feel as if supervisors have done their work, it comes at an expense. When supervisees feel brave and valued in their supervisory relationship, a commitment to the organization and the team can occur. Inman (2006) suggests that supervisors who do not have awareness around their identities tend to overlook aspects of problems that may be related to identity. For example, I (Shruti) was supervising a Black man who was one of two in the division. He always felt the need to overcompensate through his work and in turn, struggled to meet deadlines and manage his workload. I had a sense of this as I was one of three Asian women in the division. If I had practiced identity-neutral supervision, I would not have had him reflect on how being one of two Black men was affecting his work or felt the need to help him find a mentor on campus. When I did ask him to reflect on this lonely dynamic, he was vulnerable and explained the impact on his sense of self as well as belonging. Identity-neutral supervision tends to exacerbate problems because supervisors cannot acknowledge their own biases and prejudices while identity-conscious supervision understands that identity and workplace challenges often go hand in hand.

Self-awareness, self-authorship, and developing a strong sense of self all go hand in hand. These skills and traits lead to a capacity to reflect and pause to take in someone else's viewpoint as opposed to reacting and responding. These qualities also lead to cultural humility. Cultural humility supports identity-conscious supervision when partnered with a strong sense of self.

CULTURAL HUMILITY

Cultural humility and identity-conscious supervision work together as it allows for vulnerability, learning edges, and curiosity. Hook, Davis, Owen, Worthington Jr, and Utsey (2013) describe cultural humility as the "ability to maintain an interpersonal stance that is other-oriented (or open to the other) in relation to aspects of cultural identity that are most important to the supervisee" (Hook et al., p. 354). In other words, a supervisor who demonstrates cultural humility holds the capacity to know their supervisee's values at the intersection of identity or culture. This also means a supervisor has done enough work to separate their own needs for affirmation with the desires of their supervisee. For example, if a member of the team is from a different faith tradition, it is worth understanding what holidays that individual may celebrate and how the role of a supervisor can support time off for those holidays.

Covarrubias (2017) defines cultural humility as a process of engaging in a regular reflection to make meaning of areas of personal challenges and strengths around identity and inclusion. Covarrubias (2017) goes onto discuss the impact of humility, empowering supervisors, and advisors to know their limits and name power to impact the team they oversee positively. Cultural humility is an ongoing work and involves having a strong sense of self-awareness.

The relationship is the core of identity-conscious supervision. Ladany, Brittan-Powell, and Pannu (1997) and Bhat and Davis (2007) found that supervisors with a stronger sense of self around their racial identity than their supervisees showed the most substantial supervisory relationship both in cohesion and emotional bond when compared to other supervisory interactions. This means that supervisors who had done their work around their social identities and integrated their identities had stronger supervisory relationships than those that did not. Another study suggests that supervisors who were less racially aware than their supervisees did not understand the full depth of a problem (Inman, 2006). This creates an opportunity for misunderstanding and feelings of not being seen by the supervisee.

Further investigation of cultural humility provides a greater understanding of its components. Characteristics of culturally humble supervisors include exhibiting a more precise understanding of themselves and individual areas of growth. Supervisors also demonstrate an others-focused framework and continual respect (Davis et al., 2011; Davis, Worthington, & Hook, 2010). A consistent pattern begins emerging about managing self and focusing on others regarding cultural humility. Cultural humility also impacts the relationship. Covarrubias (2017) found that white, female supervisors' level of competency in social justice and inclusion was the most influential aspect of the quality of relationship (positive or negative) with men of color supervisees. In other words, students valued supervisors who valued equity and inclusion more than supervisors who led with their organizational checklists. Men of color could be seen and heard when white women had looked in the mirror and worked on themselves.

When a supervisor is aware of their own biases and limitations, they can share with a team member to create vulnerability as well as role modeling self-awareness and the need for self-work. For example, I (Shruti) was supervising a Black man, and he was discussing his frustrations with finding a mentor who shared identities. I listened and responded by acknowledging that I did not understand what it meant to be Black in America or on campus but would be willing to serve as a mentor and connect him with others in the field if that proved helpful. He took me up on that opportunity. Cultural humility allowed for a different connection, and I (Shruti) did not claim to be an expert in supporting Black men. I also knew that as an Asian woman, I am inundated with anti-Black messaging and had to unlearn.

Further, understanding that just because I am a person of color does not mean that I understand the lived experiences of all people of color. Engaging in these conversations with vulnerability can be challenging, mainly when cultural competence is practiced and not cultural humility. Self-work regarding identity is iterative and learning happens through practice and reflection.

54

COMMUNITIES OF PRACTICE AND REFLECTION

Self-awareness does not occur in a silo. Magolda and King (2004) offer the Learning Partnership Model (LPM) as a model promoting self-authorship and intercultural maturity. This model validates learners as knowers who create their perspectives based on their lived experiences. The strategy of a learner as knower repeats in *Pedagogy of the Oppressed* (2018), which advocates for mutual learning and knowledge construction. LPM adheres to the idea that learning occurs in an individual's experience or this idea that individuals are their meaning-making structures. The third component of LPM is that individuals learn collaboratively. These three components can be utilized to create communities of practice in which each individual brings their thoughts and perceptions as well as a willingness to learn from one another. Magolda and King (2004) also underscore that the LPM's authority is built through mutual knowledge construction; it is not based on one individual. This partnership model builds on the idea that multiple perspectives create a greater depth of knowledge and allow for a nuanced understanding of how social identities impact views. This type of learning community promotes accountability and vulnerability to support progression through the stages of self-authorship.

Rogoff (2014) also has a model for communities of practice. This model underscores the value of shared understanding within communities of practice where members work together to build a common goal and a shared set of exercises—for example, when working toward implementing a racial equity framework in residential life. The team broke into three types of groups. Two were affinity groups, one for People of Color and one for white staff. The third group gathered across race to talk about what was going well, what skills were growing, what needed evaluation, and priorities for growth for the next meeting. Creation of this community of practice occurred after seeing a need after two days of training around racial equity. This monthly meeting allowed for vulnerability and perspective sharing as well as mutual learning and accountability. Without this community, there would not have been as much sustained change in the department. Communities can happen across and within identity but must offer shared goals and mutual learning. Supervisors also participated in these groups, which demonstrated several essential values. The first value was a commitment to this work across the hierarchy, the second a willingness for vulnerability and building self-awareness, and the third, modeling for individuals so they would also be willing to take risks and participate. These groups allow for reflection on an individual level as well.

Reflection as a Practice

When instilling reflection as a practice on an organizational, supervisory, and individual level, it allows for a deeper and more meaningful conversation and, in turn, continued growth. Bolton (2010) defines reflective practice as opportunities to question self through interrogating attitudes, thought processes, values, habits, and relationships with others. Reflection is more than just writing down or discussing thoughts and feelings, but it also involves a questioning of these thoughts and feelings. Francis (2018) writes, "reflective practice cultivates more ways of knowing that draw from a deeper place: your intuition, imagination, and innermost being." Through reflection, you examine your assumptions and biases and contemplate "failures" to apply those insights in the future. Reflective practice is more than taking time to think about process, learnings, or data. When we reflect on our true self, trust, and community, "we can gain insight on how our inner lives are informed by our outer circumstances and vice versa" (p. 26). This statement mimics the stages of self-authorship and allows for the development of true self or a strong sense of self. Often in student affairs, reflection is prioritized for students, but this practice is dismissed at a professional level but is necessary for identity-conscious supervision.

Further, developing the practice of reflection also is a component of mindfulness. This practice allows a response from a place of being grounded as opposed to stress or anxiety. Responding intentionally is an indicator of a strong sense of self.

Schön (1983) offers two types of reflection: reflection-in-action and reflection-on-action. Often time's professionals wait until after an action is complete to reflect. This creates a too little, too late effect. Reflection-in-action builds an opportunity to pause and edit if needed. Reflection-on-action requires a sustained commitment to reflect. The completion of an event allows for continued reflection as opposed to a quick course correction reflection. Reflecting on action can be done through journaling, communities of practice, or an internal contemplation. Reflection-on-action allows for consideration of impact, intention, and learning (1983). Consideration of impact, intention, and learning can lead to self-growth and a continued conversation through a supervisory relationship. Bolton (2010) suggests making a reflection activity part of regular supervisory meetings so it does not become an afterthought. Also, by creating an ongoing loop of a reflective student affairs practice, it allows for a continual unpacking of values and beliefs that individuals hold that may be impacting the supervisory relationship and the larger department.

CONCLUSION

Change does not happen solely through compliance. The culture must shift to create sustained change. To move the needle around inclusion and equity, a group of supervisors working in a community through reflection to develop a strong sense of self, self-authorship, self-awareness, and cultural humility can lead to dismantling systems of oppression. Supervisors can hold their privileged identities and not spiral in shame, guilt, or rage, pay attention to their bodily cues, and remain present because they have done their healing work. Leverage that healing and work to advocate for equity for individuals in the margins. When supervisors have not done their self-work the shame, guilt, and anxiety silences voices and allows duplication of oppressive systems and practices. Brown (2018) writes, "Integrity is choosing courage over comfort; it is choosing what's right over what's fun, fast, and easy; and it's practicing your values, not just professing them." (p. 220). Creating a strong sense of self means becoming uncomfortable and curious about the messages we have received and how that impacts the way we supervise as well as taking risks to practice our values knowing that it will be imperfect the first few times. This risk, discomfort, and practice all lead to a method of identity-conscious supervision.

Case Study
Meghan Reyonne Griggs

Magnolia University (MU) is a private, highly selective, predominately white, mid-sized research university. The students of MU represent 49 U.S. states and over 55 countries. Fifty-nine percent of the student body identify as men, 38% identify as women, and 3% gender nonconforming and 28% Students of Color. Located in the northeastern region of the United States in Speakertown, Pennsylvania, a bustling metropolis, Magnolia is known for producing the most female Ph.D.'s.

Sampson, the Vice President of Student Life, identifies as a white, upper-class, 58-year-old, heterosexual, cisgender, Christian, able-bodied male. Sampson has spent his entire career at Magnolia. As the VP, Sampson prides himself on being a supervisor who works to create an inclusive and equitable environment for the campus community. As a supervisor he considers the added labor his employees take on to assist students of marginalized populations for promotion and raises opportunities during annual performance reviews to create dialogue for this additional labor. Sampson has cultivated relationships with organizations specializing in promoting diversity. Most recently, he lauched an annual climate survey. The intention of the survey was to center the voices of students. This data was also analyzed through the demographic information provided. Data allows the Division of Student Life to measure student experiences and make data-driven decisions. Sampson has a passion for ensuring that the Division of Student Life meets its programming goals, particularly for students of the LGBTQAI+ community. He also openly advocates and supports LGBTQAI+ initiatives outside of work through attending PRIDE events and making supportive posts via social media, as his daughter identifies as queer. Sampson feels a personal call to LGBTQAI+ equity due to this important relationship.

In an all staff meeting, the Dean of Student Success, Kris, and the Director of Diversity and Inclusion, Yvette, presented findings from the most recent campus climate survey. Yvette identifies as Black, 29-year-old, upper-middleclass, cisgender, nonconformist, bisexual, able-bodied, female. Chris identifies as a 42-year-old, Latino, middle-class, cisgender, gay, Christian, able-bodied, male. Through the presentation, Sampson is made aware of the alarming numbers of LatinX and Black cisgender women experience an uncivil campus environment. Additionally, the graduation rate of these groups has declined by 5% over the past two years. Both Yvette and Kris explain their concern for these specific groups of students and how recently there has been a decline of racial minority students participation in university social events as well as overall applications for admission. This information prompts Sampson to consider the decisions that he has made toward creating a more inclusive student life experience and if he, indeed, was making those decisions through a lens that centered marginalized identities. He is also reflecting upon the data of the decline in women graduates. This decline is a major concern for the university.

Sampson is also concerned about the decline of minority student participation in campus events. All of this impacts retention of current women of color to not transfer out.

After the meeting, Sampson asks Dena, the Assistant Vice President of Student Life, to prepare a benchmarking report on all programming progress to date. Dena is a 39-year-old, white, upper-middle class, able-bodied, gender-queer person. Dena is the only member of the leadership team and the individual Sampson relies on to be his thought partner. After reviewing the report, Sampson realizes that each portfolio has met their goals based on the strategic plan. However, he also notes that the majority of this plan was skewed toward programming for international students, white women, and the LGBTQAI+ community. This plan reflects the areas he feels passion and competence. This left other marginalized student groups (students of color, undocumented, etc.) unengaged and underserved in programming. Additionally, Sampson notices a salient request expressed in these reports from his mid-level administrators for opportunities to share their ideas and start new initiatives, so programming is more inclusive. Further, the comments of marginalized staff members spell out how though they are recognized for going above and beyond, there is still a need to be heard by upper-level leadership to prevent burnout. Sampson is now positioned to consider his own biases and how they show up in his role as the VP of Student Life. Sampson considers how to move forward to create a better environment for racial minority students and staff.

KEY QUESTIONS

1. What stage is Sampson in self-authorship and what could help him progress to the next stage?
2. How has Sampson demonstrated self-awarenss and cultural humility?
3. What are some next steps Sampson can take to address the inequities on the campus and how can he engage others to help him accomplish these steps?

REFERENCES

Bhat, C. S., & Davis, T. E. (2007). Counseling supervisors' assessment of race, racial identity, and working alliance in supervisory dyads. *Journal of Multicultural Counseling and Development, 35*(2), 80–91.

Bolton, G. E. J. (2010). *Reflective practice: Writing and professional development* (3rd ed.). Thousand Oaks, CA: Sage Publications.

Brown, B. (2018). *Dare to lead: Brave work. Tough conversations. Whole hearts.* New York, NY: Random House.

Covarrubias, A. (2017). *Exploring the racial and gender identity formation of men of color in student leadership roles who have white women supervisors and advisors in higher education* (Unpublished doctoral dissertation), University of San Francisco, San Francisco, CA.

Davis, D. E., Hook, J. N., Worthington Jr, E. L., Van Tongeren, D. R., Gartner, A. L., Jennings, D. J., & Emmons, R. A. (2011). Relational humility: Conceptualizing and measuring humility as a personality judgment. *Journal of Personality Assessment, 93*(3), 225–234.

Davis, D. E., Worthington Jr., E. L., & Hook, J. N. (2010). Humility: Review of measurement strategies and conceptualization as personality judgment. *The Journal of Positive Psychology, 5*(4), 243–252.

Francis, S. L. (2018). Cultivating a campus culture of courage. *About Campus, 23*(3), 23–30.

Freire, P. (2018). *Pedagogy of the oppressed.* New York, NY: Bloomsbury Publishing.

Hook, J. N., Davis, D. E., Owen, J., Worthington Jr., E. L., & Utsey, S. O. (2013). Cultural humility: Measuring openness to culturally diverse clients. *Journal of Counseling Psychology, 60*(3), 353.

Inman, A. G. (2006). Supervisor multicultural competence and its relation to supervisory process and outcome. *Journal of Marital and Family Therapy, 32*(1), 73–85.

Kegan, R. (1994). *In over our heads: The mental demands of modern life.* Cambridge, MA: Harvard University Press.

Ladany, N., Brittan-Powell, C. S., & Pannu, R. K. (1997). The influence of supervisory racial identity interaction and racial matching on the supervisory working alliance and supervisee multicultural competence. *Counselor Education and Supervision, 36*(4), 284–304.

Lopez, A. S. (2008). Making and breaking habits: Teaching (and learning) cultural context, self-awareness, and intercultural communication through case supervision in a client-service legal clinic. *Washington University Journal of Law & Political Science, 28,* 37–69.

Lorde, A. (2012). *Sister outsider: Essays and speeches.* Crossing Press.

Luthans, F., & Avolio, B. J. (2003). Authentic leadership development. In K. S. Cameron, J. E. Dutton, & R. E. Quinn (Eds.), *Positive organizational scholarship* (pp. 241–258). San Francisco, CA: Berrett-Koehler.

Magolda, M. B. B. (2008). Three elements of self-authorship. *Journal of College Student Development, 49*(4), 269–284.

Magolda, M. B. B., & King, P. M. (2004). *Learning partnerships: Theory and models of practice to educate for self-authorship.* Sterling, VA: Stylus Publishing.

martinez, b., & Ardoin, S. (2019). *Straddling class in the academy: 26 stories of students, administrators, and faculty from poor and working-class backgrounds and their compelling lessons for higher education policy and practice.* Sterling, VA: Stylus Publishing.

Obear, K. (2007). Navigating triggering events: Critical skills for facilitating difficult dialogues. *Generational Diversity, 15*(30), 23–29.

Rogoff, B. (2014). Learning by observing and pitching in to family and community en-deavors: An orientation. *Human Development, 57*(2–3), 69–81.

Schön, D. (1983). *The reflective practitioner: How professionals think in action.* London: Temple Smith.

Sodowsky, G. R., Kuo-Jackson, P. Y., & Loya, G. J. (1997). Outcome of training in the philosophy of assessment: Multicultural counseling competencies. In D. B. Pope-Davis & H. L. K. Coleman (Eds.), *Multicultural counseling competencies: Assessment, education and training, and supervision* (pp. 3–42). Thousand Oaks, CA: Sage.

Soheilian, S. S., Inman, A. G., Klinger, R. S., Isenberg, D. S., & Kulp, L. E. (2014). Multicultural supervision: Supervisees' reflections on culturally competent supervision. *Counselling Psychology Quarterly, 27*(4), 379–392.

Stewart, D. L. (2012). Promoting moral growth through pluralism and social justice education. *New Directions for Student Services, 139*, 63–71.

Tyler, J. M., & Guth, L. J. (1999). Using media to create experiential learning in multicultural and diversity issues. *Journal of Multicultural Counseling and Development, 27*, 153–165.

Watt, S. K. (2007). Difficult dialogues, privilege and social justice: Uses of the privileged identity exploration (PIE) model in student affairs practice. *College Student Affairs Journal, 26*(2), 114–126.

Chapter Four

Managing Power

In *The Book of Joy* (Lama, Tutu, & Abrams, 2016), the Dalai Lama says "When we meet anyone, first and foremost we must remember that they, too, have the same desire to have a happy day, a happy month, a happy life. And all have the right to achieve it" (p. 203). We apply this sentiment to the workplace and the supervisory relationship. The supervisory relationship has a built-in power dynamic that significantly influences job satisfaction and happiness by creating a sense of value and belonging. When supervision is performed well, it creates opportunities to be seen, known, and understood. Supervisors have more power due to access to information, structured hierarchy, salary level, and evaluative implications. These factors develop an expert and novice dynamic as well as a boss and employee dynamic. In a traditional supervisory structure, the expert is the supervisor, and the learner is the supervisee, similar to the external focus of the Self-Authorship Model discussed in Chapter 3. Coupling inherent power with the systems of oppression and privileged social identities creates an overlay of power that should be identified and discussed. Managing power as an identity-conscious supervisor has to be a cyclical process of addressing power and then dismantling it to make an organizational culture and supervisory relationship satisfying.

Earlier in my career, I (Shruti) was in a mid-level residence life role and transitioned to a new supervisor, James. James exuded privilege in every identity. He would interrupt people and was unwilling to hold a differing opinion. He was an alum of the university, white, upper-middle class, had multiple degrees, and so on. I was disappointed and anxious with the organizational change, as I felt valued by my previous supervisor. Rumors swirled about James's commitment to diversity. He had academic credentials that demonstrated knowledge around social justice but would often defend the dominant structures of the university instead of embracing the harm these systems caused. People gossiped about James's privilege and that he was a micromanager. As I prepared for my first one-on-one with him, I created a list of my needs and expectations and also thought about what my other new supervisors have asked for in the past such as budget, priorities, and student issues. But when we sat down for the meeting, he asked me something that I did not expect. He stated, "Shruti, I've heard this department is hard on People of Color, and you have done a lot of the work toward changing this culture. Can you help me understand why we lose People of Color so often?" Because I had done some of my self-work, and I prepared well for this first meeting, I felt courageous and was able to share honestly about my experiences and perceptions. James listened empathically and humbly, and I felt like he valued my perspective and viewed me as an equal. This initial dialogue interrupted my assumptions of how James would use his power, and it served as the foundation for examining power and privilege in the department.

Although addressing the power dynamic both within relationships and as individuals is vital, it is often easier said than done. Because of how it is structured, a supervisory relationship does not necessarily allow for equal footing as one person is evaluating the other. Higher salary levels, access to knowledge, an elevated title, and organizational structures give power to supervisors. Naming and identifying power differential in the relationship is critical, as is developing the commitment between all parties to offset it. The undoing of power requires vulnerability of the supervisor and supervisee, consistent dialogue, and naming (explained further in Chapter 9). It also requires the supervisor to lead the way. When supervisors consistently role model these traits in practice and self-work, it shifts the organizational culture toward change and identity-consciousness. This chapter identifies theories and strategies to addressing power as a supervisor through an identity-conscious lens, discussing power as a supervisory dyad, and the benefits of distinguishing these dynamics.

DEFINING POWER

Power has a surplus of definitions including a degree of influence in a relational context, passing down of information as opposed to mutuality, and a system of hierarchy (Nelson & Holloway, 1990; Markham & Chiu, 2011). Power in a supervisory relationship has additional dimensions. There are implications in a supervisory relationship that a supervisor knows more and supervisees know less (Nelson & Holloway, 1990). The expert and novice dynamic comes from a power structure in place as well as a structure of evaluation and top-down communication. For generations, supervision practices allow for assessment, evaluation, observation, and measurement (Marsten & Howard, 2006) of supervisees by supervisors. This hierarchy and the tools used to reinforce that hierarchy build a power dynamic of an observer and an observed.

The observer and observed structure mimic the imperial gaze of privileged identities consuming as well as imposing a set of values that reflects the dominant power structures and norms. For example, talking in large group settings is valued, which is a dominant Western value. The transference of what is right and valuable in the broader culture automatically gets replicated in organizations and teams. Markham and Chiu (2011) suggest a supervisee's success stems from assimilating to both social rules and professional standards. The default of power, social norms, and professional standards privilege the dominant identity groups.

In the example of working with James, my preparation for our one-on-one included preparing expected items. Through this preparation, I disregarded the anxiety that our team and I felt about the changes to keep business as usual. Slowing down and being curious about the anxiety would have allowed for reflection, which would have created space for the exploration of expectations of the supervisor and how to build a relationship as opposed to assuming what "prepared" meant based on prior understandings or cultural norms. Choosing "business as usual" as the regular operation instead of critical reflection, growth, and evolution of department practice reflects a patriarchal and colonial view on emotions in the workplace. No one told me I needed to prepare budgets and priorities, but that was my first instinct. My supervisor had a different agenda. If James had sent me an e-mail saying, please don't prepare anything, I want to have an honest dialogue about the state of the department, my preparation and anxiety would have decreased. The norms of the workplace instilled in me came to life, and I conspired with them by not interrogating my own feelings and the anxiety of the department. James could have role modeled leading change by creating a clear path and bringing in his direct reports early on as a group to distinguish priorities. Understanding and disrupting these inherent power structures is critical in identity-conscious supervision.

RELATIONSHIPS AND POWER

Relationships provide opportunity for conversation around power and expectations. Disrupting dominant norms in organizations and relationships happens in the context of supervisory relationships. Cook, McKibben, and Wind (2018) found that supervisors excelled at identifying interventions, setting goals, and providing feedback. These all are observer traits and allows supervisors to be content experts, not relationship experts. Supervisors get the mission and purpose moved forward through activity and programming. This pushing of priorities, often leveraged through the use of supervisory power, comes at a cost to the retention and job satisfaction of caring for people who are also incredibly competent and reliable professionals. Retention and job satisfaction often decreases when the supervisor holds dominance, and the supervisee is from a minoritized background (Nilsson & Duan, 2007). Goal setting early on in a supervisory relationship can start the process of owning and undoing power.

Brown (2018) empowers us to think about three types of power: power with, power to, and power within. *Power with* is the notion of finding common ground to build solidarity. It makes space for inclusion and multiple perspectives (Brown, 2018). For example, community organizers often work across agencies to create progress toward shifting policies and protocols. *Power to* underscores the idea that the distribution of power elevates minoritized individuals (Brown, 2018). It supports the idea that every individual can make an impact, and collaboration brings a sustained and powerful effect. Identity-conscious supervision requires sharing power with a supervisee to create mutual trust and respect. Often for individuals with privileged identities, it means refusing the power that comes with the privilege. Finally, *power within* is defined by "an ability to recognize differences and respect others, grounded in a strong foundation of self-worth and self-knowledge" (Brown, 2018, p. 97). Power within embraces the idea behind self-authorship: despite what society thinks, an individual makes a decision based on their values and ethics. In other words, you cannot give what you don't have. To mitigate or manage the impact, power has to be shared in our daily practice of infusing identity-focused conversations into systems and methods.

COMMUNICATION AND POWER

Communication patterns are often a telltale sign of how the supervisor, and more importantly, the supervisee, relates to and experiences power. Nelson and Holloway (1990) describe several communication patterns on a scale of high power to low power and describe behavior that defines each level of power. As Figure 4.1 indicates, specific behaviors are related to high power, low power, and high involvement. One individual (supervisor) demonstrating high power communication and another individual (supervisee) exhibiting low power communication indicates a traditional, hierarchical supervisor. Traditional supervisory relationships perpetuate the high power (supervisor) and low power (supervisee) norm. When this conventional model intersects with identity, it reflects traditional messaging around who belongs in power positions and who does not. For example, this traditional messaging would have us believe that only men become presidents and

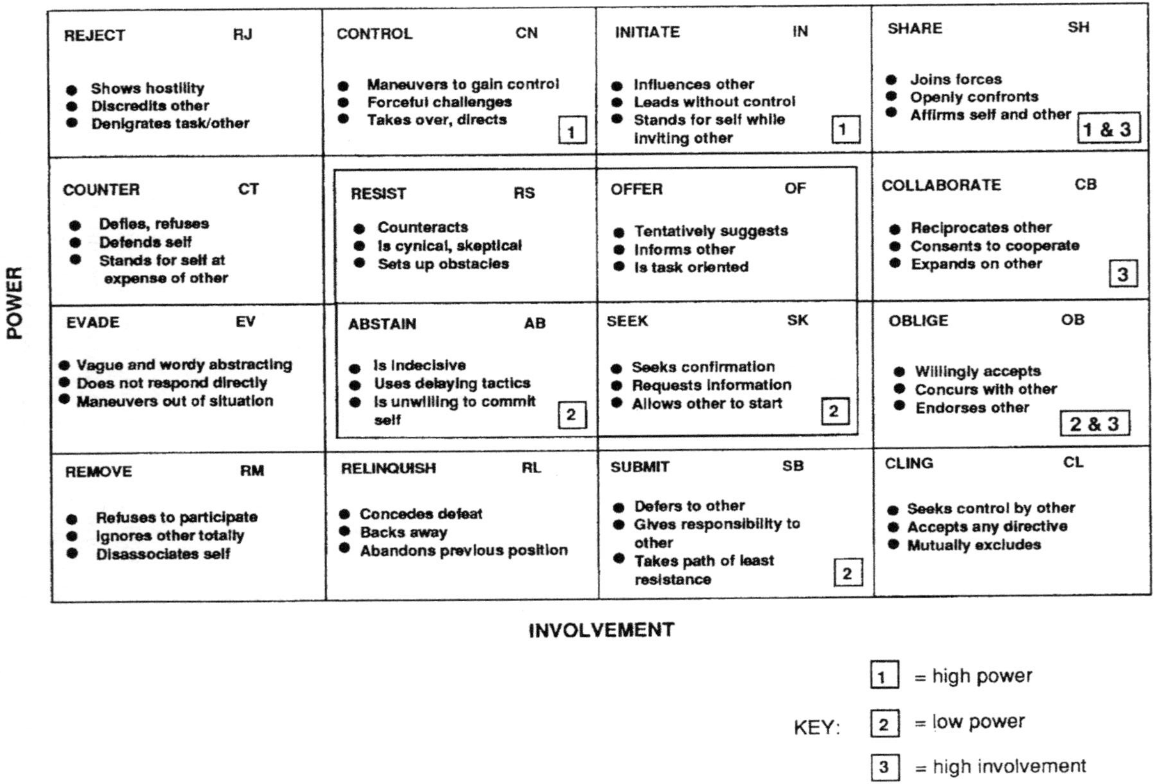

REJECT RJ	CONTROL CN [1]	INITIATE IN [1]	SHARE SH [1 & 3]
• Shows hostility • Discredits other • Denigrates task/other	• Maneuvers to gain control • Forceful challenges • Takes over, directs	• Influences other • Leads without control • Stands for self while inviting other	• Joins forces • Openly confronts • Affirms self and other
COUNTER CT	RESIST RS [2]	OFFER OF	COLLABORATE CB [3]
• Defies, refuses • Defends self • Stands for self at expense of other	• Counteracts • Is cynical, skeptical • Sets up obstacles	• Tentatively suggests • Informs other • Is task oriented	• Reciprocates other • Consents to cooperate • Expands on other
EVADE EV	ABSTAIN AB [2]	SEEK SK [2]	OBLIGE OB [2 & 3]
• Vague and wordy abstracting • Does not respond directly • Maneuvers out of situation	• Is indecisive • Uses delaying tactics • Is unwilling to commit self	• Seeks confirmation • Requests information • Allows other to start	• Willingly accepts • Concurs with other • Endorses other
REMOVE RM	RELINQUISH RL	SUBMIT SB [2]	CLING CL
• Refuses to participate • Ignores other totally • Disassociates self	• Concedes defeat • Backs away • Abandons previous position	• Defers to other • Gives responsibility to other • Takes path of least resistance	• Seeks control by other • Accepts any directive • Mutually excludes

POWER

INVOLVEMENT

KEY:
[1] = high power
[2] = low power
[3] = high involvement

Figure 4.1 Power and Communication Styles

CEOs or that dress codes only allow for two options along a gender binary in the "professional workplace." Communication of high and low power includes behaviors such as the high power individual controlling, initiating, and sharing (Nelson & Holloway, 1990). These behaviors are not harmful at the surface level, but when intersecting with high power communication, it reinforces dominant norms and dynamics of oppression. High power communication mimics individualistic and patriarchal norms in the United States.

The low power behavior in a high power-low power dyad can look like abstaining, seeking, submitting, or obliging (Nelson & Holloway, 1990). In detail, these behaviors include delaying tactics, needing constant affirmation, following the path of least resistance for results, and sacrificing self. For example, I (Shruti) had a staff member who would need to check every conduct decision with me even after being in his role for two years. He would always apply the same sanction to the same behavior and would need affirmation. We talked through this behavior, and I learned that he had a previous supervisor who did not trust him and often overturned each decision he made. This dynamic showed up in our relationship, and I set up more time in our regular meetings to talk through conduct cases until he believed in his decision making and to shift the power dynamics in our relationship. Behaviors of low power are not indicators of health or mutuality.

How a supervisor utilizes inherent power in a relationship can be positive or negative. Neutralization of power is integral for identity-conscious supervision. Subdued power is not synonymous with apathy or silence. When asked, supervisees stated they valued a supervisor's authority when power was used for the facilitation of a discussion of power, sharing of ideas, empowerment, and defining expectations (Murphy & Wright, 2005). Power is a choice; it is conferred based on a title, but it depends on the individual on how to utilize it effectively and positively. Power can be used to transform a relationship and transform organizational culture. For a supervisor to use their energy to empower others, create mutuality, or build healthy relationships creates a significant impact, and it diminishes power as a tool of coercion and threat and reframes it as healing and partnership. Power used in this way transforms particular alliances, but it also has a profound influence on workplace culture and productivity.

When power is used negatively, it also has a profound impact. Supervisees were also asked about the harmful use of a supervisor's power and named these behaviors: preferential treatment, imposing of style, gossip, and prioritization of the supervisor's agenda (Murphy & Wright, 2005). These behaviors dismantle trust and utilize power for selfish gain. It also indicates a scarcity mentality as opposed to functioning from abundance,

67

an indicator of U.S. capitalism, patriarchy, and dominant social norms. Self-awareness in supervisory behavior is needed for identity-conscious supervision and power management. In the example, at the start of the chapter, James came into the first one-on-one with self-awareness and created a space where I felt empowered. His positive and productive use of power allowed for a partnership through listening instead of getting defensive. That built safety in our supervisor-supervisee relationship. This first impression built the foundation of the relationship and allowed us to talk across identity differently. The supervisors' communication pattern in the study indicated mutuality, understanding, and shared power as opposed to a power structure that mimicked dominant and subordinated norms.

In unhealthy and ineffective workplaces, individuals in the margins often diminish their power and influence because of unsafe conditions and trauma. The traditional power dynamics perpetuate built-in dominant norms around communication, evaluation, and mattering which sends a message that minoritized identities do not belong. Proctor and Rogers (2013) discuss how racial identities impact the comfort level of communication, which influences employees' job satisfaction. When trauma has occurred in minoritized identities, this harm often replicates in supervisory relationships. A supervisee shrinking their power and influence to match the needs of a supervisor does not support identity-conscious supervision dynamics. It is important to name these harmful behaviors as they do occur in supervision practices. Calling out these dynamics often falls to the supervisee, which causes harm and perpetuates challenging power dynamics. It mimics the norms of supervisors having high power and supervisees having low power. Thinking back to James, if in our first one-on-one he said, "I heard this department is hard on People of Color and our work is not diversity and inclusion, but residential life," the relationship would have started with identity-neutral supervision. The communication pattern would have been one of low power and high power as he dictated the priorities, and there would be little sharing or visioning.

The optimal power dynamic in identity-conscious supervision practice is where both the supervisor and supervisee have high power communication styles. Relationships built from high power communication style exhibits sharing behavior, which allows for coalition building, an empowered self, an empowering relationship, and behavior that affirms each other (Nelson & Holloway, 1990). This style also encourages healthy behavior in the workplace and enhances satisfaction. Another behavior exhibited in this style is a collaboration that shows up through reciprocation, a desire and willingness to cooperate, and obliging each other. In this context, oblige means enthusiasm to endorse and support (Nelson & Holloway, 1990). This relationship pattern creates mattering and mutuality and diminishes power dynamics that reflect dominant cultural norms.

James demonstrated this pattern initially, and in turn, I (Shruti) felt seen, valued, and respected for my work, my extra contributions, and my professional competency.

BRINGING LIGHT TO POWER

Power is often immeasurable and unidentifiable. Power and privilege go hand in hand, and both often surface in a supervisory relationship but go unnamed. Power and privilege lead to discontentment and disenfranchisement for marginalized supervisees. As a child of immigrants, my (Shruti) parents were very intentional about building an Indian community that created belonging and reflected their values. If James had been an Indian man, perhaps my initial response would have been different due to my socialization from my family and my Indian culture. This socialized messaging taught me to trust people that share cultural identities, and view everyone else as an outsider. This messaging also creates an initial level of trust not shared across all relationships. Socialization of trust impacts supervisory relationships. It is essential to understand what behavior is about the specific supervisory relationship and what is about the group identities individuals hold.

Identity-conscious supervision allows for discussion of this invisible power. Researchers have found that making the hidden power dynamic visible leads to open and honest communication (Dressel, Consoli, Kim, & Atkinson, 2007; Gloria, Hird, & Tao, 2008; Hays & Chang, 2003). Naming these dynamics, or creating space for them to be named, falls to the supervisor and creates opportunities to demonstrate courage. For example, vulnerability and shame come up when I (Shruti) supervise someone who holds a minoritized identity where I carry privilege. As a supervisor, I need to name it and continue to learn and own my mistakes. If an individual feels marginalized because of how we behave, it affects both the supervisor's and supervisee's self-value and undermines the mission and department. Often our privileged identities go unexamined (Nilsson & Duan, 2007). Prioritizing the acknowledgment and deconstruction on our privilege creates space and mutuality for marginalized identities. Naming power creates an opportunity to directly address the dynamic as opposed to dancing around it. This will allow for effective dismantling.

Naming Power

Another critical step in managing power is naming power. Cook et al. (2018) found that identifying power can impact a supervisory relationship in both tangible and intangible ways. If the power goes unnamed, it

69

causes harm; conversely, highlighting power empowers others to leverage power in productive ways. For example, I (Shruti) was working with a staff member who was struggling with depression and anxiety, and they were worried people would not understand why they were absent or could not take on additional requests. I offered as a supervisor with influence and ability privilege to talk to the team with them. This allowed me to name my power and not cause them to do additional labor by feeling like they had to share with the team alone. Ellis et al. (2014) indicated that failure to adequately address power dynamics in supervisory relationships could result in inefficiencies or ethical dilemmas. Discussing power one time is not enough; consistent dialogue must occur. A mutual decision to engage in dialogue about power supports the effectiveness of the conversation. Merely naming the power in a supervisory relationship is a step; in identity-conscious-supervision, one must also address the identity dynamics of dominance. Otherwise, the persistence of the dynamics of dominance within a relationship results in silencing and further marginalization. Gatmon et al. (2001) note that disregarding cultural variables such as race, ethnicity, ability, gender, and sexuality can increase conflict between the supervisor and supervisee. As discussed in Chapter 8, prolonged conflict in a supervisory relationship due to disregarding cultural identities creates a sense of invisibility and erasure. It also results in a perpetuation of dominance and privilege. Identity-neutral supervision practices further perpetuate dominance as well. Tension also occurs because the decisions and meaning-making of a supervisee often directly tie to their identities. For example, not allowing a case-by-case decision neutralizes the impact of identities. When a supervisor does not understand how an individual relates to their identities and makes sense of the world, they cannot understand the individual. Naming power as part of an identity-conscious supervision practice allows for individuals to be known in their whole self, provides a foundation for respect and empowerment, and helps contain conflict. It is a continued and mutual process.

However, naming the power is not enough. Proctor and Rogers (2013) found that within supervisory relationships, particularly across white supervisor and supervisee of color relationships, supervisees were often more knowledgeable about issues of diversity than their supervisors. In the previous example, James could have come into the office owning his privilege but behaving in ways that perpetuated problematic norms. This naming, but not owning of identity creates a conflict of individual and group levels. For example, I (Shruti) can name my identity as a middle class person but do not hold the harm I cause to working-class individuals due to perpetuation of unexamined socialization. The inherent power in supervisory relationships presents an opportunity to create shared space and mitigate power by learning from each other, as I can own my class identity; it allows a supervisee also to own their identity, which enhances the conversation. Each individual is an expert in their experiences, and these stories create learning to challenge systems of oppression. If we do not create this space to learn, we negate voice and devalue others through our unwillingness to learn and listen. We want to add an important note here: often, people with marginalized identities are looked to be experts on diversity. Just because a supervisee or supervisor holds a marginalized identity does not mean they speak for an entire group. No one is an expert of the whole.

Further, it is also essential that a supervisor demonstrates their growth through their continued self-work. Self-work can happen by reading, writing, traveling, participating in identity dialogue groups, or researching identities not held to understand the lived experiences better. It is essential that we understand who we are in relationship to our identities, understand others concerning their identities, and understand how the system operates. But identity-conscious practice does not happen in a vacuum. It requires mutuality. Supervisees must be willing to engage with a supervisor and provide experience, perspective, and education when necessary, and vice versa. When a supervisor creates opportunities for supervisees to become content experts, it leads to empowerment.

When there is no mutuality, and a supervisee does not share openly, it is because they believe their voice will go unheard (Sullivan & Conoley, 2002) because of lack of trust in the other person or a pattern of dismissiveness from another. This devaluing results in low power, high power communication pattern mentioned previously. The model also results in job dissatisfaction and high turnover. The impact of dissatisfaction is the loss of human capital, institution time, money, and resources due to low-performance and/or an eventual rehiring to fill the vacant position.

The mitigation of power through listening and humility is critical. Hernandez and Rankin (2008) found that supervisees of color feel disempowered when their contributions are minimized. When this occurs, programs, services, and processes continue to remain culturally irrelevant due to power and a reflection of dominant societal norms. Hernandez and Rankin (2008) also found that when white supervisors encouraged supervisees of color to discuss racial, ethnic, and cultural issues, they built a blueprint for empowerment. Empowerment involves making the invisible visible by acknowledging and developing supervisee's voices and allowing content expertise. These behaviors create mattering if the supervisee wants to serve in this manner. However, not all individuals in the margins wish to perform this extra labor. A trusted supervisory relationship allows for this

71

discussion and behaviors indicating mattering, and a trusted relationship leads to identity-conscious supervision.

NEUTRALIZING POWER IN RELATIONSHIPS

To build an identity-conscious supervision practice we must neutralize power. Supervisors can neutralize power by creating mutual and trusting relationships (Nelson & Holloway, 1990). A straightforward way to do this is by going to the supervisees' office every other one-on-one. Another way to build equitable structure is empowering the supervisee to take the lead in setting the agenda and using the majority of time in the one-on-one. The supervisor can then focus on listening as opposed to starting with our agenda and task list. As discussed previously in the chapter when a supervisor prioritizes their plan, it creates a harmful use of power. Think about opportunities to invite the supervisee's voice in the conversation. While some people are most comfortable with the supervisor taking the lead (low power style), this practice will help develop capacity in team members. Priorities typically come down the hierarchy pipeline, but it is vital to allow for priorities to come up from those we supervise as well. It increases buy-in at every level for the decision to be made, or clarity when a decision is nonnegotiable.

This communication creates transparency and trust. For example, in a one-on-one or weekly report, we can ask the supervisee what they are proud of this week and how their identities influence what caused that pride. It builds confidence and allows positive rapport building as opposed to the tasks of student issues and programming details. Many researchers have indicated that supervisors must be the first to initiate dialogues around diversity and inclusion (Tohidian & Quek, 2017; Duan & Roehlke, 2001; Lopez, 2008). These small things will catalyze an initial blueprint of a trusting relationship. Markham and Chiu (2011) suggest the idea of reflection in teams as a part of the meeting schedule. A lunch or space to reflect on what is going well and identifying challenges helps gain feedback and also for building trusting engagement within the team. This space should not just be a venting session but provide prompts for reflection. These questions could revolve around identity as long as individuals do not feel taxed due to tokenization. Thoughtful dialogue builds a practice of honest conversation, which requires relational safety.

Supervisory Alliance

Relational safety is a critical piece of power management. Hernandez and Rankin (2008) described relational welfare as "the co-construction of a dialogical context in which students and supervisors can raise questions, challenge points of view, ponder issues, confront opinions, articulate ideas, and express concerns" (p. 255). The intentionality of co-construction requires work and thoughtfulness around how meetings are structured. Think back to the style of high power communication: it takes cooperation and sponsorship of one another. Safety does not mean the absence of being uncomfortable. Hernandez and Rankin (2008) clarify that relational security does not equivocate to supervisors offering supervisees blanket validation and emotional support. Instead, supervisors support supervisees to develop "critical thinking in a caring environment" (Hernandez & Rankin, 2008, p. 255). Identity-conscious supervision and mitigating power require a constant commitment to living in the ambiguity of "both-and." Adapting from the counseling world supervisors and supervisees must have a supervisory working alliance (Proctor & Rogers, 2013). This is another way to say a robust supervisory relationship or, in the world of diversity and inclusion, allyship. A robust supervisory alliance is demonstrated by mutual trust, liking, and an emotional bond between the supervisor and supervisee (Bordin, 1983). When the time spent together feels valuable, and honoring it creates a sense of belonging and mutuality. This alliance is formed by shared expectations and goals as well as a mutual understanding of the project and tasks ahead (Bordin, 1983). In identity-conscious supervision, both parties should share expectations and goals on a group and individual level. One-way communication creates a continued, problematic power dynamic. Finally, a robust supervisory alliance facilitates a vulnerable and authentic environment for supervisees to talk with their supervisors, and in turn, supervisees demonstrate more professional growth (Mehr, Ladany, & Caskie, 2010). A willingness to disclose learning edges means an opportunity to retain a staff member and troubleshoot problems proactively. Increased professional growth allows for greater responsibility and peer leadership. Both of these are benefits of identity-conscious supervision.

Consistency

Managing power is not a one-time event. In my (Shruti) example with James, if he had only discussed diversity and inclusion that one time, the relationship would have been dramatically different. The first one-on-one created an opportunity for vulnerability, trust-building, and alliance versus a one-on-one that was solely based on transaction and reiterated that I was just another cog in the wheel. The continued back and forth, and his initiation, made our relationship one that permitted identity-conscious supervision. Moderating power means a consistent expression of the supervisor and supervisee to take risks involved in creating honest and open communication.

This consistency also allows for individuals in the margins to create a different narrative of the dominant culture. Supervisees with marginalized identities often experience silencing and invalidation of their voices. This silencing often creates a need for more depth regarding relational safety, and it may take more time to develop this safety (Proctor & Rogers, 2013). This is why the adage of treating everyone the same does not always work as messaging around identities is entangled with messaging around professionalism. It is also vital for supervisors to bring up issues of diversity and inclusion early and often. Duan and Roehlke (2001) researched supervisors and supervisees, and they found that 93% of supervisors believed they discussed diversity and inclusion regularly and frequently, but when researchers asked their supervisees only 50% of supervisees agreed that diversity and inclusion were routinely addressed. This discrepancy leads to frustration and mistrust. Supervisors feel as if they are prioritizing and valuing diversity and inclusion, while supervisees feel as if the surface is barely scratched. Creating a consistent, regular, and semi-structured dialogue is very important in managing power.

These consistent conversations should not just be about the individual or the supervisor and supervisee relationship but also about the broader landscape. It is essential to use an equity and inclusion lens and dialogue in the group and individual meetings to discuss policy, protocol, programs, student issues, supervision, and team dynamics. Building this dialogue into everyday conversation creates a shared language, which manages power. Further, it elevates some tokenism if everyone is conversing and prioritizing. However, in these conversations, the supervisors and leaders of the organization must make space for role modeling how to manage and navigate microaggressions and other symptoms of prejudice and lack of understanding. Sue, Lin, Torino, Capodilupo, and Rivera (2009) define microaggressions as "brief and commonplace daily verbal, behavioral, and environmental indignities, whether intentional or unintentional, that communicate hostile, derogatory, or negative slights and insults to the target person or group" (p. 273). A microaggression is the small and regular verbal and nonverbal cues devaluing or discriminating an individual based on social identity. The intent is typically not to harm, and harm happens when individuals are in a relationship with one another.

A large piece of managing power means ownership of mistakes. When a supervisor takes responsibility for errors and is accountable to learning and behaving better in the future, it role models vulnerability and humility for the broader team, it allows the supervisee to continue to take risks and build trust, and it increases the strength of the relationship. This empowers the supervisee, which leads to shared power. It is essential when admitting a mistake to balance accountability and shame. We need to be cautious of asking the supervisee to take care of us or appease us. We need to admit the error, have a conversation, and trust the relationship to move forward. There is power in naming something, dialoguing, and continuing to believe and evolve the relationship.

PRACTICAL STEPS

Earlier in the chapter, this notion of naming the power dynamic was addressed. How we do this in practice can be challenging. Naming dynamics is not just about calling the power but authentically and honestly naming expectations, challenges, hopes, and other pieces to practice identity-conscious supervision. First, name our role. Often we hear professionals talk about wanting a supervisor also to be a mentor. We also hear supervisors wishing they were also mentors to the supervisee in addition to their formal relationship. Combining both roles is usually not possible and should not be a goal for everyone. The assumption that it is (or should be) can lead to mismanaged expectations and conflict.

Markham and Chiu (2011) address this dynamic by challenging supervisors and supervisees to name their roles and clarify expectations. A mentor is different from a supervisor, and that is different from a colleague. The power in each one of those relationships varies by the role and the context. We cannot manage power if we do not have an understanding of the inherent power due to expectations and roles. We need to name the expectations. As a supervisor, it is vital to be clear about our position because not all supervisees can effectively manage a supervisor shifting hats, and it creates role confusion. It is also essential that a supervisor navigate power by setting clear and healthy boundaries. As discussed in Chapters 1 and 2, we need to discuss this early on and revisit it regularly.

Another vital component is identifying behaviors without adding our judgments, assumptions, or stories. For example, "I notice you do not often speak in staff meetings, can you help me understand why that is?" identifies the behavior and asks a question to understand the intentions behind it. This approach is a much different statement than "I notice you do not often speak in staff meetings, is that because you are the only person with X-identity in the room?" The first question allows the centering of the supervisee's voice, and the second question centers the supervisor's story and assumptions which violates trust and eliminates any opportunity for empowerment. When supervisors ponder with their supervisees about how power is entering a space, it allows for power and relationship dynamics to be brought into the discussion rather than remain hidden or taboo (Markham & Chiu, 2011). This modeling creates the opportunity for power to be engaged as a continued dialogue instead of a one-time check-list item.

CONCLUSION

A good strategy for managing power for supervisors is "initiate, invite, instill" (Lopez, 2008, p. 37). We need to initiate the conversation around power and identity. The inherent power dynamic built into a supervisory relationship is layered with privilege and oppression, and it is not an easy conversation to approach. Since the supervisor holds power, we model how to engage it when we make it our responsibility. This process will be imper-fect, but that imperfection allows for trust-building and vulnerability. In the example with James, he started the conversation and was imperfect at times. But that conversation helped me (Shruti) feel seen and valued, and it provided a little breathing space. When we invite our supervisees' voice into the conversation, it allows them to feel known and respected. Next, we need to ask our team members how their identities may impact and influence their supervisory relationship or their role on a team. Then we need to listen, practice humility, understand when it is our responsibility to learn more, and practice accountability for initiating that learning and growth. James stated what he had heard and then created an opportunity for my voice and narrative to be centered. He also reiterated that he needed to deepen his understanding of a few identities and organizational patterns and showed that he was actively engaged in doing so.

Finally, we need to instill conversations about power and regularly identify where it is showing up in our staff and committee meetings, one-on-ones, and other contexts. This shows our continued commitment and authenticity in dismantling and mitigating power, and it is central to our identity-conscious supervision practice. The conversation James and Shruti had at their first one-on-one ended up being one of many opportunities to explore and engage how power was present. The work is challenging and worth the investment. Managing our power is central to identity-conscious supervision and required to enhance retention and job satisfaction.

Case Study
By Kathy Sisneros, Ed.D.

You are a new director and have responsibility for a unit over-seeing student leadership opportunities, social justice retreat, and volunteer opportunities. You feel like you are gaining a good sense of your team and their individual styles and have been observing group and individual dynamics. You have had multiple one-on-one meetings with each of the staff and feel that overall good work is being done on behalf of the students. You feel confident in your relationships. Based on these meetings and your observations you notice other dynamics as well:

> Erica is a program coordinator and is a cisgender, het-erosexual, African American woman. She has been in her position for 1.5 years fulltime, previously worked in the center as an undergraduate. She shared that she doesn't feel supported in the office, and the support for students is rooted in whiteness. You have challenged her to think about why she took the position and how she can shift the narrative, but she spends a lot of time mentoring students and doesn't feel as if she has the time to do larger scale work.

Erin is a program coordinator and a cisgender, queer, white woman who has been in her role for four years. She feels like she is expected to do more work than Erica, and that Erica often gets a pass for doing substandard work. She complains to you about her during your weekly meetings.

The other members of the team are Rob and Marisol. Rob is biracial, cisgender, heterosexual man and uses a hearing device. He has been in his role for five months and is the only person hired by you. He serves in the program coord-inator role. Marisol is a graduate assistant. She is gender-nonconforming, Latinx woman, been in the role for one month and was selected prior to your arrival.

During staff meetings, there is a lot of silence when team members ask for input and an avoidance to work together. There is also a limited relationship between Erica and Erin.

Jennifer served the interim director for close to a year and is a cisgender, lesbian, white woman, has been in her position for four years. Jennifer is conflict adverse and confirms that some of these tensions have been in place, and that she finds Erica to be intimidating, so she avoided addressing concerns. Jennifer does not feel it was her place to address a "personal conflict."

You plan a retreat for your team to do some team building and long-term vision setting. During the morning you all focus on more personal sharing of stories. Everyone seemed comfortable sharing and talking about most of their identities as it relates to themselves and supporting students. You think that this has set a solid foundation to dig into work as a team for the afternoon. During lunch you notice that Erica and Erin seem to mostly avoid each other but don't think too much of it.

As you shift into the afternoon session and begin mapping out everyone's roles and responsibilities, Erin gets upset by some of the tasks listed because she is tired of doing programs that are mostly for white students. You share that everything being listed is from the position descriptions that correspond with job duties, and that it is a way for the team to gain a better collective understanding. Erica interjects that Erin's programs are with mostly white students because she is white, and that's all the students she recruits. Simultaneously, Rob is enthusiastic and volunteers to take on some of the tasks that Erin is complaining about. Marisol also jumps at the chance. Erica interjects and tells Rob and Marisol to not let Erin dump work she doesn't want to do onto them. Next thing you know Jennifer is coming to Erin's rescue and saying that she has been assigned a lot of extra work prior to your arrival, and that Erin hasn't had time to recruit Students of Color. As the back and forth between Erica and Erin continues, you observe Marisol visibly begin to shut down and withdraw. Rob again interjects with experience he's had at a previous campus on how maybe the team could recruit more diverse students.

Erica says, "that all sounds great, but will never happen if Erin is the point person." On that note, you realize that you need to take a break, regroup, and figure out next steps.

KEY QUESTIONS

1. What type of communication power dynamics are occurring (low power/high power, high power/ high power, etc.) and how are they impacting team relationships and functioning?
2. How can power be named and neutralized based on identity and hierarchy?
3. As a new supervisor, what ideas do you have to continue to build the team and share power?

REFERENCES

Bordin, E. S. (1983). A working alliance based model of supervision. *The Counseling Psychologist, 11*(1), 35–42.

Brown, B. (2018). *Dare to lead: Brave work. Tough conversations. Whole hearts.* New York, NY: Random House.

Conoley, J. C., & Sullivan, J. R. (2002). Best Practices in the Supervision of Interns. In A. Thomas & J. Grimes (Eds.), *Best practices in school psychology IV* (pp. 131–144). Washington, DC, US: National Association of School Psychologists.

Cook, R. M., McKibben, W. B., & Wind, S. A. (2018). Supervisee perception of power in clinical supervision: The power dynamics in supervision scale. *Training and Education in Professional Psychology, 12*(3), 188–195.

Dressel, J. L., Consoli, A. J., Kim, B. S. K., & Atkinson, D. R. (2007). Successful and unsuccessful multicultural supervisory behaviors: A Delphi poll. *Journal of Multicultural Counseling and Development, 35*, 51–64. doi:10.1002/j.2161-1912.2007.tb00049.x

Duan, C., & Roehlke, H. (2001). A descriptive "snapshot" of cross-racial supervision in university counseling center internships. *Journal of Multicultural Counseling and Development, 29*(2), 131–146.

Ellis, M. V., Berger, L., Hanus, A. E., Ayala, E. E., Swords, B. A., & Siembor, M. (2014). Inadequate and harmful clinical supervision: Testing a revised framework and assessing occurrence. *The Counseling Psychologist*, 42(4), 434–472.

Gatmon, D., Jackson, D., Koshkarian, L., Martos-Perry, N., Molina, A., Patel, N., & Rodolfa, E. (2007). Exploring ethnic, gender, and sexual orientation variables in supervision: Do they really matter? *Journal of Multicultural Counseling and Development*, 29(2), 102–113.

Gloria, A. M., Hird, J. S., & Tao, K. W. (2008). Self-reported multicultural supervision competence of White predoctoral intern supervision. *Training and Education in Professional Psychology*, 2, 129–136. doi:10.1037/193 1-3918.2.3.129

Hays, D. G., & Chang, C. Y. (2003). White privilege, oppression, and racial identity development: Implications for supervision. *Counselor Education & Supervision*, 43, 134–145. doi:10.1002/j.1556-6978.2003.tb01837.x

Hernandez, P., & Rankin, P. (2008). Relational safety in supervision. *Journal of Marital and Family Therapy*, 34, 58–74.

Lama, D., Tutu, D., & Abrams, D. C. (2016). *The book of joy: Lasting happiness in a changing world*. New York, NY: Penguin.

Lopez, A. S. (2008). Making and breaking habits: Teaching (and learning) cultural context, self awareness, and intercultural communication through case supervision in a client-service legal clinic. *Washington University Journal of Law & Policy*, 28, 37–69.

Markham, L., & Chiu, J. (2011). Exposing operations of power in supervisory relationships. *Family Process*, 50(4), 503–515.

Marsten, D., & Howard, G. (2006). Shared influence: A narrative approach to teaching narrative therapy. *Journal of Systemic Therapies*, 25(4), 97–110.

Mehr, K. E., Ladany, N., & Caskie, G. I. (2010). Trainee nondisclosure in supervision: What are they not telling you? *Counselling and Psychotherapy Research*, 10(2), 103–113.

Murphy, M. J., & Wright, D. W. (2005). Supervisees' perspectives of power use in supervision. *Journal of Marital and Family Therapy*, 31(3), 283–295.

Nelson, M. L., & Holloway, E. L. (1990). Relation of gender to power and involvement in supervision. *Journal of Counseling Psychology*, 37(4), 473.

Nilsson, J. E., & Duan, C. (2007). Experiences of prejudice, role difficulties, and counseling self-efficacy among U.S. racial and ethnic minority supervisees working with White supervisors. *Journal of Multicultural Counseling and Development*, 35, 219–229. doi:10.1002/j.2161 1912.2007.tb00062.x

Proctor, S. L., & Rogers, M. R. (2013, March). Making the invisible visible: Understanding social processes within multicultural internship supervision. *School Psychology Forum*, 7(1).

Sue, D. W., Lin, A. I., Torino, G. C., Capodilupo, C. M., & Rivera, D. P. (2009). Racial microaggressions and difficult dialogues on race in the classroom. *Cultural Diversity and Ethnic Minority Psychology*, 15, 183–190. doi:10.1037/a0014191

Tohidian, N. B., & Quek, K. M. T. (2017). Processes that inform multicultural supervision: A qualitative meta-analysis. *Journal of Marital and Family Therapy*, 43(4), 573–590.

Chapter Five

Engaging With Courage

The work of identity-conscious supervision takes commitment, hard work, and involves vulnerability and challenging of self and others. When identity-conscious supervision occurs, it creates the potential for movement of an organization toward identity-consciousness. Systems of oppression and privilege exist in a way that makes entering and shifting the system and patterns of the system incredibly tiring and frustrating. To create sustainable and systemic change, we must have reservoirs of resilience, rooted investment to engage through resistance and courage. Courage, however, cannot be singularly sustained. Courage requires coalition building and clarity of values.

I (Shruti) was working in a mid-sized department and supervised five professional staff members. I had heard anecdotally from our student and professional staff that they were often asked to perform additional work in their minoritized identities. As a part of my role, I also chaired the assessment committee. In that role, I oversaw our annual survey gauging satisfaction with students regarding programs and services. When it came time to analyze our data, we found our Students of Color were statistically less satisfied with their experiences than their white peers. I brought this to our team and my supervisor and did not get much traction to do additional focus groups, training, or programming. We also presented this data to the more extensive department. This data pattern continued for one more year and again received limited resources for training or additional data collection. At our annual presentation, individuals in the department became concerned. I continued to have Staff Members of Color leave at a faster rate than their white peers and continue to express concerns about the culture. Not surprisingly, the same data came back in the third year. Finally, in this third year, a white colleague agreed to advocate with me for additional resources. We received the go-ahead to do other focus groups as well as hire a consultant to work with our team to do training and an audit of position descriptions and programming to look for opportunities to shift the culture.

This example demonstrates the need for courage. I was told no twice before we achieved additional resources. I could not give up asking as my supervisees needed to see someone advocating for them and their colleagues. As one of the leaders in that department, I also had a responsibility to help us live the values in our diversity statement. Getting to that yes required coalition building, vulnerability, fear, resilience, and a clear and committed focus on integrity and the organization. Innovation and disruption need courage.

DEFINING COURAGE

Social movements have been impacted by courage in life-altering and powerful ways. Reviewing history from the civil rights movement, the suffrage movement, Black Lives Matter, and current movements such as the March for our Lives and immigration rights, all demonstrate opportunities to show up with courage in the face of inequity. Each of these also highlights the power of coalition building and community engagement to spark courage and change. None of these movements would have happened without numerous acts of courage. Courage is contagious.

Brown (2018) describes courage as "the willingness to risk hurt or failure" (p. 115). Courage is not effortless, and stepping into courage can lead to pain. This is why so many shy away from it! Merriam-Webster defines courage as "mental or moral strength to venture, persevere, and withstand danger, fear, or difficulty" (2003). This definition underscores the necessity of mental or moral strength and an ability to withstand. It is not just psychological or moral strength or never being afraid, but it is both strength and an ability to hold uncomfortable feelings such as fear and difficulty and still act. Utilizing courage to stand up against inequity both on an individual and systems-level is often distressing. Courage juxtaposes with vulnerability; you can't have one without the other.

As many chapters throughout this book discuss, socialization occurs around whom to trust based on identities and power structures. Vulnerability is easier for some relationships and identities than others. For minoritized individuals who face consistent microaggressions and messaging of value, shame around identity often already exists. Asking a supervisor or supervisee to discuss identity involves vulnerability, but even more so when it requires dialogue around a minoritized identity. Why should professionals in the margins exhibit courage only to bring on more potential shame? It allows the practice of empathy and in turn, a demonstration of identity-conscious supervision. Empathy and vulnerability lead to opportunities for courage and identity-conscious supervision.

COURAGEOUS LEADERSHIP

In Brene Brown's (2018) book, *Dare to Lead*, her research identifies courage as a set of four skills: rumbling into vulnerability, living into our values, braving trust, and learning to rise (Brown, 2018). In other words, willingness to risk failure, clarity and focus of "the why," mutual trust, and resilience necessitate getting up after a defeat. If systems are going to change, an exhibition of courage occurs. The courage comes not in the first rise after a no, but the second, third, and fourth rising after a no. This continual ascension is why Brown (2018) emphasizes learning to rise. It is a skill that requires practice and intention, and that skill helps us develop courage. Courage is necessary for genuinely becoming an identity-conscious supervisor and a leader in shifting culture.

Rumbling Into Vulnerability

Nelson et al. (2006) shared an example about a group of women gathered across race, sexual orientation, class, faith traditions, and came together to create a feminist multicultural framework for supervision. Frustrations spurred within the dialogue from the tension of the continual centering of white women's experience in traditional feminism. They did not develop a framework due to the pain and identity politics within the group. They needed to engage this pain first. These women spent several days embarking in challenging dialogue across identity about their experiences as supervisors and researchers. They demonstrated courage in this process of engaging with each other, although it did not result in their hoped-for outcome. In their reflections, the group stated that the time together helped them heal by doing their self and collective work, become stronger professionals by practicing empathy, and build relationships where they could be seen and valued. Courage was essential for these outcomes to happen. Acting with courage creates an opportunity for internal reflection and dialogue across identities.

Their reflections offer two strategies for difficult conversations, which are a critical part of identity-conscious supervision and requires bravery. The first is the courage to be anxious (Nelson et al., 2006). The courage to be anxious refers to the nervousness that comes with being uncomfortable. In the United States, depending on class backgrounds, the default is for people to seek harmony and actively avoid discomfort. Avoidance shows up in supervisory relationships by focusing on the standard checklist of supervision such as budgets, programming, and tasks instead of embracing the uncomfortable conversation of identity, vulnerability, and authentic dialogue. Honegger (2018) writes:

> We spend our energy in defense mode, trying to avoid disappointment, betrayal, and pain. Something in us clings to these places of safety and makes it difficult to stand—even as something deeper within us longs to stand up, to eventually rise.
>
> (p. 1)

When energy shifts to taking risks with courage changes occur, stronger relationships exist, and values clarity comes to fruition. Taking risks comes with anxiety around discomfort. Systems change, however, when individuals and organizations can hold both fear and courage and act. The return on courage is significant.

Another lesson, Nelson et al. (2006) provided, is how to embrace the tension. Tension is bound to happen when there is a push against the status quo. Brown (2018) refers to this as the rumble. Systems and humans avoid tension because it creates discomfort as well. Brown writes (2018):

> Because talking about trust is tough, and because these conversations have the potential to go sideways fast, we often avoid the rumble. And that's even more dangerous. First, when we are struggling with trust and don't have the tools or skills to talk about it directly with the person involved, it leads us to talk about people instead of to them. It also leads to a lot of energy-wasting zigzagging. Both are significant values violations in our organizations, and I bet they conflict with most of our values too.
>
> (p. 222)

Individuals often feel the most vulnerable in a supervisory relationship when there is an admission of a mistake. When a supervisor admits an error, it counteracts the natural power within the relationship. It creates an opportunity for humility and honesty. It is asking for forgiveness and acceptance from a supervisee who has less power than you. This is counter to dominant norms and allows for a different cycle of events. Courage and vulnerability also lead to liberation instead of perpetuating continued oppression.

The core of the cycle of socialization is fear, ignorance, confusion, and insecurity (Harro, 2000). These emotions and traits keep systems of oppression alive. The cycle of liberation functions on self-love, self-esteem, balance, joy, security, support, and a spiritual base (Harro, 2000). When we, as supervisors and leaders, choose courage over fear and truth over ignorance, we can bring liberation to ourselves, organizations, and those with whom

85

we supervise. Brown (2018) writes that the core of vulnerability is shame and fear, but vulnerability can also be the catalyst for joy and belonging. The reframe of vulnerability bringing both pain and happiness is courage. Choosing courage creates a transformation in a supervisory relationship as well as the work culture and, eventually, the more extensive system.

Living Into Our Values

Many institutions of higher education indicate that they value diversity, equity, and inclusion, yet there is often a disconnect between those values and consistent, demonstrated action. Practicing identity-conscious supervision and dismantling systems necessitates activating our values. As Brown (2018) writes:

> Living into our values means that we do more than profess our values, we practice them. We talk our talk—we are clear about what we believe and hold as important, and we take care that our intentions, words, thoughts, and behaviors align with those beliefs.
> (p. 186)

Equity and justice work does not happen when there is no change in behavior; it is only when that behavior aligns with values and is consistent and constant that sustainable and equitable change occurs. As the image of our model indicates, this change must occur on an individual, supervisory, and organizational level.

Many professionals enter the field due to shared values. These can range from cherishing education to attaching importance to mentoring relationships within identities. This is where the socialization of professionals occurs. Supervisors are responsible for much of the socialization that happens to new and existing employees. Orientation, training, staff meetings, evaluations, and policies reinforce socialization and values. Traditions of a department or university reinforce values messaging. Referring to Harro's (2000) cycle of socialization, the messaging is kept alive by insecurity, confusion, fear, and ignorance. These feelings show up in maintenance of new professional's socialization through not communicating unspoken rules or fear of trying something new. To live into values, all of these socialization methods demand examination.

Saunders, Hirt, and Tull (2009) discuss socialization for new professionals occurring at three levels personal, departmental or divisional, and institutional. These levels create opportunities to demonstrate a commitment to values. The individual-level starts at orientation and continues throughout their time at the institution. For example, as a supervisor, I (Shruti) genuinely value getting to know team members early on in the relationship. I create an abundance of check-in points, so new team members can feel a sense of belonging and value as well as create opportunities to ask questions about culture and the unwritten rules. This also builds a relationship to allow for dialogue around identity more quickly than a normal once a week, one-on-one meeting schedule.

The next opportunity to live into values is at the departmental or divisional level. The subculture of a department takes time to infiltrate and understand (see Chapter 10 for further explanation). Student affairs units struggle to align values with action and regularly tout treasuring professional development. Definitions of professional development vary from one professional and department to another, all of which clearly articulates priorities. At one institution, only "job related" professional development directly associated with a person's job description receives funding, which is an identity-neutral practice. This strict interpretation limits opportunities, and it continues to marginalize professionals with subordinated identities. It also sends a socialization message of the process before people. For example, many Professionals of Color continue to be the "only one" in their department or division. This interpretation does not allow these professionals to attend professional development experiences that bring a community that they need but do not have at work because it is not directly related to job functions. This misalignment is often unseen by those with dominant identities or that hold positions of power.

Finally, there is socialization at an institutional level. College and university mission statements often include statements of valuing diversity or inclusion, yet many institutional actions work against the creation of diverse and inclusive campus communities. For example, many universities have the statements mentioned earlier, but looking closely at their wages for nonexempt employees or their endowment investments indicates a value of capitalism. Further, what happens at a microlevel is more paramount (Saunders et al., 2009) and gives greater insight into what the institution truly values. Scanning the external representation of the university while having clarity at the macrolevel creates an opportunity to measure these values. Instruments such as the *Multicultural Organization Development Model* or the *AAC&U model of Inclusive Excellence* are both tools to help organizations and institutions live into their mission statements. In all cases, courage is needed to address the misalignment at each level.

Braving Trust

Trust has been referred to in several chapters and is a core component of identity-conscious supervision. Feltman (2011) defines trust as "choosing to risk making something you value vulnerable to another person's actions" (p. 72). Trust happens in micro- and macro-moments, and it is ambiguous and nuanced. Trust is affected by socialization, organizational factors, and the environment. Socialization, trust, and actions impact supervisory relationships.

Smith (2010) writes thoroughly about trust-relevant conditions. Of Smith's terms, number two states, "Trust situations are those in which trustees have the decision to choose between multiple options. They can either act in ways consistent with the trusters' interest, or they can frustrate the trusters' ambition" (p. 454). In this model, the trustee is the supervisee and the truster, the supervisor. In creating trust, the supervisor must allow for some autonomy in how individuals perform their role. Micromanaging dismantles confidence. It creates a narrative that there is only one correct way to do anything, and critical thinking and individuality are not necessary. Micromanaging also perpetuates traditional supervisory patterns—as mentioned in Chapter 4—when power is used to promote the supervisor's agenda over the supervisee's. It creates a perception of leveraging power for harm. Humility in the relationship allows for trust. Smith (2010) goes on to write an argument for the foundational need for trust in a supervisory relationship, particularly around identity.

Trust is most relevant in situations where the consequences of a negative outcome are far more significant than those of a positive result (Smith, 2010). In other words, having a supervisor resent a supervisee or give a poor performance evaluation costs more than having a great supervisor and a fantastic performance evaluation. At conferences, it is common to hear statements regarding not enjoying the job but needing to pay the bills, or not having any respect for a supervisor but being unable to quit a job due to citizenship sponsorship, health insurance, supporting family, or needing the tuition benefit. This need to access resources allows the supervisor to continue to have more power and leverage than the supervisee. This adds to the dynamic that a supervisee, by default, must trust a supervisor to continue to utilize benefits and resources. This pattern can create frustration and feelings of disrespect both for the supervisor and supervisee. Lack of clarity and respect builds ambiguity in relationships around constructing trust, and how identity intersects with trust. Brown (2018) writes, "Rather than rumbling generally about trustworthiness and using the word trust, we need to point to specific behaviors. We need to be able to identify exactly where the breach lies and then speak to it" (p. 223). Specific behaviors that define trust vary from identity to identity and involve tough conversations.

A 1997 study by Smith measuring trust found that individuals belonging to a marginalized racial identity reported significantly higher levels of mistrust than those who were white. Further, 51% of Black participants said that they felt most people are trustworthy, and 81% of white participants indicated that they thought most people are honest (Smith, 1997). This stark contrast creates a dramatically different starting point around trust. Supervisors who utilize an identity-neutral approach to building trust may quickly grow frustrated when the same attempts are not creating symmetrical movement in the relationship. Historical and contemporary issues of discrimination and racism attribute to the differences of generalized trust in these populations (Smith, 1997).

I (Shruti) was working in the St. Louis area when the killing of Michael Brown occurred. Trust levels for Black colleagues shifted due to the messaging received around who was safe and trustworthy. The mistrust eventually leveled out, but only after some critical conversations and dialogue and continued investment of colleagues. As a supervisor, I intentionally checked in with all of my supervisees but did so more often with the Black supervisees. We talked about how to reduce workload, the need to take a day off, and boundary setting. I made myself available outside of work hours for these team members and would also try to volunteer or offer services so Black supervisees could say no. Pinch-hitting for my team created trust and an opportunity for respite. The strategies used for trust creation must ebb and flow based on identity, current issues, and department and institutional culture. Creating trust is a continual process and requires courageous actions.

One of the ways to build trust and demonstrate courage is through dialogue across identities. Engaging in these conversations can be painful and must be embraced to practice identity-conscious supervision. Difficult discussions allow for a demonstration of courage and reframe the difficulty as courageous conversations. Courageous conversations allow for learning and healing. When these conversations do not occur, pain and microaggressions are left unnamed, and learning does not take place. When these conversations do occur, it can be uncomfortable for both the supervisor and supervisee. The decision to engage or not engage in challenging a microaggression or a hard conversation often leaves minoritized individuals in a double-bind (Sue, Capodilupo, & Holder, 2008). Both options of engaging or disengaging can cause harm or pain. If an individual chooses to challenge or question a microaggression regarding an oppressed identity, it will ignite a challenging dialogue that could create painful adversity (Sue et al., 2008).

Naming a microaggression requires trusting a relationship, showing up vulnerably, and acting courageously. If a minoritized individual decides not to address a microaggression, it can lead to questioning of being "enough" (Sue et al., 2008). Addressing a microaggression for minoritized identities

89

is an option of two challenging choices, being vulnerable or feeling like a sellout; other options exist. These options create difficult dialogues for individuals involved because identity-based conversations are personal. Personal conversations go against the traditional model of supervision and are necessary for identity-conscious supervision. These difficult dialogues require skill-building as referenced in Chapter 6. The first time an individual engages in a challenging conversation across identity can be awkward and shaky, but over time individuals learn to trust their skills and the relationships around them. Covarrubias (2017) names the attributes of not being afraid to participate in dialogue across differences as authenticity, having an intersectional lens, and courage. The task of not being afraid takes time and a relationship that provides reassurance when taking a risk. Comfort in a supervisory relationship regarding conversations around microaggressions and identity will take patience but will be a valuable step in practicing identity-conscious supervision.

Authenticity creates trust in a relationship as it creates a consistent pattern of behavior that allows someone to believe the person is communicating honestly and transparently. In other words, if a supervisor continuously demonstrates consistency and honesty, it provides trust to a supervisee; they will regularly behave that way. Functioning from an intersectional lens enables story creation beyond a single narrative. It also creates an opportunity for empathy. Covarrubias (2017) writes, "The conversations must be intersectional, honoring the experiences that stem from marginalization and pushing on how privilege manifests on the individual and group levels" (p. 212). This fluid approach allows for both challenge and support for growth to occur. Finally, courage is a crucial component in serving as a catalyst for diving into a challenging conversation. Brown (2018) mentions that it only takes a few seconds of bravery to make a difference. These difficult dialogues and courageous conversations make an impact.

Learning to Rise

In the example provided at the start of this chapter on Black students' significant dissatisfaction, the challenge was trying again each time a "no" occurred. It was exhausting and frustrating, and it mattered. Each time, refining occurred; it created opportunities for the empowerment of those who participated as well. Another word for learning to rise is resilience. Resilience is defined as "achievement when such achievement is rare for those facing similar circumstances or within a similar socio-cultural context" (Gayles, 2005, p. 250)—shifting systems of higher education attempt to make the priority diversity and inclusion expansive and ingrained. These attempts for change bring frustration and exhaustion on an individual and systemic level. Exhaustion and frustration occur because it is often the same group of individuals doing the painstaking work of liberation and change. Change brings fear and anxiety for individuals and systems. This fear and anxiety are often more pronounced when it comes to identity-based work. Literature indicates that dominant group members often hold onto cultural beliefs without examination (Adams, Bell, Griffin, & Joshi, 2016). Often when conversations of identity occur, individuals with dominance have not had as much experience becoming curious about their identities while marginalized individuals have spent a significant amount of time understanding and discussing their identities. Although individuals have depth understanding their minoritized identities, bringing them into a professional conversation comes with substantial risk. Student affairs administrators of color often experience an intense sense of fear of retaliation or backlash for challenging the culture toward a more just one (Elliott et al., 2013). In turn, they remain silent, which replicates systems of oppression, identity-conscious supervision offers liberation.

The rising has to happen for both the supervisor and supervisee, but the supervisor must model it. Resilience is a skill, and just like many other skills, it must be fine-tuned and practiced.

Several components make up resilience. Desai (2017) found that elements such as meaning-making, relationship building, and mentoring, focusing on the locus of control and having a strong sense of self all impacted resilience in women of color in senior student affairs officer roles. Meaning-making happens on an individual and systems level. The stories supervisors and supervisees create can often differ. Processing the objective facts of a situation followed by the impact of the same situation helps create a more objective meaning as opposed to a one-sided story. Also, the mentors and relationships allow for opportunities to add perspective to a narrative. Supervisors should pay attention to what the identity composition is of those whose voices they trust the most and how that impacts their perception. For example, I (Shruti) intentionally have mentors who do not share identities with me to help me think about different perspectives and angles. These voices have helped paint a broader picture and provide freedom to rise again versus only holding a singular narrative personally created and valued.

The capacity to take perspective also means understanding the locus of control. Focusing on what a supervisor can shift will help narrow the scope of the work it takes to create change. Supervisors should work with supervisees to develop goals and priorities together, as this will create a roadmap that builds priorities. Clearly stated objectives would help clarify when and where to rise instead of taking on every adversity and challenge. There is value in playing the long game and staying true to values. Clarity of values also comes from a strong sense of self.

91

To create dynamic change, embracing power and privilege cannot be a one-time checklist item. It requires profound rewiring at a personal and systemic level and a sustained commitment. Often in student affairs, we change one piece of the electrical system such as scholarships or reallocating funding, but what is needed is an entirely new rewiring and electrical system. Changing one wire and changing an electrical system as a whole require a different set of commitment and resilience.

The sustained ability to rise is challenging for individuals who hold mostly dominant identities, mainly white individuals, because of the social need for comfort. D'Angelo's (2011) also notes this in her research on white fragility, "White people in North America live in a social environment that protects and insulates them from race-based stress" (p. 54). Resistance to change is not new for People of Color but often takes time for dominant identities to adapt to and understand. For example, as a queer woman, I (Shruti) have been historically told no regarding marriage and shared medical benefits, straight married individuals have not had to encounter this as much. I decided to interrogate these speed bumps instead of colluding with and accepting these policies as my reality. My ability for sustained interrogation came from my consistent confrontation with discrimination. Individuals in their dominance do not face these regular challenges, so the required skill-building is more intensive. Serious rewiring means continuing to rise in the most challenging moments while incorporating our identities.

Brown (2018) challenges the historical notions of supervision by embracing vulnerability and courage through four components; rumbling into vulnerability, living into our values, braving trust, and learning to rise. Identity significantly impacts these four practices as well as the power dynamic inherent to a supervisory relationship. This consistent decision to choose courage over fear also requires community, clarity of values, and time to reflect and learn. When we adopt courage, it allows for curiosity and hard conversations regarding patterns in relationships and organizations. The interrogation of the repetition of dominance can allow for shifting of relationships and in turn, authentic dialogue regarding the impact of policies, culture, and socialization. Conversation can create different decisions or revamp of current structures. These adjustments provide a foundation for identity-conscious supervision and identity-conscious organizations. Communities and relationships play a vital role in sustaining movement toward identity-consciousness

COALITION BUILDING

Coalition building helps sustain courage and helps maintain an action. Critical race theory identifies relationships as a form of coalition building and underscores the singular way to change systems is to do it together (Solorzano & Yasso, 2002). Desai (2017) found that having one relationship on campus where one can talk about racism or sexism or the joys of life significantly impacted resilience. The opportunities for coalition building is something to keep at the forefront of priorities when supervising individuals, developing identity-conscious supervision, and moving an organization to embrace identity-consciousness. As discussed in Chapter 10, systems are resilient and self-preserving, and they will adapt to maintain functionality. We also know from history that systems of oppression in the United States have not changed much either. Even when courage prevails and systems shift, cycles of oppression can return. Overcoming the resistance and sustaining the resolve and action to challenge such pervasive systems requires our courage and strong coalitions with other communities. No significant movement in history happened alone; all build on strong alliances across communities, with some people serving as leaders and some as followers but all people playing a role. This leadership requires a strong sense of self, courage, and an understanding of cultural wealth (Yosso, 2005).

Building relationships builds a strong sense of self, a counternarrative, and it assembles courage. As a supervisor, it is necessary to build communities to help support sustained courage and action to shift systems and engage in difficult dialogues. It is also vital to connect supervisees with individuals to build strength and capacity to navigate dominant systems. When we, in a coalition, employ multiple strategies across a variety of contexts, we can have an impact on policies and influence change.

CONCLUSION

Identity-conscious supervision is not for the faint of heart. It takes courage to do the work necessary for identity-conscious supervision: practicing sustained commitment, reliable support, and consistent action. If courage were an easy task, we would have already done the work necessary to address the wide variety of issues affecting minoritized staff on our campuses. We would also have already transformed oppressive systems into just ones as well. Reflecting on the example earlier in the chapter regarding Students of Color in our department, this change took multiple attempts, strategies, and individuals to accomplish this goal. The effort required courage to try again and demonstrated tenacity in a coalition and the willingness to leverage privilege to help achieve the goal. When a demonstration of courage and change occurs (even small adjustments), it creates hope and healing, which leads to investment and retention of employees. We may not know the impact of the work we are a part of, and it is essential to remember that seeds planted in a supervisor's tenure may not bear the fruits of that seed until further down the road. Courage does not mean immediate results, but it means a willingness to take risks to stand for something. Showing up in courage while practicing identity-conscious supervision has a profound ripple through the trajectory of any department, university, and field of higher education if it is intentional and communal. Identity-conscious supervision takes courage as it goes against the grain, and it also sets a precedent for others to rise. It creates inspiration, which leads to action, and action leads to shifts in systems. Courage must be nonnegotiable.

Case Study
Viraj Patel and Rhina Duquela

Luz (a cisgender, heterosexual, woman, agnostic, born in the Dominican Republic) serves as a hearing officer for the Office of Student Conduct at a small private coeducational institution. She is the only person of color in the office and one of three people of color out of approximately 60 people in the division.

An annual review of the student conduct handbook occurs with all hearing officers along with Jacob, the Director for the Office of Student Conduct (a cisgender, heterosexual, white, man, Methodist, U.S. born). The campus hearing officers include Luz, Brad (a cisgender, heterosexual, white, man, Catholic, U.S. born), Jen (a queer, white, woman, atheist, U.S. born), and Sandy (a cisgender, heterosexual, white, woman, Catholic, U.S. born). As they go through the handbook, the office administrative assistant, Jen, revises appropriately. Luz has a collegial relationship with her coworkers and a strictly working relationship with her supervisor, Jacob.

Today's meeting is to review sanctions and policies with a particular focus on the Alcohol and Other Drugs Policy. When they get to the "Smoking," Brad states that there has been an increase in cases involving smoking of tobacco in the residence halls. He explains that the resident advisors confronting the incidents grew tired of smelling cigarette smoke. He advocates to have harsher sanctions to reduce repeat offenses.

In the past year, the International Office created a student exchange program for 15 students from Saudi Arabia who are required to live on campus. However, there was no orientation for the exchange students regarding on-campus policies. Sandy attributes the rise of conduct cases to "the Saudis," saying they have three offenses each and other students typically correct their behavior after their first offense. Currently, students receive a written warning for their first offense, a $50 fine for a second offense and an educational sanction, and a $100 fine and housing probation for a third offense. Brad recommends that students found responsible for violating the policy be removed from on campus housing after their second offense. Brad states "$100 to the Saudis is no big deal," With little hesitation, everyone agrees.

Luz notices that Jen, the administrative assistant, didn't revise the sanction under the smoking policy and kindly reminds her to edit. Jen looks to Brad to respond. Brad explains that this is not a policy that should be written in the handbook, as the sanction will be administered on a case-by-case basis. Luz suggests this policy should be stated explicitly so all students are aware of the possibility of removal from housing. Luz also suggests proactive policy education for short-term international students.

Brad states, "Luz, what you want, will not happen. Someone like Jen, for instance will not be kicked out of housing for her second offense. The Saudis need to learn their lesson." Luz retorts, "This sounds like discrimination." Sandy states, "That's fine with me." Luz waits for someone to advocate on behalf of the exchange students, but no one does. She states, "As the only Person of Color, I no longer feel safe in this space." Luz packs up her things and leaves. After Luz leaves, there is a few moments of silence before Brad says, "Wow, that was very unprofessional of Luz." Nobody responds to Brad's statement, including Jacob. Jacob ends the meeting early.

After consulting with mentors, Luz decided to schedule a meeting with Karen, the Vice President of Student Affairs (VPSA) (a cisgender, heterosexual, white, woman, identifies as spiritual, U.S. born), who is Jacob's supervisor. Luz stated she did not feel safe in the office anymore and expressed disappointment at her colleagues and her supervisor for not speaking up or following up with her. She is disappointed in her colleagues for speaking in such an exclusionary way. She told the VPSA that the lack of advocacy for the exchange students made her fearful for their rights as students, and she wanted to know how to ensure accountability.

Luz talked about the possibility of sitting down with the coordinators of the exchange program to discuss the ramifications of moving students off campus on their visas and eligibility for institutional aid. The VPSA agreed that this would be a helpful step into the right direction. She also asked if Luz would like to meet with Jacob to brainstorm ways to change the office culture. The VPSA challenges Luz to think about how to manage her emotions while also continuing to be an advocate.

KEY QUESTIONS

1. Of the four values of courageous leadership, which ones did Luz demonstrate and how did that impact her and the team?
2. What are strategies discussed in the chapter that Jacob can use as tools for critical reflection and building resiliency?
3. How can Karen challenge and support the team to do their self-work, deepen their identity-conscious practice, and invest in their relationship? How can she hold them accountable in effective ways?

REFERENCES

Adams, M., Bell, L. A., Griffin, P., & Joshi, K. (2016). *Teaching for diversity and social justice: A sourcebook*. New York, NY: Routledge.

Brown, B. (2018). *Dare to lead: Brave work. Tough conversations. Whole hearts.* New York, NY: Random House.

Courage. (2003). *Merriam-Webster's dictionary* (11th ed.). Springfield, MA: Merriam Webster.

Covarrubias, A. (2017). *Exploring the racial and gender identity formation of men of color in student leadership roles who have white women supervisors and advisors in higher education* (Unpublished doctoral dissertation), University of San Francisco, San Francisco, CA.

D'Angelo, R. (2011). White fragility. *International Journal of Critical Pedagogy*, 3(3), 54–70.

Desai, S. P. (2017). *Defiance: Resilient women of color as senior student affairs officers* (Unpublished doctoral dissertation), Maryville University, St. Louis, MI.

Elliott, C., Stransky, O., Negron, R., Bowlby, M., Lickiss, J., Dutt, D., . . Barbosa, P. (2013). Institutional barriers to diversity change work in higher education. *Sage Open*, 3(2). doi:2158244013489686

Feltman, C. (2011). *The thin book of trust: An essential primer for building trust at work*. Bend, OR: Thin Book Publishing.

Gayles, J. (2005). Playing the game and paying the price: Academic resilience among three high achieving African-American males. *Anthropology & Education Quarterly*, 26, 250–264.

Harro, B. (2000). The cycle of liberation. In M. Adams, W. J. Blumenfeld, C. Castañeda, H. W. Hackman, M. L. Peters, & X. Zúñiga (Eds.), *Readings for diversity and social justice* (2nd ed., pp. 52–58). New York, NY: Routledge.

Honegger, J. (2018). *Imperfect courage: Live a life of purpose by leaving comfort and going scared*. Colorado Springs: WaterBrook.

Nelson, M. L., Gizara, S., Hope, A. C., Phelps, R., Steward, R., & Weitzman, L. (2006). A feminist multicultural perspective on supervision. *Journal of Multicultural Counseling and Development*, 34(2), 105–115.

Saunders, S. A., Hirt, J. B., & Tull, A. (2009). *Becoming socialized in student affairs administration: A guide for new professionals and their supervisors* (1st ed.). Sterling, VA: Stylus Publishing.

Smith, S. S. (2010). Race and trust. *Annual Review of Sociology*, 36, 453–475.

Smith, T. W. (1997). Factors relating to misanthropy in contemporary American society. *Social Science Research*, 26(2), 170–196.

Solorzano, D. G., & Yosso, T. J. (2002). Critical race methodology: Counter storytelling as an analytical framework for education research. *Qualitative Inquiry*, 8, 23–44.

Sue, D. W., Capodilupo, C. M., & Holder, A. M. B. (2008). Racial microaggressions in the life experience of Black Americans. *Professional Psychology, Research and Practice*, 3, 329–336.

Yosso, T. J. (2005). Whose culture has capital? A critical race theory discussion of community cultural wealth. *Race Ethnicity and Education*, 8(1), 69–91.

Part II

Action at the Supervision Level

Chapter Six

Fostering Identity Exploration

I (Robert) worked in multicultural affairs for several years as a mid-level professional, where I had the opportunity to discuss social justice issues with students, faculty, and staff on campus. While engaging these conversations were the norm in my office, I quickly learned that was rarely the case for my colleagues working in other areas in our division of student affairs or other units across campus. Many of them sought out programming within our Center and relationships with our staff in order to find space for community and respite from marginalizing work environments. These colleagues even shared how their supervisors found conversations about identity to be unprofessional, political, and not a topic to be discussed in the workplace. At times their supervisors would specifically share that it was the responsibility of my staff in multicultural affairs to do "that work," not that of financial aid, first year experience, or career services, or every office on campus. These messages not only neglect the role of identity-conscious perspectives across the field of student affairs, but they often leave supervisees feeling disempowered, disconnected, and angry.

As we build and develop our supervisory relationships, we must incorporate conversations about the role and impact of identity in our work. Departments and units often experience shifts in their team composition as practitioners navigate staff turnover, new leadership, and organizational restructures. The seemingly constant change can create relational challenges as staff adjust to new people, different working styles, personalities, and identities. For supervisors and leaders, the constant change of team members makes it hard to sustain progress along a vision. Supervisors need to hold the expectation that teams engage in conversations around identity in our work.

While we tend to see these changes as an opportunity to deepen our understanding of the team, the focus of our team development retreats prioritizes training on communication, personality types, and community building. When we do bring conversations about diversity and inclusion into professional development opportunities or annual retreats, it is sporadic, and we seldom infuse these efforts and insights throughout the year. Engaging in this work from time to time is not enough; we must normalize identity-consciousness throughout our work and foster identity exploration within conversations about supervision and team dynamics. All of us must do our part. As supervisors, we have the responsibility to incorporate opportunities for reflection about identity in times of transition, at the start of a new academic year, within performance review, and as a part of team development efforts.

While it is critical to articulate job duties and expectations in initial supervisory conversations, these expectations must be coupled with dialogue on the role of identity. By doing so, we can demonstrate that identity exploration is critical to the work of the team and department emphasizing that both the job and the individual performing the job hold value. Identity-centered dialogue can serve as a mechanism to enhance supervisory relationships and create the foundation for effective dialogue across difference. By holistically empowering and supporting staff through centering the role of identity exploration, supervisors can maximize personal and professional growth (Bailey & Hamilton, 2015). An identity-conscious supervision practice builds upon that holistic empowerment and support adding a focus on identities, organizational dynamics, and systems change. It is important to develop skills to foster open dialogue about the impact of identities in the workplace and embrace the role of critical self-reflection as a foundational element of our supervisory relationships. This chapter will review the diverse ways to center identity exploration within the supervisory relationship offering strategies that invite dialogue, acknowledge defensiveness, and deepen relationships.

CENTERING IDENTITY IN SUPERVISION

Effective supervision does not rest solely in the hands of the supervisor; the supervisee also has agency and can have a significant impact on the relationship (Winston & Creamer, 2002). Much of the literature about supervision in student affairs references the synergistic supervision model, created by Winston and Creamer (1997), as the preferred model to guide student affairs practice (Hirt & Strayhorn, 2011; Jenkins, 2015; Morgan, 2015; Shupp & Arminio, 2012; Tull, 2006). Their model is characterized by joint-effort, two-way communication and a focus on competence and goals (Winston & Creamer, 1998). However, due to the hierarchical power differences within the supervision relationship, the supervisor carries more of the responsibility to make the relationship a positive and productive one.

Tull (2006) explained that synergistic supervision "involves establishing open lines of communication, building trusting relationships, supervisory feedback and appraisal, identification of professional aspirations of staff and identification of the knowledge and skills necessary for advancement" (p. 466). His study, which examined the relationship between synergistic supervision and job satisfaction in new professionals, found that a "lack of synergistic supervisory relationship could lead to greater intentions to turnover among new professionals" (Tull, 2006, p. 474). Additionally, Shupp and Arminio (2012) found that new professionals in student affairs desire synergistic supervision in the workplace. A limitation in the literature, however, is that these models of supervision do not consider the role of social identity. In fact, Shupp and Arminio (2012) interviewed participants who were all white—not one Person of Color was included in the research—while Tull (2006) had a participant sample where less than 10% of the sample were People of Color.

To address these limitations, Jenkins (2015) argued that supervisors must go beyond learning about the characteristics of synergistic supervision and focus on cultural sensitivity and "how to have conversations about race, personal biases, and any lack of understanding" (p. 56). Similarly, White-Davis, Stein, and Karasz (2016) emphasized that supervisors need to be trained to create comfort and openness in supervisory relationships, specifically when it comes to addressing issues of identity. In order to address these issues, we must realize the importance of self-reflection in order to work through areas of bias and discrimination (Singh & Chun, 2010). These scholars challenge us to extend our understanding of synergistic supervision through a more holistic, identity-conscious lens, considering the complexity of multicultural and social justice issues.

Supervision is a challenging task and becomes even more so when done within the harmful context of inequitable and oppressive campus and workplace environments. Social justice issues and the development of identity-consciousness are "at once, enormously complex and deceptively simple. We need to see people as individuals and, at the same time; we need to recognize that a person's core being may rest in their social group membership" (Pope, Reynolds, & Mueller, 2019, p. xxi). As we begin the relationship-building process with supervisees, it is essential that we learn how to embrace both of these truths. Supervisors have a responsibility to initiate dialogue to explore the nuances and potential impacts of identity in the workplace both individually within the supervisory relationship and broadly within the organization.

103

FACILITATING IDENTITY EXPLORATION

Within a professional context, few, if any of us, have received adequate training to address the myriad of social justice concerns in higher education today. To increase our consciousness and competence, it is critical that we first be willing to take risks and admit what we do not know (Pope et al., 2019). As supervisors, we consistently build and cultivate relationships with supervisees who have a broad variety of cultural frames and lived experiences, who also need to deepen their understandings and awareness. Because of the power differential between supervisor and supervisee, it is important for supervisors to initiate conversations and let their supervisees know that identity-based issues are an important topic within the relationship and are central to doing quality and effective work (Pope et al., 2019). By doing so, the relationship-building process cements itself in an identity-conscious framework that takes into account both the supervisor's and supervisee's identity lenses, positionality, and divergent perspectives. Engaging these conversations at the start offers opportunities that can bring greater insight to later conversations considering the impact of identity on workload, team dynamics, staff support and overall performance. This section will provide supervisors with a process for engaging in these conversations.

Proactive Engagement

Often supervisors neglect to bring identity into conversations proactively because of insecurity, discomfort, and a fear of where these conversations may lead. It is important to consider the unintended consequences of our silence and what might be communicated from a lack of proactive engagement. In their study on dialogues about race within cross-cultural supervisory relationships, White-Davis et al. (2016) noted that microaggressions are more likely to occur when supervisors have an identity-neutral view of race. Additionally, the authors noted the importance of understanding power and its role in supervision, as well as the importance of open communication and appreciating individuals' multiple identities. They noted, "It is of utmost importance that supervisors create a supervisory relationship characterized by safety and comfort" (White-Davis et al., 2016, p. 354). While we have previously shared our concerns about the notions of safety and comfort within identity-conscious supervision practice, we echo White-Davis' et al. (2016) assertion that discussions around identity are central to effective supervision. Markham and Chiu (2011), who looked at power in supervisory relationships, echoed these findings. The authors highlighted the importance of supervisory practices that "render whiteness visible" and facilitate discourse that explores both dominant and

104

subordinated dimensions of identity within the relationship (Markham & Chiu, 2011, p. 513).

It is important to explore the impact of identity to discover how supervisees make meaning of their environmental contexts. Even though initiating conversations about identity is countercultural to identity-neutral paradigms that hold these conversations as crossing professional boundaries, we must realize that "identity is not just a private, individual matter [but] a complex negotiation between person and society" (Josselson, 1996, p. 31). The construction of our identities happens as we negotiate cultural contexts, interact with other people, and absorb the cultural messages that surround us (Davis & Harrison, 2013). Therefore, identity-centered dialogue in the workplace creates the space to explore the nuances of our career history and socialization, acknowledging the successes and pains of staff members' past supervisory experiences.

Throughout our careers, we have found that practitioners bring distinctly positive or negative supervisory experiences that provide an immense amount of insight on the expectations, harms, and "rules" they are bringing to a work context. Exploring the underlying dynamics embedded within these experiences offers key insights in how best to support and operate from a place of empowerment rather than disempowerment with each of our supervisees. As supervisors, we must develop a strong sense of staff members' unique work histories, avoiding simplistic binary and essentialized understandings of identity, in order to enhance our ability to empathically ask questions and listen to diverse perspectives (Davis & Harrison, 2013). To engage in reciprocal narrative sharing with supervisees, we can facilitate dialogue using the following questions:

- What social identities have the greatest effect on how you see yourself?
- How have your social identities affected your career choices and development?
- Which social identities have the greatest effect on how others see you or interact with you?
- How did identity manifest itself within your past work experiences, particularly in your supervisory relationships?
- Do you have any triggers I should be aware of? How can I help you feel included and a part of the team?
- What aspects of identity and inclusion would you like to learn more about?

By engaging in these conversations during the relationship-building process, we can gain a deeper understanding of our staff members' identity-based experiences in the workplace—how often has identity been centered in their work environments? What is their socialization and relationship to hierarchy and power? What types of supports are helpful for them?

As supervisors, we must approach conversations about identity through the lens of multiple identities—"if we see individuals in terms of only one identity, we minimize the complexity of who they are" (Pope et al., 2019, p. 55). Too often we simplify our supervisees' identities and make them singularly Asian, Trans, wealthy, differently abled, etc., as opposed to holding their multiple and intersecting identities in a broader context that comprises who they are within their wholeness. Engaging these complexities is at the heart of what it means to be a culturally sensitive and identity-conscious supervisor. It is essential that we move beyond narrow conceptualizations because they do an injustice to the complexity of identities, statuses, and power dynamics that exist within our working relationships. While those holding subordinated identities are generally more conscious of institutional oppression and are certainly more likely to suffer the material and psychological consequences of those systems, they also possess dominant identities that limit their consciousness of other systems or intersections. Similarly, those predominantly advantaged with power and privilege typically have a foundation for empathy based on identity dimensions that may be subordinated (Davis & Harrison, 2013). These early conversations create space to explore marginalizing and privileged aspects of identity for both you and your supervisee, preemptively exploring the possibility of their impact on relationship building, trust, and conflict.

Acknowledging Defensiveness

Cultural values define how a campus does its work, how faculty, students, and staff behave, and how they receive rewards. In some places on campus, the rules are explicit and obvious to any community member. Others are far subtler and not as easily detected. Supervisors may not be explicit about the rules because we assume that everyone knows them, particularly when the rules align with our ways of being (Saunders, Hirt, & Tull, 2009). In order to make the campus equitable and just, we have a responsibility to ensure that everyone we supervise has knowledge of these unwritten rules (Pope et al., 2019). The rules we hold most closely to tend to reinforce privileged aspects upheld by our positionality and identities. These rules may be in relation to attire expectations at certain campus events, how to approach senior leaders, expectations to attend happy hour, and many others that can have a detrimental impact when lacking transparency. It is important that supervisors not only explain the unwritten rules and norms but also listen to their supervisees as they challenge rules that marginalize and possess negative impacts.

To reconstruct environments to become more inclusive, we must be able to identify defensive reactions that arise in others and ourselves (Stewart, 2012). We tend to become most defensive when engaging and responding from a place of dominance and privilege. As outlined in Chapter 1, privilege is a social and political construct that references how individuals with dominant culture identities (i.e., white, male, cisgender, heterosexual, Christian) experience fewer obstacles and more benefits because of their identity (Adams & Bell, 2016). To better acknowledge our own defensiveness, we can look to Watt's (2007) privilege identity exploration model. The model explains various defenses that arise as individuals recognize, contemplate, and address experiences of dissonance. According to the model, our defensive reactions to dissonance can show up in eight ways: denial, deflection, rationalization, intellectualization, principium, false envy, benevolence, and minimization (Watt, 2007). These defenses are common when it comes to conversations about identity, social justice, and inequitable environments. As supervisors, we must work to identify these common reactions within others and ourselves as we attempt to create inclusive and equitable environments.

Developing the skills to identify defensive reactions rooted in internalized dominance and oppression can help us incorporate new knowledge and improve our supervisory practice. Supervisees may bring forward experiences with a particular colleague or process that conflict with our perspective. For example, when I (Robert) was an entry-level professional in residential life helping with the professional staff recruitment process, I shared my frustrations with the lack of diversity on staff and identified our recruitment process as a contributing factor to the issue. My supervisor Sally, a straight, white woman with seven years of experience in the department, led our recruitment team. As we were preparing for the upcoming national recruitment events, I shared my frustrations with the lack of diversity on staff and identified inequitable elements of our recruitment process. Throughout the conversation, Sally shared defensive rationalizations about our limited diversity related to geography, principled arguments about her commitment to and the intentionality of our recruitment process and shared how far we have come as an office minimizing my experience. While it is completely normal to have a defensive reaction to staff feedback, it is important to acknowledge the silencing effect of these interactions, especially when related to identity, and develop skills to engage in critical dialogue. The Privileged Identity Exploration model serves a great template to reflect on these conversations gauging where we may be asserting our own power and privilege when engaging with feedback from supervisees. Depending on the context and environment, it may be best to circle back and reengage the conversation with openness, humility, and a commitment to being more responsive in the future.

Deepening Our Dialogic Praxis

Throughout our careers, we have immersed ourselves in dialogic spaces as a tool to explore our identities, practice vulnerability, and cultivate humility to engage effectively across difference. The history of dialogue finds its roots with Freire (1970) in critical pedagogy (discussed further in Chapter 9), as well as in the field of international relations and reconciliation (Androff, 2012). Allport's (1954) Intergroup Contact Theory suggested that the more people connect across lines of difference, the more likely they are to build mutual trust, work through conflict toward reconciliation, and build bridges to greater understanding. Higher education research also explores the role of dialogue, often focusing on the experiences of participants (DeTurk, 2006; Nagda, 2006) or facilitators (DeTurk, 2006; Khuri, 2004; Zúñiga, Nagda, Chesler, & Cytron-Walker, 2007) within a formal setting. The utility of dialogue praxis can also be extended to interpersonal relationship building. In this section, we extend the utility of dialogue facilitation for supervisors as a tool to facilitate identity exploration within supervisory relationships.

In my (Robert) work as a social justice educator, my campus serves as a member of the Campus Network branch of the Sustained Dialogue Institute (SDCN). SDCN teaches dialogue through the work and theories of the organization's founder, Hal Saunders, who described dialogue as "a process of genuine interaction through which human beings listen to each other deeply enough to be changed by what they learn" (Saunders, 1999, p. 82). The distinctive feature of dialogue emphasized in Sustained Dialogue workshops centers on the differences between debate, discussion, and dialogue. With dialogue, participants hold differences in tension, "where no participant gives up [their] identity, but each recognizes enough of the other's valid human claims so that they will act differently toward the other" (Sustained Dialogue Institute, 2016, p. 1). More importantly, dialogue is not considered as "better than" debate or discussion, where relationships are decentered in the process of reaching a definitive solution to the issue. Rather, through dialogue, change becomes possible through relationship building.

The dialogue process focuses on first transforming relationships that cause problems, create conflict, and block change (Sustained Dialogue Institute, 2019). SDCN frames the concept of relationships around five key components: identity, interests, power, perceptions, and interactions. Utilizing this framework, we can engage in self-reflection by utilizing the following questions to explore our own practices:

1. *Identity*—How do your supervisee(s) define themselves across their multiple identities?

2. *Interests*—What motivates your supervisees (goals, aspirations, and desires)?

3. *Power*—Who holds significant or disproportionate influence in the norms, values, and culture of your department or institution? How might systems of power & privilege be surfacing within a given situation?

4. *Perceptions*—What assumptions, misconceptions, or stereotypes might you be holding about an individual or group?

5. *Interaction*—What patterns exist in how groups and individuals interact, including the frequency, tone, and rules (written and unwritten) of their interaction?

(Sustained Dialogue Institute, 2019)

These five elements frame the process of dialogue toward relationships and connections, looking to these elements as moments to interrupt conflict or misunderstanding. Through this mapping, similar and diverging perspectives become apparent in ways that point to interventions for change (Flint, 2019). As supervisors, we can apply this framework to address identity-related conflicts that emerge within supervisory relationships.

Engaging Conflict

Along with assessing the role of relationships in the process of exploring identity in supervisory relationships, it is critical to consider the role of conflict. As issues related to power, identity, and perception surface in dialogue, conflict will inevitably emerge as a factor worth paying close attention. The LARA methodology serves as useful tool in moving through moments of tension and disagreement, making it highly relevant in the context of staff supervision. The LARA methodology is introduced in Gordan's Leadership Effectiveness Training and the University of Michigan's Program on Intergroup Relations (Gordon, 2001; Tinker, 2004). LARA is an acronym that stands for Listen, Affirm, Respond, and Add Information. The first element, *Listen*, incorporates a focus on needs, cultural values, interests, emotions, and meaning of word choice. *Affirm* acknowledges listening occurred by paraphrasing the supervisee communication. Agreement is not necessarily a part of affirmation. *Respond* includes clarification of information to assure understanding. *Add information* offers space for additional views and context to be shared. The LARA methodology can provide an optimal tool for the supervisor and supervisee to share perspectives and understand each other's point of view.

During my (Robert) time working in multicultural affairs, our office experienced multiple staff changes and high turnover within a short period.

During one of our transitions in staffing, we had an open Assistant Director position that we filled with a cisgender man, thus making our three-person leadership team all cisgender men. As a member of the leadership team, I initiated dialogue about this dynamic to explore the impact of our leadership composition on cisgender women supervisees. There were several apprehensions and concerns raised throughout these conversations, which caused me to exert heightened attention to how gender dynamics would unfold on our team and in our work with students. Early on, one of my staff members, Sonya, a queer, Asian, cisgender woman, shared their frustrations about the men in leadership focusing on "big picture" work and leaving other forms of work to women on staff. The LARA method served as a helpful resource in making sense of the feedback, allowing us to deepen dialogue about our work and my impact as a supervisor.

As I heard Sonya's comment, I initially became defensive feeling frustrated that my work, beyond big picture thinking, was not being noticed. It was important that I listened more deeply to process the underlying emotion, values, and principles embedded in their comment. As our dialogue continued, I affirmed the comment, acknowledging where I found connection in the statement. I followed up to seek clarity by asking where they noticed the greatest amount of unequal work. Sonya responded by describing a disproportionate amount of emotional labor in how students sought out support and processing space. As we continued to process further, we were able to explore their direct needs and address the feedback both personally and departmentally. The patterns we experienced on our team are not unique and often affect minoritized practitioners, particularly Nonbinary and Women of Color professionals. It is critical to normalize dialogue as a consistent pattern of practice remaining open to disagreement and varying perspectives. We explore the dynamics of conflict and identity-conscious supervision further in Chapter 8, offering further perspective and tools to utilize in your supervisory practice.

MAINTAINING A CULTURE OF IDENTITY EXPLORATION

Too often, when discussing identity-consciousness in supervisory relationships, the assumption is that the supervisor is a person with privilege by race or gender or some other identity who is working with a supervisee from a marginalized identity. This assumption is one of the many ways that student affairs Professionals of Color, LGBT student affairs professionals, and other marginalized professionals are further marginalized or erased. Creating or contributing to climates that foster dialogue and breaking the silence are everyone's responsibility.

Regardless of our role or identity within an organization, we contribute to the climate of our office, division, and institution. We all have work to do and learning to explore. Recommendations in this area begin with improving trust with individuals and across the team (discussed in Chapter 2), understanding the experiences of individuals with marginalized or underrepresented identities in our office or workplace, and becoming familiar with dialogic tools that are available to process concerns with workplace inequities.

Regardless of our role on a team, it is important that we know how to respond when concerns are shared with us. Identity-conscious practices include an awareness of how to recover from oppressive errors and incorporate cultural learning in new situations (Pope et al., 2019). If we misgender someone, for instance, how do we respond with cultural humility that minimizes our defensiveness and treats the other person with dignity? For both new as well as seasoned professionals working in the field, organizations must continue to create opportunities for individuals to hone their skills to practice identity-conscious supervision.

CONCLUSION

College campuses are fluid and evolving microcosms of the larger society. Finding ways that higher education administrators, faculty, staff, and student affairs professionals can continue to develop skills to manage difference constructively is important and necessary (Watt, 2015). As we build and develop our supervisory relationships, we must incorporate conversations about the role and impact of identity in our work. Dialogue provides a useful tool to engage and learn at the interpersonal level. It is important to remember that there can be an adverse burden placed on supervisees to do all of this learning together. We must seek additional resources, relationships, and self-reflection tools to hold up the mirror to our own practices without placing the burden on supervisees to prompt or further our learning. Supervisors committed to exploring identity with their supervisees must realize that this is an iterative process worth initiating and returning back to establish relationships that invite dialogue, acknowledge defensiveness, and deepen relationships.

Case Study
Gustavo Molinar and Antonio Duran

Victor (he/him), a gay, Latino man, serves as the program coordinator for Latinx Initiatives in the Office of Multicultural Student Services at Pillar University. Victor has served in his role for three years and is known as an advocate for Latinx students across campus. He has started a community mentoring cohort that explores Latinx issues and students seek him out to consult about personal, academic, and professional concerns. This is the first year that Victor has the opportunity to supervise a graduate assistant for Latinx initiatives named Juan (he/him). Juan is a heterosexual, Latino man in his first year of the Higher Education Administration program.

Victor and Juan established a strong relationship at the beginning of the year. During their first meeting, Victor outlined his expectations as a supervisor; these expectations included his hope that Juan would learn how professionals' social identities influences the work practitioners do and how they engage with students. To model this, Victor shared his story as a student affairs professional, including the multiple challenges he has faced as a Latino man in the field. Juan decided to share his own journey into the field, detailing how he is excited to have a similar background as an out-of-state, first-generation student who is from a low-income background. In subsequent meetings, Victor disclosed his identity as a gay, Latino man.

It is now the spring semester and Victor feels disappointed. As both Juan and Victor shared stories at the beginning of the year, Victor wanted to continue their conversations about identity and the profession during their one-on-one meetings. Admittedly, Victor was eager to help mold an emerging student affairs professional. Instead, Juan always seems focused on what tasks need to be accomplished. When Victor attempted to communicate how he has wrestled with his identities in working with undergraduate students, advising student organizations, or the programs that he holds, Juan quickly changes the topic or states that "There's plenty of time to have those discussions! We have two years together." Later, Victor learns from other graduate students that Juan has voiced that Victor is one of the first gay people that he has met. Although Juan mentioned that he wants to learn from Victor about how to navigate the field, Juan worries about saying the wrong thing and offending him. With this knowledge, Victor wants to say something in their next one-on-one meeting but does not know how to proceed.

KEY QUESTIONS

1. What dialogue tools or questions would you utilize to address this situation?
2. What power dynamics or identities are important to consider if you choose to have this discussion?
3. How may this scenario impact the work and relationships Juan has with students? As Victor, how would you address these concerns?

REFERENCES

Adams, M., & Bell, L. A. (Eds.). (2016). *Teaching for diversity and social justice* (3rd ed.). New York, NY: Routledge.

Allport, G. (1954). *The nature of prejudice*. Reading, MA: Addison Wesley.

Androff, D. K. (2012). Reconciliation in a community-based restorative justice intervention. *Journal of Sociology and Social Welfare, 39*(4), 73–96.

Bailey, K. W., & Hamilton, J. (2015). Supervisory style. In M. J. Amey & L. M. Reesor (Eds.), *Beginning your journey: A guide for new professionals in student affairs* (4th ed., pp. 67–94). Washington, DC: National Association of Student Personnel Administrators.

Davis, T., & Harrison, L. M. (2013). *Advancing social justice: Tools, pedagogies, and strategies to transform your campus* (1st ed.). San Francisco, CA: Jossey-Bass.

DeTurk, S. (2006). The power of dialogue: Consequences of intergroup dialogue and their implications for agency and alliance building. *Communication Quarterly, 54*(1), 33–51.

Flint, M. A. (2019). Healing a divided nation: Transforming spaces through sustained dialogue. *The Review of Higher Education, 42*(Suppl), 337–361.

Freire, P. (1970). *Pedagogy of the oppressed.* New York, NY: Continuum.

Gordon, T. (2001). *Leader effectiveness training, L.E.T: Proven skills for leading today's business into tomorrow* (1st Perigee ed.) New York, NY: Berkley.

Hirt, J. B., & Strayhorn, T. L. (2011). Staffing and supervision. In J. H. Schuh, S. R. Jones, & S. R. Harper (Eds.), *Student services: A handbook for the profession* (5th ed., pp. 372–384). San Francisco, CA: Jossey-Bass.

Jenkins, T. C. (2015). *Why keep us here? Perceptions of workplace supervision among African American men in student affairs* (Doctoral dissertation). Retrieved from ProQuest Dissertations and Theses Global database. (UMI No. 3739606)

Josselson, R. (1996). On writing other people's lives: Self-analytic reflections of a narrative researcher. In R. Josselson (Ed.), *The narrative study of lives,* Vol. 4. Ethics and process in the narrative study of lives (pp. 60–71). Thousand Oaks, CA, US: Sage Publications, Inc.

Khuri, M. L. (2004). Facilitating Arab-Jewish intergroup dialogue in the college setting. *Race, Ethnicity, and Education, 7*(3), 229–250.

Markham, L., & Chiu, J. (2011). Exposing operations of power in supervisory relationships. *Family Process, 40,* 503–515.

Morgan, D. (2015). *An examination of the relationship between perceived level of synergistic supervision received and key job performance indicators within midlevel student affairs administrators* (Unpublished doctoral dissertation). Colorado State University, Fort Collins.

Nagda, B. A. (2006). Breaking barriers, crossing borders, building bridges: Communication processes in intergroup dialogues. *Journal of Social Issues, 62*(3), 553–576.

Pope, R. L., Reynolds, A. L., & Mueller, J. A. (2019). *Multicultural competence in student affairs: Advancing social justice and inclusion* (2nd ed.). San Francisco, CA: Jossey-Bass.

Saunders, H. (1999). *A public peace process: Sustained dialogue to transform racial and ethnic conflicts.* New York, NY: St. Martin's Press.

Saunders, S. A., Hirt, J. B., & Tull, A. (2009). *Becoming socialized in student affairs administration: A guide for new professionals and their supervisors* (1st ed.). Sterling, VA: Stylus Publishing.

Shupp, M. R., & Arminio, J. L. (2012). Synergistic supervision: A confirmed key to retaining entry-level student affairs professionals. *Journal of Student Affairs Research and Practice, 49,* 157–174.

Singh, A., & Chun, K. Y. S. (2010). "From the margins to the center": Moving towards a resilience-based model of supervision for queer people of color supervisors. *Training and Education in Professional Psychology, 4*(1), 36–46.

Stewart, D. L. (2012). Promoting moral growth through pluralism and social justice education. *New Directions for Student Services, 139,* 63–71.

Sustained Dialogue Institute. (2016). *Sustained dialogue campus network moderator manual.* Retrieved from http://sustaineddialogue.org/wp-content/uploads/150812-Final-ModManual-2015-2016.pdf

Sustained Dialogue Institute. (2019). *SD focuses on relationships.* Retrieved July 24, 2019, from http://sustaineddialogue.org/our-approach/

Tinker, B. (2004). LARA: Engaging controversy with a non-violent, transformative response. In *The program on intergroup relations* (pp. 1–22). Michigan: University of Michigan. Workshop handout available by request from info@LMFamily.org

Tull, A. (2006). Synergistic supervision, job satisfaction, and intention to turnover of new professional in student affairs. *Journal of College Student Development, 47,* 465–480.

Watt, S. (2007). Difficult dialogues, privilege and social justice: Uses of the privileged identity exploration (PIE) model in student affairs practice. *College Student Affairs Journal, 26,* 114–126.

Watt, S. (Ed.). (2015). *Designing transformative multicultural initiatives: Theoretical foundations, practical applications, and facilitator considerations.* Sterling, VA: Stylus Publishing.

White-Davis, T., Stein, E., & Karasz, A. (2016). The elephant in the room: Dialogues about race within cross-cultural supervisory relationships. *International Journal of Psychiatry in Medicine, 51,* 347–356.

Winston, R. B., & Creamer, D. G. (1997). *Improving staffing practices in student affairs.* San Francisco, CA: Jossey-Bass.

Winston, R. B. & Creamer, D. G. (1998). Staff supervision and professional development: An integrated approach. *New Directions for Students Services, 84,* 29–42.

Winston, R. B. & Creamer, D. G. (2002). Supervision: Relationships that support learning. In D. L. Cooper, S. A. Saunders, R. B. Winston, Jr., J. B. Hirt, D. G. Creamer, & S. M. Janosik (Eds.), *Learning through supervised practice in student affairs* (pp. 65–96). New York, NY: Routledge.

Zúñiga, X., Nagda, B. A., Chesler, M., & Cytron-Walker, A. (2007). Intergroup dialogue in higher education: Meaningful learning about social justice. *ASHE Higher Education Report, 32*(4).

Chapter Seven

Critical Authentic Leadership
A Pathway to Balancing Identity and Expectations

As a young professional, I (Robert) worked as a Resident Director (RD) on a large residential life staff. While my RD colleagues and I shared many of the same job expectations, our identities brought additional expectations for some of us, particularly the RDs of Color. There was an increased burden and obligation on us to join institutional and departmental diversity committees, advise minoritized student groups, and hold the emotional weight of supporting our RAs and residents of Color as they navigated race and racism on campus. My colleagues and I sarcastically named these unspoken expectations the "race tax."

My supervisor, Aria, identified as a Woman of Color, which made her intimately aware of the "race tax" dynamics on our team and within her own experience as well. Because she understood the dynamics and had done her own work, she provided me with support that was authentic and empowering, often creating space to process the fatigue of these expectations throughout our supervisory relationship. The reality of disproportional labor reverberates throughout higher education for People of Color (Smith, Yosso, & Solórzano, 2006), particularly Women of Color and Queer People of Color. As supervisors, we have a responsibility to engage the impact of identity-driven expectations and job responsibilities when working to create a more equitable environment for minoritized staff. Despite the need to enhance workplace environments, there are very few models or frameworks providing a guidepost for identity-conscious supervision and management development.

As discussed in Chapters 2 and 3, supervision, at its most basic, is a relationship between a supervisor, a person who holds more power and responsibility, and a supervisee, who reports to the supervisor. In practice, there is a wide range of how student affairs practitioners define and enact supervision across the field. Perhaps this dynamic is due in part to the fact that, despite its ubiquitous nature, there is a disproportionately small amount of literature available to guide supervisory practice (Perillo, 2011; Winston & Creamer, 1997). What we do know from the limited research, however, is that effective supervision has the immense potential to propel employee growth (Tull, 2009; Winston & Creamer, 1997) and reduce attrition of new professionals in the field (Barham & Winston, 2006; Tull, 2006). Given this shortage of scholarship, we have found that leadership theory, particularly authentic leadership theory (Avolio & Gardner, 2005), can provide a useful guide for supervisory practice. A central premise to authentic leadership theory is that authentic leaders foster the development of authenticity in followers and centers efficacy, hope, optimism, and resilience (Avolio, Walumbwa, & Weber, 2009).

Even so, authentic leadership theory has significant limitations that must be addressed to better inform our identity-conscious supervision practice. Most notably, the theory neglects to acknowledge or address the impact of social positionality and thereby reinforces dominant ideologies and ways of being (Dugan, 2017). Applying authentic leadership theory without an identity-conscious lens creates an environment where all too often supervisors do not recognize or understand the impact of emotional labor, racial battle fatigue, and marginality on minoritized supervisees. Aria's ability to incorporate a race-conscious approach within her leadership created space to acknowledge and address many of these dynamics. Therefore, it is necessary to integrate leadership theory with critical race perspectives to enact identity-conscious supervision. In this chapter, we will share a conceptual supervisory framework for Critical Authentic Leadership to help reduce systemic racial bias in the workplace and provide a pathway for supporting supervisees as they balance identity and job expectations.

WHAT IS AUTHENTIC LEADERSHIP?

One of the aspects I appreciated most about Aria's supervision was her ability to lead with authenticity through centering relationships and modeling vulnerability. These values are mirrored in authentic leadership theory, offering an opportunity for further exploration. Authentic leadership theory is one of the more recent leadership theories to emerge, and the body of research is steadily growing (Avolio & Gardner, 2005; Avolio et al., 2009; Dugan, 2017). It is distinguished by the deep levels of leaders' awareness of their own and others' moral values and perspectives, knowledge and strengths, and of the context in which they operate (Northouse, 2018). It is an often cited and supported model for student leadership development by student affairs professionals. Its applicability in the field is well suited for identity-conscious supervision as it frames leadership as

117

a joint practice between leaders and followers centering relationships and self-awareness as key components.

Core Components

The four key constructs of authentic leadership, as first introduced by Luthans and Avolio (2003), include:

1. Self-awareness: demonstrated understanding of how one makes meaning of the world and how that meaning-making process impacts one's internal view over time
2. Relational transparency: presenting one's authentic self as opposed to a fake or distorted self to others
3. Balanced processing: objective analysis of all relevant data before coming to a decision
4. Internalized moral perspective: internalized and integrated form of self-regulation, guided by internal moral standards and values versus group, organizational, and societal pressures.
   (Avolio & Gardner, 2005; Luthans & Avolio, 2003)

Luthans and Avolio's (2003) work anchors authentic leadership in values, character, and moral capacity. Core capacities of authentic leaders include possessing and modeling confidence, hope, optimism, and resilience. A key element is the notion that authentic leadership requires heightened levels of self-awareness (Avolio & Gardner, 2005). Goffee and Jones (2005) suggest further that authentic leaders foster trust and followership. Walumbwa, Christensen, and Hailey (2011) assert that "authentic leadership is founded on the notion of trust and transparency, which is a vital element that enables people who work together to know they can rely on each other implicitly" (p. 113). Leaders cannot successfully operate on their own (Northouse, 2018). Given that trust, transparency, and self-awareness are necessary for identity-conscious supervisory relationships, it is reasonable to suggest authentic leadership builds from aspects that could become a leadership theory that equips supervisors for sustainable practice.

Limitations

In spite of authentic leadership theory being a promising framework for student affairs supervisors and leaders, there is a need for further research and development. Given the relatively young nature of the theory, there is little empirical research validating the legitimacy (Dugan, 2017; Northouse, 2018). Additionally, the theory is leader-centric, furthering differentiations among leaders and followers. Dugan (2017) posits that some attention is focused on follower authenticity as directed and influenced by the leader's role in development, which may further the paternalistic nature of supervisory relationships. There is also the ambiguity of defining authenticity to consider along with answering the question of what is fundamentally moral (Avolio & Gardner, 2005). Given the power dynamics at play within supervisory relationships, as discussed in Chapter 3, it is troubling to position the supervisor as the definer of what and who is "authentic" or moral for their supervisees. Doing so not only limits the fluidity of how we define our "true self," it also upholds a false binary of good and bad, moral and immoral, and authentic and inauthentic.

Dugan (2017) implores us to consider how authenticity might reflect dominant norms based on social location and proximity to power. We must also consider the role of sociopolitical context that creates risks and consequences for minoritized people to be, live, and express as their authentic selves. If the standard for leaders and authenticity are linked to dominant norms, "being perceived as genuinely authentic becomes a much more challenging and complex task for women, People of Color, and members of the LGBTQ community whose expressions are often judged against dominant norms" (Dugan, 2017, p. 285). Individuals must then take on the added burden of masking their expressions to perform within the dominant group norms or face negative consequences. Adding to the complexity is the reality that the dominant group may still fail to recognize them even after adopting masks and performative expression (Dugan, 2017). It is imperative that we apply a critical race lens to our understanding of authentic leadership in order to challenge these complexities within our roles as supervisors, particularly when supervising and mentoring Staff of Color.

TOWARD CRITICAL AUTHENTIC LEADERSHIP— INTEGRATING CRITICAL RACE THEORY

In order to center the needs of Supervisees of Color and identity-consciousness in supervision, a critical race theory (CRT) perspective serves as our guide for the development of a conceptual framework for critical authentic leadership through this chapter. CRT was originally conceptualized as a framework to critique the U.S. legal system's role in upholding white supremacy (Delgado & Stefancic, 2017). Scholars utilize CRT to recognize the permanency and endemic nature of race in American education (Delgado & Stefancic, 2017; Ladson-Billings & Tate, 1995). In their pioneering article that outlined a critical race theory for education, Ladson-Billings and Tate (1995) theorized education as rife with racialized and racist cultural constructs and demarcations. Assuming such, critical race scholarship challenges dominant ideologies that support racialized inequalities stemming from dominant educational practices. Through its use, scholars seek to promote increased equity and social justice for People of Color (Bell, 1987; Delgado & Stefancic, 2017; Solórzano & Yosso, 2002).

Core Tenets

Solórzano (1998) identified five tenets of CRT that can and should inform theory, research, pedagogy, and policy: 1) intercentricity of race and racism; 2) challenge to dominant ideology; 3) commitment to social justice; 4) centrality of experiential knowledge; and 5) a utilization of interdisciplinary approaches. CRT foregrounds race and racism throughout the research process but also acknowledges that other systems of domination intersect with race and racism (Solórzano & Yosso, 2002). Therefore, the third tenet of CRT encourages a focus on intersecting systems of domination and the ways in which these systems influence the everyday, identity specific experiences of individuals with multiple minoritized identities (Crenshaw, 1991). An intersectional approach to research allows for the interrogation of racism, sexism, classism, and other interlocking systems of oppression that work to influence lived experiences (Crenshaw, 1991).

Applying the Theory to Supervision

By challenging dominant ideologies, critical race theory moves academic inquiry beyond frameworks of individual responsibility and success to discussions that center the unexamined institutional and systemic factors that leave oppressive power dynamics intact (DeCuir & Dixson, 2004; Patton, 2006). In this way, a critical race perspective illuminates the ways dominant ideologies manifest in social narratives. Social narratives operate to normalize oppressive conditions within society by telling stories from the perspective of the dominant social group in order to sustain their racial and class privilege (Dixson & Rousseau, 2007).

Supporting this move from individual to institutional and systemic responsibility, CRT often draws on narrative data to examine discursive understandings of lived experience (Delgado & Stefancic, 2017). As such, CRT values the voices and experiences of those who are least heard in education, especially as they provide counter-understandings to dominant ideologies (Solórzano & Yosso, 2002). They often take shape as assumed rules, folk knowledge, and stereotypes that people cling to, draw from, or resist in order to make sense of their place in the world.

A critical race perspective on supervision recognizes that racism is a normal and common aspect that shapes workplace environments. Race is deeply embedded in our social, cultural, and political structures, thus making it difficult to recognize and address within organizations (Delgado & Stefancic, 2017; Ladson-Billings, 1998). Furthermore, race is socially constructed with historical interpretations that marginalize People of Color (Delgado & Stefancic, 2017). If we are to apply a CRT perspective to address patterns of marginalization within supervisory relationships, the voices and experiences of People of Color must be considered central, legitimate, and relevant in contextualizing race and racial realities (Solórzano, 1998). This practice is central to our understanding of identity-consciousness challenging us to engage race and its intersections as a primary lens in making meaning of supervisory practice.

Minoritized voices serve as counter narratives that challenge universality and conventional interpretations of the workplace experience. In addition, identity-neutrality and racial indifference are consistently challenged through exposing the manner in which racial advances often come at the cost of promoting or feeding into white self-interests (Delgado & Stefancic, 2017). Forman (2004) noted that race-neutral ideologies ignore the systemic nature of race, excuse accountability for racial injustices, and promote apathetic, covert acts of racism, which ultimately place power and privilege with the dominant group, as framed in Chapter 3.

Racial Battle Fatigue

Distributing a job description and organizational chart helps employees understand their role within the department and broader institution. As supervisors, we must prioritize discussions that set shared expectations for successfully accomplishing a particular job (Career Press, 1993). Unfortunately, emotional weight and fatigue often complicate and distract from the ability of Supervisees of Color to accomplish direct job responsibilities, while holding additional burdens, obligations, and expectations (Erickson & Ritter, 2001). The normalized and common existence of racism as experienced through racial microaggressions often develops a cumulative impact for People of Color.

Drawing from CRT, educator William A. Smith (2004) coined the phrase *racial battle fatigue* as a mechanism to increase understanding of this phenomenon. Smith (2004) describes racial battle fatigue as the anxiety experienced by racially underrepresented groups as well as those engaged in race work with a focus on the physical and psychological toll

121

taken due to constant and unceasing discrimination, microaggressions, and stereotype threat. Racial battle fatigue is similar to the stress that soldiers experience from battle and references the psychological, physiological, and behavioral stress response that comes from perpetually fighting and coping with racism (Smith, 2004; Smith, Yosso, & Solórzano, 2006).

The everyday manifestations of racial battle fatigue surface from expectations to serve as a representative for your entire race, the need to cover core aspects of yourself to perform "professionalism," and expectation to support students and colleagues of color as they also navigate their own experiences with racial battle fatigue. It is important for us to explore strategies to interrupt this pervasive pattern in our supervisory practices. This chapter will introduce a conceptual framework that takes up Smith's concept and extends it as a means of understanding how supervisor-supervisee relationships operate with respect to racial battle fatigue and expectations for authentic leadership.

CONCEPTUALIZING CRITICAL AUTHENTIC LEADERSHIP FOR IDENTITY-CONSCIOUS SUPERVISION

The key factors in our conceptual framework for this chapter are authentic leadership, critical race theory, and racial battle fatigue. Authentic leadership theory serves as the foundational theoretical framework advanced through the addition of a critical race theory lens. Our model serves as a new framework for student affairs supervisors and supervisees to engage in Critical Authentic Leadership (CAL) as a tool to increase consciousness and decrease racial battle fatigue. Our conceptual framework places critical authentic leadership at the center and interconnects the four key components with critical perspectives:

1. Identity-conscious self-awareness in relation to the intercentricity of race and racism
2. Racialized relational transparency, which foregrounds experiential knowledge of self and others
3. Multipartial balanced processing, holding a rejection of dominant ideology
4. Internalized moral perspective rooted in a commitment to social justice values.

The model connects core components of authentic leadership and CRT to address the necessity of practicing supervision in a way that is connected and grounded with multiple supports.

Identity-Conscious Self-Awareness

The first component of CAL refers to the personal insights of leaders and followers within a context that holds the relevance and intercentricity of race and racism. The intercentricity of race and racism suggests that race and racism are central factors in the experiences of People of Color at their intersections such as gender and class (Delgado & Stefancic, 2017). The intercentricity of race and racism prompts us to acknowledge the premise that race and racism are central, endemic, permanent, and a fundamental part of defining and explaining how U.S. society functions (Solórzano, 1998), most notably within workplace environments and supervisory relationships.

Self-awareness is key here. Supervisors must understand that their own process of deriving and making meaning of the world shapes their perspective of self over time (Avolio & Walumbwa, 2014). In order to adopt a more critical perspective, authentic leaders must hold the context of race, racism, and white supremacy in their analysis of self and the world around them. For instance, supervisors should foreground their racial identity and positionality as a primary dynamic to explore within their supervisory relationships. For white supervisors, it is important to acknowledge their white privilege and seek to understand how white fragility affects their ability to engage in racial dialogue (DiAngelo, 2018). Conversely, Supervisors of Color should explore their own racial socialization, marginalization, and internalized racism as a tool increase their identity-conscious self-awareness. By doing so, critical authentic leaders deepen their awareness of their own racial identity and positionality with an awareness of the broader sociopolitical context existing around them.

Self-awareness through the lens of CAL includes reflecting on our core values, identities, emotions, motives, and goals (Northouse, 2018), while acknowledging and taking ownership of our racialized history and temporalities (Solórzano & Yosso, 2002). We encourage engaging in intergroup racial dialogue, intragroup affinity space dialogue (i.e., caucusing), and personal reflection to explore these core aspects of self. Many campuses offer dialogue spaces for faculty and staff, but these opportunities can also be pursued through professional development experiences, like the Social Justice Training Institute (SJTI), White Privilege Conference (WPC), National Conference on Race & Ethnicity (NCORE), and many more. As we discuss in Chapter 3, Northouse (2018) echoes that authentic leaders know themselves and have a clear sense of who they are and what they stand for. Critical authentic leaders engage in the leadership process with clarity of their own socialization narratives, deconstructing the impact of internalized white supremacy and internalized racism. By doing so, we

123

develop a critical consciousness motivating our willingness to work in solidarity and community to advance social justice.

Applying the Concept

Self-awareness is an essential skill to develop for effective supervisory relationships (Winston & Creamer, 1998). Identity-conscious supervisors apply this core component of CAL by demonstrating an awareness of their strengths and weaknesses related to advising, coaching, and inclusion. We can start this process by sharing our strengths and weaknesses with supervisees creating space for open dialogue that articulates our own self-awareness in relation to identity and inclusion. Identity-conscious supervisors also create the space for their supervisees to adopt a similar growth mindset, where they focus on shared development through authentic and honest feedback. These initial conversations help to normalize vulnerability, authenticity, and open dialogue within the relationship. As we discussed in Chapter 2, developing relationships grounded in trust and transparent communication allows both parties to exhibit a mindfulness of their impact on others, particularly through the lens of identity.

By applying the concept, we can develop an ability to assess racialized dynamics (Delgado & Stefancic, 2017) developing within the relationship and address potentially harmful behaviors. In our practice, we have found it useful to pause conversations to name the impact of race and racism on our decision-making. For instance, one of my (Robert) supervisors held anxiety about budget decisions always making sure every detail was considered. As we reflected together about her heightened caution, she was able to name her internalized fear that her departments would suffer heightened scrutiny because of mistrust in her leadership as a Woman of Color on a predominately white leadership team. The conversation created clarity that helped me understand what felt like micromanagement and scrutiny on my practices. It also provided her with an opportunity to process the impact of her own internalizations on her supervisees. Identity-conscious self-awareness create opportunities to explore additional dynamics that surface as disproportionate labor patterns, microaggressive behavior, favoritism, and identity-driven patterns of mistrust and micromanagement.

Racialized Relational Transparency

The second component of CAL refers to the ability and willingness to present one's authentic self to others centering the validity of experiential knowledge. Authentic leadership theory projects the importance of relational transparency while ignoring a relationship to social positionality (Dugan, 2017). By doing so, it limits relational transparency to those possessing dominant identities and ideologies. A Critical Authentic Leadership perspective, however, centers the lived experiences and realities of People of Color by acknowledging the impact of race and racism (Delgado & Stefancic, 2017; Solórzano & Yosso, 2002). By centering the voices and narratives of People of Color, supervisors can create space for racialized relational transparency. Identity-conscious supervisors practicing this form of transparency reject inauthentic manifestations of allyship and solidarity that lead to white silence and horizontal hostility. Racialized relational transparency also creates the opportunity for reflection and shared dialogue, as discussed in Chapter 6. Through dialogue, a racialized understanding of relational transparency acknowledges the power differential in disparate abilities to present oneself as fully "authentic."

Applying the Concept

Racialized relational transparency provides the greatest opportunity to address the impact of racial battle fatigue in supervisory relationships. Relational transparency is about communicating openly and being real in relationships with others (Northouse, 2018). One aspect of racial battle fatigue derives from the cumulative stress of coping with racism, which is exacerbated when done in isolation (Smith et al., 2006). As discussed in Chapter 3, increasing transparency of racial dynamics in supervisory relationships alleviates the weight of this burden and creates opportunities for support among supervisors and supervisees. Given the power dynamics at play within the relationship, we must be willing to initiate and model conversations that engage racialized relational transparency with vulnerability and empathy.

It is important to note that supervisors and supervisees can identify in similar and disparate ways across racial and ethnic lines. At times, showing up authentic can be more difficult when racial identities are shared depending on a person's socialization and level of safety within and across a particular racial dynamic. For instance, we have supervised professionals with the same racial identities and across identities. Our levels of authenticity have varied with staff, as has the level of authenticity our staff felt with us. Despite the fluidity and salience of identity, there remains a need for supervisors to acknowledge how our power or marginalization influences our lens and lived experience. The centrality of lived experience (Solórzano & Yosso, 2002) is crucial in ensuring these conversations spark validation, affirmation, and change.

Multipartial Balanced Processing

The third component of CAL interrupts objective and neutral analyses by challenging dominant ideologies. Authentic leadership theory projects an individual's ability to analyze information objectively and explore other people's opinions before making a decision (Northouse, 2018). By doing so, it upholds dominant ideology by centering objectivity over mutipartiality. Objectivity and neutrality often skew toward dominant ideologies given the context of race and racism in U.S. society and must be critically considered (Delgado & Stefancic, 2017). A Critical Authentic Leadership perspective challenges white supremacy, and refutes claims of objectivity, meritocracy, and race neutrality. There is no such thing as objective research or practice (Yosso, 2005). Such approaches serve as camouflage for the interests of dominant groups.

Multipartiality, as opposed to objectivity, is a practice drawn from intergroup dialogue facilitation that focuses on balancing social power, *independent of* and *in contrast to* dominant norms in society (Gurin, Nagda, & Zuniga, 2013). A multipartial balanced processing rejects dominant ideologies that ignore the systemic nature of race, excuse accountability for racial injustices, and promote apathetic, covert acts of racism, which ultimately place power and privilege with the dominant group (Forman, 2004). The conceptual framework maintains the need to consider information and perspectives that challenge deeply held positions (Avolio & Walumbwa, 2014) but advances the balanced processing component through a critical race analysis. Critical authentic leaders with multipartial balanced processing assess multiple viewpoints within a broader structural power analysis to conduct decision making that will ultimately create social and institutional change.

Applying the Concept

As supervisors, we face challenging decisions that require us to engage in perspective taking and balanced decision-making (Tull, 2009; Winston & Creamer, 1997). Numerous situations and issues arise where we are required to engage in decision-making related to hiring and promotion, policy change, and performance review. These encounters can have racial undertones depending on the staff and policies involved. Through multilateral affirmation, multipartiality "dissipates symmetrical, tug-of-war interactions by establishing *both/and* ecological striving" (Butler, Brimhall, & Harper, 2011, p. 195). Student affairs supervisors apply multipartial balanced processing by rejecting binary ways of thinking that uphold dominant ideologies (Smith et al., 2006).

For instance, when balancing job expectations for our staff, there are often additional needs that arise in relation to childcare, continuing education, self-care, ADA accommodations, and disproportionate workload. It is common to have staff turn to us for support with flexible working hours or other support mechanisms. We can apply this concept by asking questions related to disproportionate impact, representation, mission/values alignment, and identity-consciousness prior to making a decision. Multipartial balanced processing prompts us to consider the role of identity, labor, and staff needs instead of strict, hard and fast policies consistent for all staff across the board regardless of nuance. Identity-conscious supervisors acknowledge the power dynamics at play in their decision-making processes by assessing the who, what, and why behind their decisions with an inclusion lens. Developing supervisory practices grounded in equity-driven decision making creates an opportunity for increased trust, transparency, and collective impact.

Internalized Moral Perspective

The final component of CAL refers to a self-regulatory process where individuals use their social justice values to guide their behavior. Critical authentic leaders assess the influence of external pressures driven by institutional racism and white supremacy and work to resist pressures that limit equitable approaches. The approach centers the agency of each individual in determining how much they want to allow external pressure to drive their actions and decisions (Northouse, 2018). These external pressures may stem from top down decisions that we have to pass down to our supervisees such as a need to produce more with less and conform to dominant ways of being. Given this scenario, a strong internalized moral perspective prompts leaders to weigh the rewards and consequences of their decision to conform to pressures for production from leadership. Within these reflections, leaders question either/or thinking and realize the agency to advocate for the needs of their team. We must demonstrate congruence between our internalized values and behaviors (Avolio & Walumbwa, 2014) by prioritizing values related to social justice and inclusion. Critical authentic leaders must first establish and then articulate their values for social justice to their team infusing accountability measures (discussed in Chapter 3) that support consistency and congruence.

Applying the Concept

As student affairs supervisors, we experience a variety of pressures from supervisees, supervisors, institutional leaders, and political dynamics within the institution (Holmes, 2014; Perillo, 2011). These challenges can create a variety of internal conflicts, where moral perspective taking becomes integral to sustainability within the field. It can be challenging to decipher which stakeholder or priority should drive our decision making and internal processing. Applying the concept allows supervisors to approach complex decisions grounding themselves in their values. Student affairs professionals often espouse a value of diversity and inclusion but fall short of being in congruence with those values. Supervision is complex and challenging. CAL is not suggesting that perfection is the expectation from you as a supervisor. Rather, it attempts to provide a framework where supervisors pause to reflect on critical questions related to decision making as they engage in complex processes and leadership challenges. We can consider the following questions when exploring decision-making processes:

- Have we defined the problem accurately?
- How would we define the problem from our supervisee's perspective?
- How is power and privilege manifesting in our decision-making process?
- How could our decision cause harm? Would this harm conflict with our values?
- How might our decision affect other supervisees, colleagues, or fellow supervisors?
- Who might be disproportionately affected by our decision?

CONCLUSION

Critical Authentic Leadership provides a framework for us to take action in addressing issues of exclusion, domination, and social injustice in the workplace. Naming issues of racism and oppression and merely espousing commitments to diversity and inclusion are not sufficient to dismantle systems of domination (Smith et al., 2006). We need to move beyond addressing racism solely in the context of our students and push to address dynamics that surface throughout all the work we do in higher education. Supervision continues to serve as one of the most frequent tasks engaged in student affairs work and must be critically examined (Tull, 2009). As supervisors, we have a responsibility to reshape human resource practices to address systems of domination within workplace environments. Leaders must also push white supervisors, in particular, to interrogate white supremacy, acknowledge the histories and experiences of Staff of Color, and integrate intersectional perspectives through their supervisory practices. Our framework centers race intentionally in its utilization of critical race theory and racial battle fatigue, but similar conclusions can be drawn and applied when exploring feminist theory, queer theory, and critical disability theory to enhance our practice through a more intersectional lens.

Authentic leadership offers a useful framework to engage supervision within a complex and turbulent social context (Dugan, 2017; Northouse, 2018). In management development initiatives, trainers must problematize the uncritical use of authentic leadership theory with differing staff populations and racialized contexts. Our conceptual framework for Critical Authentic Leadership seeks to serve as a model to interrupt dominant ways of being and leading. It supports the need for the development of an intersectional approach to supervision and management. Student affairs supervisors must stop relying on and positioning Staff of Color as experts on all things diversity and inclusion. It is not the responsibility of People of Color to teach their white colleagues and supervisors about racism and white supremacy in higher education and the workplace. Relying on People of Color to provide these educational interruptions to normative supervisory practices does little to interrupt the isolation and racial battle fatigue experienced throughout society and in higher education. Critical authentic leadership offers a model to spark further leadership development for student affairs supervisors.

Case Study
Brandi Scott and Braelin Pantel

You supervise several competent staff at a mid-sized, predominately white institution (PWI). One of your staff members, Lacy, is a skilled and capable leader who has several direct reports of her own. She is a strong performer in her role as the Director of the Student Health Center with many accolades and accomplishments. She identifies as a white, cisgender woman and a single mother. Lacy has disclosed to you that she struggles with a chronic illness. Lacy is also the parent to a child with a disability that requires a heavy degree of involvement with the school and specialized therapy that often occurs during work hours. Lacy has been made aware of her rights and resources under both the Americans with Disabilities Act

(ADA) and the Family Medical Leave Act (FMLA) but has not availed herself of accommodations at this time. Lacy has followed the specified channels to communicate about her absences. The institution has a very generous leave policy, and Lacy has used her allocated sick or annual leave time for her many absences.

Over the course of the past semester, Lacy has needed to miss a lot more work and has shared with you that this has been related to her or her daughter's conditions. Several of these absences have been during major departmental events or meetings, so other employees have been asked to cover for her and/or have otherwise been adversely impacted by her absences. Many of the individuals covering for her are staff Lacy supervises who hold minoritized identities, including several People of Color.

Javior is supervised by Lacy and identifies as a Latino man who is also a parent. Unbeknownst to Lacy or his colleagues, Javior has a nonapparent disability. Javior shares with you that he has been socialized to hide his disability and not receive accommodations for fear that he will be perceived as lazy or trying to take advantage of the institution as a Person of Color. Chavon, another supervisee of Lacy, comes to you to share her concerns about Lacy's absences. Chavon, a Native American woman who is the Coordinator of Health Services, is often tapped with multiple requests to offer voice to the experiences and needs of Native American students. Chavon serves on multiple committees and task forces outside of her formal role to help contribute to student support. Chavon is the primary caretaker for her three young children and drives for a car sharing service at night. With Lacy's absences, Chavon has been asked to stay late for events, preventing her from earning extra money for her family from her side job.

You have a good rapport with both Javior and Chavon and they have come to you to express their concerns about Lacy's absences. They share that they have already tried speaking with her about their concerns, but they left those conversations without a plan to resolve the impact that her absences have on the department or on them. Separately, both Chavon and Javior have expressed to you that they feel exhausted and overwhelmed on campus at times, particularly as they have experienced countless racial microaggressions and a climate that Chavon describes as "prickly" for People of Color. Chavon was quick to share with you that generally her own experiences in the Health Center have been positive and in fact better than what she has experienced elsewhere on campus. Chavon appreciates that Lacy has worked to engage the Health Center team in anti-racist trainings and similar initiatives to better the climate for Staff of Color within the department; yet, despite this, the overall climate still weighs heavily on the Staff of Color in their day-to-day work.

KEY QUESTIONS

1. As the supervisor overseeing the department, and Lacy's direct supervisor, how do your own identities factor into your approach?

2. While many individuals have come to you and disclosed personal and confidential information about their own identities and experiences, this is not information you can readily share with others. How do you navigate knowing the information about each staff member while addressing the concerns?

3. What is your responsibility as an identity-conscious supervisor to navigate the various needs and identities of your staff? What considerations does Critical Authentic Leadership prompt you to factor into your response?

REFERENCES

Avolio, B. J., & Gardner, W. L. (2005). Authentic leadership development: Getting to the root of positive forms of leadership. *The Leadership Quarterly*, 16(3), 315–338.

Avolio, B. J., & Walumbwa, F. O. (2014). Authentic leadership theory, research, and practice: Steps taken and steps that remain. In D. V. Day (Ed.), *Oxford handbook of leadership and organizations* (pp. 331–356). Oxford: Oxford University Press.

Avolio, B. J., Walumbwa, F. O., & Weber, T. J. (2009). Leadership: Current theories, research, and future directions. *Annual Review of Psychology, 60,* 421–449.

Barham, J. D., & Winston Jr., R. B. (2006). Supervision of new professional in student affairs: Assessing and addressing needs. *The College Student Affairs Journal, 26*(1), 64–89.

Bell, D. (1987). *And we are not saved: The elusive quest for racial justice.* New York, NY: Basic.

Butler, M. H., Brimhall, A. S., & Harper, J. M. (2011). A primer on the evolution of therapeutic engagement in MFT: Understanding and resolving the dialectic tension of alliance and neutrality. Part 2-recommendations: Dynamic neutrality through multipartiality and enactments. *The American Journal of Family Therapy, 39*(3), 193–213.

Crenshaw, K. (1991). Mapping the margins: Intersectionality, identity politics, and violence against women of color. *Stanford Law Review, 43,* 1241–1299.

DeCuir, J. T., & Dixson, A. D. (2004). "So when it comes out, they aren't that surprised that it is there": Using critical race theory as a tool of analysis of race and racism in education. *Educational Researcher, 33*(5), 26–31.

Delgado, R., & Stefancic, J. (2017). *Critical race theory: An introduction* (3rd ed.). New York, NY: New York University Press.

DiAngelo, R. (2018). *White fragility: Why it's so hard for white people to talk about racism.* Boston, MA: Beacon Press.

Dixson, A. D., & Rousseau, C. K. (Eds.). (2007). *Critical race theory in education: All God's children got a song.* New York, NY: Routledge.

Dugan, J. P. (2017). *Leadership theory: Cultivating critical perspectives.* San Francisco, CA: Jossey-Bass.

Erickson, R. J., & Ritter, C. (2001). Emotional labor, burnout, and inauthenticity: Does gender matter? *Social Psychology Quarterly, 64*(2), 146–163.

Forman, T. A. (2004). Color-blind racism and racial indifference: The role of racial apathy in facilitating enduring inequalities. In M. Krysan & A. E. Lewis (Eds.), *The changing terrain of race and ethnicity* (pp. 43–66). New York, NY: Russell Sage Foundation.

Goffee, R. L. B. S., & Jones, G. (2005). Managing authenticity—the paradox of great leadership. *Harvard Business Review, 83*(2), 87–94.

Gurin, P., Nagda, B. (R.) A., & Zúñiga, X. (2013). *Dialogue across difference: Practice, theory, and research on intergroup dialogue.* New York, NY, US: Russell Sage Foundation.

Holmes, A. C. (2014). *Experiences of supervision skill development among new professionals in student affairs* (Unpublished doctoral dissertation). Iowa State University, Ames.

Ladson-Billings, G. (1998). Just what is critical race theory and what's it doing in a nice field like education? *International Journal of Qualitative Studies in Education, 11,* 7–24.

Ladson-Billings, G., & Tate IV, W. F. (1995). Toward a critical race theory of education. *Teachers College Record, 97,* 47–68.

Luthans, F., & Avolio, B. J. (2003). Authentic leadership development. In K. S. Cameron, J. E. Dutton, & R. E. Quinn (Eds.), *Positive organizational scholarship* (pp. 241–258). San Francisco, CA: Berrett-Koehler.

Northouse, P. G. (2018). *Leadership: Theory and practice* (8th ed.). Thousand Oaks, CA: Sage Publications.

Patton, L. D. (2006). The voice of reason: A qualitative examination of black student perceptions of black culture centers. *Journal of College Student Development, 47*(6), 628–646.

Perillo, P. A. (2011). Scholar practitioners model inclusive, learning-oriented supervision. In P. M. Magolda & M. B. Baxter Magolda (Eds.), *Contested issues in student affairs: Diverse perspectives and respectful dialogue* (pp. 427–432). Sterling, VA: Stylus Publishing.

Smith, W. A. (2004). Black faculty coping with racial battle fatigue: The campus racial climate in a post—civil rights era. In D. Cleveland (Ed.), *Broken silence: Conversations about race by African Americans at predominately White institutions* (pp. 171–190). New York, NY: Peter Lang.

Smith, W. A., Yosso, T. J., & Solórzano, D. G. (2006). Challenging racial battle fatigue on historically white campuses: A critical race examination of race related stress. In C. A. Stanley (Ed.), *Faculty of color teaching in predominantly White colleges and universities* (pp. 299–327). Boston, MA: Anker.

Solórzano, D. G. (1998). Critical race theory, race and gender microaggressions, and the experience of Chicana and Chicano scholars. *Qualitative Studies in Education, 11*(1), 121–136.

Solórzano, D. G., & Yosso, T. J. (2002). Critical race methodology: Counter storytelling as an analytical framework for education research. *Qualitative Inquiry, 8,* 23–44.

Tull, A. (2006). Synergistic supervision, job satisfaction, and intention to turnover of new professionals in student affairs. *Journal of College Student Development, 47*(4), 465–480.

Tull, A. (2009). Supervision and mentorship in the socialization process. In A. Tull, J. B. Hirt, & S. S. A. Saunders (Eds.), *Becoming socialized in student affairs administration: A guide for new professionals and their supervisors* (pp. 129–151). Sterling, VA: Stylus Publishing.

Walumbwa, F. O., Christensen, A. L., & Hailey, F. (2011). Authentic leadership and the knowledge economy. *Organizational Dynamics, 40*(2), 110–118.

Winston, R. B., & Creamer, D. G. (1997). *Improving staffing practices in student affairs*. San Francisco, CA: Jossey-Bass.

Winston, R. B., & Creamer, D. G. (1998). Staff supervision and professional development: An integrated approach. *New Directions for Students Services, 84*, 29–42.

Yosso, T. J. (2005). Whose culture has capital? A critical race theory discussion of community cultural wealth. *Race Ethnicity and Education, 8*, 69–91.

Chapter Eight

Engaging With Conflict

Not many people embrace conflict; we are socialized to either shy away from it or end it as quickly as possible. Our socialization comes from the dominant norms connected to our identities or through an institutional culture. But engaging in conflict effectively is essential to our work in identity-conscious supervision and in institutional change efforts. Mmeje, Newman, Kramer II, and Pearson (2009) write, "Conflict is inherent in cultural change" (p. 304). In order to fully embrace an identity-conscious approach, we must embrace conflict and resistance from those who intend to maintain the status quo. Even if we are thoughtfully and compassionately bringing identity into our supervision practice, we will find moments of conflict with each other, where our ways of knowing from our identities may bump with others' ways of knowing. We will also face our internal conflicts as we navigate our relationship to power, privilege, and internalized dominance and subordination. Moreover, we are bound to make mistakes in our practice that we will need to reconcile.

As supervisors engage in more just and equitable supervisory practices, conflict is bound to emerge both with individual supervisees and in the process of team development. Even when we invest in people, and create supportive work environments, people being in community with each other will create conflict at some point. Conflict is inevitable with systemic change, and if unmanaged, will lead to a return to racist, ablest, hegemonic, patriarchal, sexist, heteronormative, cisgendered practices (Pope, Reynolds, & Mueller, 2014). But in order to engage effectively across difference, managers must embrace conflict as a normative practice (Keehner, 2007). We need to develop our skills and our capacity to effectively engage and reconcile conflict using an identity-conscious lens.

We want to note that we intentionally use the term "engagement" because partnering with others across identity and experience is an active experience and being explicit about engagement reminds us of our roles as partners and supervisors. We also use "reconciliation" instead of the more common "resolution." We prefer this term because the idea of resolution of conflicts is rooted in an imagined separation from each other, and as noted in the following, the concept is rooted in gendered and racists notions of supremacy. Conflict reconciliation focuses on the positive, creative aspects of working with conflict, and the model centers relationships, love and care, and creates space for the people involved to feel valued and respected.

We want to name the importance of conflict in this transformational, identity-conscious practice so that we can embrace it, rather than running away. A great deal of learning and growth can come from the productive engagement with our conflicts (Taylor, 2003). Anytime we bump up against a new idea, a new perspective, or a new way of being, we are given an opportunity to rethink how we have been socialized, the impact of socialization on our responses and behaviors and how we continue to engage with others in alignment with our values. Dissonance is a powerful learning space for us as individuals and with others.

As we acknowledge the importance of conflict, we also understand that unresolved and poorly managed conflict resolution is a leading reason that faculty and staff leave institutions of higher education (Warters and Wendy, as cited in Watson, Rogers, Watson, & Yep, 2019). Indeed, unresolved conflict can fester into a sense of marginalization and divert energy to distract from the goals and mission of the organization. We also want to distinguish conflict from violence and abuse (Hemphill & BLM Healing Justice Working Group, date unknown). While violence and abuse are often the responses to conflicts in this society, they are separate.

Last, we note that conflict is often associated with negative experiences. We offer that conflict is a natural part of relationships and can be a powerful and profound experience. In her partnership model, Eisler (2002) described that conflict provides energy for creative exploration that results in growth and community centered solutions (Eisler, 2002). Further, Wynton Marsalis, an African American trumpeter/musician, reflecting on his process in working with other musicians, notes "there is always tensions that come up. Part of working is dealing with tensions. If there is no tension, then you're not serious about what you're doing" (Edmondson, 2012, p. 61). Tensions in art can be empowering and transcendent, helping the artist to discover new depths of beautiful expression that weren't apparent. This tension and beauty also manifest in higher education and has the potential to create space for creativity and growth.

We offer that conflict can serve us in developing and deepening our identity-conscious supervision practice in the same ways. Conflict is essential for growth to occur (Pope et al., 2014; Manning & Coleman-Boatwright, 1991). Successful conflict reconciliation also can help deepen relationships and strengthen teams (Watson et al., 2019). We will not be able to transcend oppression or transform our organizations until we learn to embrace and engage conflict and practice reconciliation in ways centered in love, respect, and justice. There is no other way.

CONFLICT DEFINED

Zarko Andricevic, a Croatian Buddhist, was interviewed in *Tricycle Magazine* (The Editors, 2003) and spoke of the Buddha's teachings on conflict: "The causes of any conflict lie in strong attachment to certain views." When we hold onto to the simplistic, and usually dualistic, understandings of conflict, we become locked into a competition where we are focused on winning. There are rarely only two solutions in conflict. This energy shuts us down from listening to one another and viewing each other with respect. In many ways, this is why we fear conflict.

Further, Smith and Berg (1997) challenge the notion that an absence of conflict should be a goal. "It is impossible to have a group without certain kinds of conflict and that the wish to have those conflicts 'resolved' stems from an imperfect understanding of the meaning that conflict has in the life of the group" (p. 11). We also offer that that notion is centered in whiteness, where the focus is on politeness and harmony at the expense of respect and the honoring of varied life experiences and differing truths.

Cohen, Davis, and Aboelata (1998, as cited in Taylor, 2003) define conflict as a "process of expressing dissatisfaction, disagreement, or unmet expectations with another person, group, or organization" (p. 526). While technically correct, this definition of conflict lacks the emotions that come with conflict. It further assumes a neutrality of perspective and that our needs aren't connected to our identities. As we discuss in Chapter 7, objectivity and neutrality often reflect dominant ideologies and can serve as entry points for oppression to show up.

Smith and Berg's (1997) definition of conflict brings in the emotion behind it, and they define it "simply as the clash of oppositional forces, including ideas, persons, interests, wishes, and drives" (p. 36). This feels more complete, but we are uncomfortable with the metaphor around fighting, war, and aggression. These concepts are very much rooted in gendered, supremacist notions (Sharoni, 2017).

We are drawn to Watson, Watson, and Stanley's definition (as cited in Watson et al., 2019): "conflict is a struggle between people with opposing needs, ideas, beliefs, values, and/or goals" (p. 252). This definition best addresses the nature of conflict, the variety of sources it can come from, including identity-based experiences and needs and provides room for emotional and spiritual connection. It also moves away from

137

gendered, supremacist language that perpetuates in a dominator model. For example, opposition between parties is not defined in violent ways (i.e., clashes, fights), and resolution is not defined in rightness of position. Marshall Rosenberg (2015) grounds it in a similar philosophy as Non-violent Communication.

Conflicts can show up with other people at the individual level, around style or personality. Conflict can show up at the group level around our many group identities (race, class, gender, ability, religion, etc.) or around our role within higher education (faculty and staff, employees and management, students and administration). Conflict can show up at the organizational level through decision-making processes, systemic treatment, or differential policies and practices. Constantino and Merchant (1996, cited in Taylor, 2003) also add competition, inefficiency, and withholding knowledge to organizational conflicts, in addition to others.

There are several limitations in these definitions of conflict when we attempt to apply them to identity-conscious supervision practices. These definitions don't always speak to how conflict shows up in an identity-conscious supervision practice. Our experience around conflict regarding identity-conscious practice and systems engagement is highly emotional. We are deeply embedded into a system rife with inequity, we have many painful experiences as a result of this system (many that are unhealed) and reconciling our relationship to this system causes dissonance in our sense of self. To reconcile our conflicts, we need to acknowledge our past, the fear that comes with engaging conflict in a vulnerable and authentic way (especially when that is different from our past), and the emotions that come with it. The only way to reconcile is through this kind of engagement.

Last, we note that successful engagement and reconciliation of conflict rests on the strength of the relationships as outlined in Chapter 2. It is imperative that supervisors take responsibility for investing in their own work, and for investing in building relationships built on authenticity and trust, particularly across difference where trust is often lacking.

LOCATIONS OF CONFLICT

At one of my former institutions, I (Craig) had a conflict with one of the directors that I supervised. Dave was director of student activities, and he identifies as a Black man. I identify as a white man. Our conflict started as feedback about the quality and timeliness of his work, and after repeated efforts to address, led to lower evaluations than Dave thought he deserved. It escalated when the institutional needs shifted, and Dave was asked to perform his work in new ways. Dave did not like the feedback and was resistant to changing and working in ways that were unfamiliar to him and out of his comfort zone. I interpreted that he felt I was challenging his competence, and he responded with aggression and calling me a racist.

Another supervisory conflict I (Craig) had at another institution was with Liam, a resident director. Liam identifies as a white, heterosexual man. Our conflict started because students were complaining about his lack of availability and support. As we explored the issues, it was clear he wasn't showing up to his office hours, nor completing any of his assignments. The main issue, however, was that he didn't care to do better; he had gotten far with marginal performance and wasn't invested in working harder than he had to. He viewed me as an annoyance and an anomaly. And I read his behavior and attitude as classic, white maleness, and I found it offensive.

Both conflicts became a really complex mix of factors and dynamics, and in both cases, it was really hard for us to reconcile. Our identities fueled our conflicts as we both became more and more uncomfortable working with each other; in stress, each of us resorted to default patterns around maleness and masculinity (yelling, posturing, using size to intimidate) and whiteness (disengagement, strict adherence to organizational norms and needs, and use of power to force the other) (Obear, 2014, personal communication) of dealing with conflict. Both conflicts also spilled out into other members of each team and created further tensions to navigate.

While both of these conflicts were interpersonal and connected to how identities showed up in supervisor/supervisee relationship, that is not the only source of conflicts within a supervisory context. Employees often act and respond in relationship to the environment in which we work (Gibson & McDaniel, 2010). Therefore, it is important for us to understand some environmental sources of conflict. In our work as supervisors, and in our work as consultants leading trainings and organizational change efforts, we have repeatedly observed these to be at the root of most conflicts.

Bolman and Deal's (2017) four frames model also offer us a helpful way to understand how and where conflicts can arise within an organization. From the structural frame, conflicts can stem from the structure of the organization, from competition for resources, disincentives for collaboration, and gaps in training or communication. From the human resources frame, conflicts can stem from needs of the employees or students that are in conflict. From the political frame, conflict can stem from the political process, which is often hidden and about power. From the symbolic frame, conflicts arise when there is a disconnect (or refusal to align) with the meaning and belief of the organization.

Conflict can show up in the unexamined identities in ourselves, especially our relationship to dominance, power and privilege. In as much as our identities drive our behaviors and shape our world view, acting out of dominance, even unconsciously, creates conflicts. A main source of conflict and misunderstanding is that we "tend to interpret others' behaviors, values, and beliefs through the lens of our own culture" (Shonk, 2014). In identity-conscious supervision, we must pay attention to our internal dissonance as well as the dissonance in our supervisory relationship. The internal conflict can often be more challenging to understand and navigate.

Conflict can be based in our individual unmet universal needs. Universal Needs, according to Rosenberg (2015) are expressions of our humanity. Universal Needs are core to who we are and don't vary by circumstance or in relationship to another. While we may share many of these universal needs, the combination of needs within each of us is unique. Rosenberg organizes these Universal Needs around 1) subsistence and security, 2) connection, and 3) meaning. We have these needs in our professional contexts, in our relationship contexts, and in our identity contexts. For example, we all want to matter, to belong, to be accepted and valued, and to be loved. We also want to be understood and appreciated. Rosenberg notes that when our Universal Needs are unmet, conflict can arise. As supervisors, arises when we don't have an identity-conscious practice and acknowledge the overlap of identity and Universal Needs with our supervisees.

Conflict can also emerge in a variety of forms between managers and staff. Conflict can arise from organizational changes that require work processes to be done differently, or from the organizational change process at any level (Bridges, 2009). Conflict most often occurs in the process of evaluation and feedback. We acknowledge the inherent problems in institutionalized evaluation systems, the tools that are used, and how pay increases or bonuses are tied to a summative label or level. The evaluation system is a complex formation of identity-neutral practices that lead to inequities in outcomes at the system level and allow for sanctioned abuse or bias at the individual level. But they are widely used. Therefore, supervisors must be diligent and honest in their assessment of poor performance in a timely and direct manner, while demonstrating care, concern, compassion, and an understanding of cultural nuance (Buckingham & Coffman, 1999). Supervisors must also sustain their identity-conscious practice and continue to name how identities are present in the relationship and in the work environment.

Space, Windows, and Doors

People have attachments to where their workplace is, and they place great value on whether they have a door and a window. Certainly, some of this is about wellness (no one wants to work in a dark basement). We have been conditioned to understand that an office symbolizes power, value, and importance. This is rooted in Western, and corporate ideology, and certainly part of the colonial view of space. A window and door are symbolic of that power, and the value one feels one has. Conflicts can occur around who gets a window or a door, if I feel my value is deserving of different space than I have, or if I have a feeling that you are not respecting my space. At one institution, the square footage allocated to various offices was based on the level or coding of the position, which perpetuated systems of inequity at that institution.

Interpersonal

Conflicts can also occur because of a clash of personalities or ego between passionate caring team members who have varied approaches, or lack of trust. Conflicts also stem from people's insecurities. Often these insecurities stem from past personal experiences that show up in the workplace. Certainly, situations, contexts, or people may be contributing to the situation, so that situation deserves attention. Encouraging and supporting employees finding healing is a longer-term, more sustainable solution.

Miscommunication and Misunderstandings (E-mail Is Not Your Friend)

Poor communication, an overreliance on e-mail (the written word), and the push for efficiency all contribute to conflicts. It is difficult to understand tone and intent in the written word because our understanding relies on verbal and nonverbal communication. With e-mail, nonverbals are absent, so we have to make assumptions about the writer's intent and tone. If we have a good relationship with that person, we are more likely to assume good intent and tone; if we have a poor relationship with someone (or lack of trust), we are more likely to assume attack. As we discussed in Chapter 4, our identities also influence how we disseminate and take in communication. Further, employees put too much in writing—we text or write an e-mail when we should talk in person or over the phone. That isn't to say that e-mail and texting doesn't have value, but it should not be used for communicating emotional topics. The writer's intent doesn't always have the intended impact, and conflicts and difficulties stem from that as well. Writing to align intent and impact takes a great deal of effort and time, mostly to consider words to effectively communicate content, and we don't often give that much time to e-mail. Conflicts stem from this misalignment.

When the University has Said "No"

Sometimes conflicts come when the institution says "no" to an idea, suggestion, or contribution, or considers it but chooses to go in another direction. Frustrations sometimes are about arrogance or an inflated sense of self-importance; other times they are founded. It is easy to write off the decisions that the president, chancellor, provost, or vice president makes because we likely have enough distance from them or do not have a personal relationship with them; when these decisions come from a peer or supervisor, they tend to be more personal. As we have been socialized within a United States colonial mentality, it means we do not like to be told "no" either.

Disrespect

Conflict also stems from disrespect: disrespect of contributions, workspace, lunch in the kitchen, who greets whom in the hallway, clothes, hair, attitude, etc. For example, "professionalism" policies often maintain dominant norms and can marginalize groups based upon appearance, tone, or attitude, rather than ability to perform the job well. There are numerous occasions of Black women being let go due to their hair choices. In other cases, disrespect can happen unintentionally, as a result of one of the other conflicts earlier, a past experience that an employee carries with them or be intended. It often carries the emotional weight from our identities—because we are all too familiar with that feeling. Sometimes it is unintended, and sometimes it is intended, either consciously or unconsciously. We think that people can't tell how we feel about them, but it is clearer than we often realize. Our nonverbals betray us. When this shows up in the supervisory relationship, it adds a complex emotional layer worth addressing before the issue can be reconciled.

Challenge and Growth

Some of us struggle to change, or grow, or aren't ready. In our supervisor capacity, we may be coaching our team members to grow and stretch. Some don't want to change (they like where they are), some aren't ready to change (they are in a comfort zone), and some don't recognize their work needs improvement (they think they are doing all that is needed). With an identity-conscious lens, sometimes challenge and growth is about the professional need at hand, and other times it is about a behavior that is associated with a group identity. For example, my (Craig)challenge with Dave was about work performance, but my challenge to Liam was about his group-level behavior around whiteness. Navigating challenge and group with an identity-conscious supervision lens is challenging for both supervisors and supervisees.

Generational Preferences

There is a greater range of generations working now, and supervisor/supervisee relationships often cross generational boundaries. "Each generation brings its own set of values, beliefs, life experiences, and attitudes to the workplace" (Lancaster & Stillman, 2002, p. 4), and it can create challenges for people working together. Some good examples of this in a supervisory context include different methods for communication, values around quality work and commitment to an organization, appropriate dress for the workplace, and the use of surnames or titles.

MODELS FOR CONFLICT RECONCILIATION

There are plenty of models for conflict resolution, many rooted in business, human resources, or peace studies. Few of these models center an identity-conscious approach in their resolution models. Edmondson (2012) offers us a good framework for how we can cool conflict. We first need to identify the nature of the conflict, then we can model good communication, identify shared goals, and last, encourage difficult conversations.

This framework is important, and we add that an identity-conscious approach also asks us to identify and explore how we have been socialized on how to respond to conflict based upon our gender, race, family dynamics, and by society. Our "cultural orientation shapes our preferences and the effectiveness of how we manage conflict, whether we rely on status or rules, use power or mutual needs, coordinate or compete, or choose to strategically display emotions" (Gibson and McDaniel, 2010, p. 456). We need to understand these conditioned behaviors and know their roots. Only then can we understand the historical impact of our conditioned behaviors and responses. We want to find ways of reconciling conflict that transcend systems of oppression.

As always, we must preliminarily engage in our self-work to understand our cultural lenses and our relationship to them. We also need to do our heart work as well. When we explored love and justice in Chapter 2, we learned that it was central to relationships. It is also crucial in engaging in conflict—we want to center reconciliation between parties as the goal rather than winning. This intention changes the interaction. The Arbinger Institute (2015) similarly offers that centering peace in our hearts while we engage in conflict because we innately respond to another based upon their "way of being" toward us (p. 39). When we respond from a place of love and peace, others respond in kind. The key to successful navigation is doing our own work and coming from a position of love, which allows us to know and honor the value in another.

Successful conflict engagement and reconciliation is a skill, and it needs to be developed and practiced. There is no one way to reconcile conflict, especially while applying identity-conscious practice. It is important for us to be aware of our cultural training, assumptions, and values. We approach situations from our own lenses, and conflict management is no different. It is important that the process and model be discussed in advance and agreed upon. A particular model or process may be culturally inappropriate or disrespectful and lead to unsatisfactory results and possibly increase the future likelihood of further conflict (Gibson & McDaniel, 2010). In an increasingly intercultural and intergenerational workplace environment, "the strategies to successfully manage conflict are crucial to understand" (Gibson & McDaniel, 2010, p. 456).

I (Craig) recently had an opportunity to practice this. I was leading a meeting with some colleagues, and I received some feedback on a project I was leading. The feedback was helpful, and I needed time to consider it so that I could incorporate it. I acknowledged the feedback and moved to the next item. I then noticed a visible shift in the body language of my colleagues. In discussing this shift, I learned that my response to the feedback came across as dismissive. As I processed this, I knew that I had not intended to be dismissive, but my quickness to get back to task created that feeling. I knew my "keeping to the agenda" is connected to the socialization I have received regarding gender and leadership, and while I have been working on this, I know I also slip back to this old training. I identified that while I had acknowledged the feedback, I failed to acknowledge the context in which it was given. I shared the insight that I had connected to my identity, and I apologized to the group for the impact this caused. We agreed to pause the work of the meeting and reschedule. Before the next meeting, I reached out to each member at the meeting to discuss and restore and reflected on how maleness was showing up in my leadership so that I could make adjustments.

Proactive conversations between supervisors and supervisee provide us the chance to explore preferences around different approaches, develop shared pathways for success, and avoid inappropriate or disrespectful processes. It also gives us a chance to name and share some of our unproductive behaviors and develop mechanisms for dealing with them when they show up.

A number of models approach conflict resolution with a notion that we can be impartial or objective. We reject this idea and clarify that an identity-conscious approach requires us to acknowledge, own, and be accountable for our identities. We apply Wilgus and Holmes' (2009) notion of *multipartiality* (also discussed in Chapter 7) where we acknowledge and explore our relationships to our own perspectives, and our identities. Our ideas for resolution are rooted in our worldviews that come from our perspectives and our identities. Multipartiality allows us, then, to understand that there are multiple ways of reconciling our conflicts.

Restorative Justice

Restorative Justice is based upon indigenous practices and has a focus on sustaining community and providing healing (Darling, 2011). It is an alternative form of justice where victims and offenders are brought together, and a contract is created by all parties to the offense to repair the harm caused and reintegrate individuals back into the community. This process focuses on repairing harm experienced by victims and community members through a commitment to fulfill all obligations (Zehr, 2002). It also holds offenders responsible for their past actions, take accountability for the healing process, and for doing the inner work that leads to a commitment to not reoffend in the future. Restorative Justice looks at offenses not as single events but contextual consequences to deeper systemic issues that must be addressed in order to decrease the likelihood of reoffending. Restorative Justice also supports mitigation of power dynamics between people or groups, and it seeks to maintain community.

Interests, Rights, and Power

Ury, Brett, and Goldberg (1993) offer us a model of conflict resolution that involves exploring three pathways for resolving conflicts between people. The first pathway involves dealing with interests. Dealing with interests is about exploring the needs of the parties, clarifying them, and exploring solutions for mutually meeting those needs. The second pathway is about determining rights. Determining rights focuses on exploring rightness of a particular position, or using rules, laws, or standards to lead to resolutions. And the third pathway, called explicating power, focuses on using power to force the solution desired. While Ury, Brett, and Goldberg offer that there is a time and place for each of these pathways in conflict resolution, the last two can very problematic. Focusing on what the rules are will quickly shut a conversation down, and using power brings compliance but not buy-in or engagement. Dealing with interests and finding mutual resolution is the most effective, longest lasting approach, and it also takes the most effort, time, and support.

Thomas-Kilman Model

The Thomas-Kilman Model, developed by Thomas and Kilman (1974) looks at behavioral styles of the people involved in addressing conflict.

The model identifies five styles based on two dimensions: level of assertiveness and level of cooperation. High assertiveness and low cooperation lead to competing behaviors, where each side seeks their own outcomes at the expense of another's. High assertiveness and high cooperation lead to collaborating behaviors where all sides work creatively to find solutions that satisfy needs of all. Low assertiveness and high cooperation lead to accommodating behaviors, where one party puts aside their needs in favor of another's. Low assertiveness and low cooperation lead to avoiding behaviors where the conflict is not directly addressed or resolved. And equal moderate levels assertiveness and cooperation leads to compromising where each side strives for partial meeting of the goals and interests. Thomas and Kilman note that all of us are capable of using all five in different situations but contend we have preferences for a particular style. The important process is to recognize the style that is best needed for reconciliation and to use that.

Feminist Models

Feminist models highlight that the concepts of conflict, resolution, peace, and power are gendered (Sharoni, 2017). All conflict resolution models reinforce dominant norms unless gender bias is intentionally addressed in our language and inequitable power structures are acknowledged and dismantled. Feminist models bring light to how we are socialized along problematic binary gender roles with narrow ranges of programmed responses to conflict and resolution, deemed "appropriate" to our gender. There is no singular feminist model (Sharoni, 2017); rather, feminist models focus on the process of conflict resolution, not the structure. In other words, *how* we resolve our conflicts matter more than *what* tool we use to resolve them. Feminist models of conflict resolution are similar to the restorative justice model, with clarity on addressing how gendered norms and power are underneath the conflict and show up in the resolution process.

Social Justice-Based Conflict Resolution

Similarly, there is no singular social justice conflict resolution model, and the focus is on infusing social justice into the entire conflict resolution process. Social justice conflict resolution is also about the process and the intentions. What is significant about social justice approaches, however, is the focus on systems and structure. Conflict resolution practices using a social justice approach attempt to highlight and name the systemic factors that drive communication, relationships, values, and ways of knowing.

Watson et al. (2019) developed a training and development curriculum based on social justice principles to build capacity in engaging in conflict. They note that some of the systemic factors behind conflict and conflict resolution in higher education is the value of debate and the privileging of intellect, particularly among faculty. These factors often are the source of conflicts within organizations and there needs to be conflict resolution practices that address these, and other, system factors. Watson et al. (2019) recommend using social justice dialogues as a mechanism to resolve conflict in equitable and sustainable ways. These dialogue groups are similar to intergroup dialogues but with a specific focus on reconciling conflict.

This is not an exhaustive list of conflict resolution models and practices. While all of them can be effective, different contexts and situations call for different approaches. Context matters in how we engage and reconcile conflicts. Considerations such as time and place can greatly affect the process, and even create conditions for one model to be used instead of another. Engaging in conflict resolution certainly should be timely, but it does not always have to be immediate. Allowing pauses in the process creates space for parties to reflect, become aware, and center energies on resolution. Finding comfortable locations for all parties to dialogue is necessary as well. We want to have these conversations in private spaces so that we can encourage and support authenticity, as well as maintain dignity and respect (Scott, 2017). Last, it is essential to find common ground with the other parties (Edmondson, 2012) as early in the process as possible. Building from places of connection is essential to finding our way to reconciliation.

RECONCILIATION AS PRACTICE

As we stated in the introduction to this chapter, identity-conscious supervision practices come with an intention for "reconciliation" instead of the more common "resolution." As discussed, resolution maintains western notions of individualism, gender roles, and white supremacy. Reconciliation centers relationships and community, through affirmative, creative, equitable practices. Engagement from the spirit of reconciliation matters, especially when we come to understand our role in the conflict. It creates space for the people involved to be valued and respected.

A significant barrier to reconciliation is defensiveness, especially as we begin to identify behaviors that have been problematic and/or led to conflict. In Chapter 6, we discussed Watt's (2007) privilege identity exploration model which addresses how defensiveness can show up in conversations about identity, social justice, and inequitable environments. The quickest way to lose trust and respect in a conflict resolution process is to show up defensively. A similar energy we want to avoid is guilt or wallow. Both defensiveness and guilt are self-serving behaviors and attitudes and are rooted in ego and arrogance. They are also endemic of our individual-centered society. Shifting toward community-focused efforts and energies allows us to move through these behaviors toward reconciliation.

One way to do this is to focus on authenticity, accountability, and vulnerability in our reconciliation practice. LeaderShape (2016) offers us some important steps in the process of reconciliation that can guide our practice. Our first step is to admit to our contributions to the conflict and take personal responsibility when we are at fault. The second step is to apologize for our wrongdoing and the impact it has made. It is important that we are authentic in our apology as well. The third step is to act and repair the damage as quickly as possible (if it is possible). We must not hesitate to act. The fourth step is to begin the process of attending to the emotions and relationships and begin the repair process. The fifth and last step is to anchor in our values and integrity to remind ourselves who we strive to be, so that we minimize the possibility of this wrong from happening again. Once done, then we can get back on track as members of our communities.

CONCLUSION

Conflict is a natural part of our identity-conscious practice, and it can be a creative energy in teams and organizations. We can't prevent conflict, especially as we are challenging systems of oppression and unproductive, unjust, and harmful behaviors. Our identity-conscious practice, therefore, is to find methods and processes to effectively reconcile conflicts between members of our community when they happen. Any of the models discussed earlier, and others, can be used in identity-conscious practice; however, any model and process must center people, connection, and a critical love in the process, and it must bring to light the systems and structures that are barriers to justice.

Engaging in conflict from an identity-conscious supervision practice means that we have intentions for justice and reconciliation, for sustaining communities, and shifting systems of oppression that may be in effect. To do that, we need to continue our reflective self-work to understand our identities, our relationship to them, and how those identities and the conditioning we receive on how to engage in conflict drive our behavior.

In both of the stories of conflict shared in this chapter, all of the parties began with conventionally male, aggressive approaches when engaging. Dave had a win-at-all-costs attitude, and Liam had a distant and dismissive attitude. Both were triggering. And I was stuck in needing to be right. The process to reconciliation was delayed because we hadn't built a relationship that would allow for identities to be named and behaviors explored (we were still in the "identities are left at the door"). Because we couldn't discuss how our identities informed how we were engaging, we couldn't discuss how the institutional cultures were at play, nor how the use of power was showing up. Sadly, neither of the conflicts were resolved: Liam left for a position at another university, and Dave minimized contact and denied that a conflict existed. Both experiences are reminders of the impact of unresolved conflict.

Conflict engagement and reconciliation can only occur when trust develops in a way that is both symbiotic and shared (Keehner, 2007). It is only after we have spent the time investing in people and developed authentic, trusting relationships that we can have a successful identity-conscious supervision and conflict reconciliation practices. This process allows us to reframe conflict to focus on developing and deepening relationships with our colleagues and those we supervise, as well as deepening our identity-conscious practice. It takes our time, energy, and investment, and it is essential to sustaining identity-consciousness in an organization.

Case Study
Tynesha McCullers

The setting of this case study is a small, predominantly white institution located in the New England region of the United States. The individuals most central to this case are Connor, Tonia, and Jim. Connor is a white, transgender man, in his junior year of college working as a Resident Assistant (RA). Tonia, Connor's direct supervisor, is a Black, cisgender woman working on a graduate degree who has a huge interest is social identities and social justice. Jim, Tonia's supervisor, is an Asian, cisgender, gay man with several years of work experience in nonprofit education and higher education.

After making a crucial duty mistake and subsequently being placed on job probation, Tonia's supervisee resigns abruptly from the RA position. Three weeks into the fall semester, Tonia, Jim, and fellow colleagues are scrambling to find a replacement that can smoothly transition into the role. After about two weeks, Connor is hired and expected to begin working promptly. As his direct supervisor, Tonia must onboard Connor by introducing him to the staff team and residential community and providing him with continual quasi-training that will help him be successful in the position. Tonia worries that Connor may struggle forming bonds with his fellow RAs because they have already established relationships after summer training and a month and a half of working together. The majority of the RAs are white, cisgender women and men and some of them identify as gay, bisexual, or questioning; Tonia is aware that none of them identify as transgender, and she worries that this will be a barrier for Connor feeling understood and accepted. In addition, Tonia recognizes that as a Black woman, her desire to make systemic changes within her role will breed resistance due to the oppression internalized by her and those she works the closest to.

While meeting with her supervisor, Tonia requests that she and Jim reconsider who her direct supervisees are, after three weeks of working with Connor. Tonia is seeking to switch supervisees because of multiple challenges she has been experiencing with Connor. She informs Jim that she has been unable to build trust and develop a relationship with Connor because he refuses to acknowledge her presence or communicate with her in any capacity. Tonia describes feeling completely rejected and disrespected by Connor; she notes previous times when he has only taken direction when given to him by Jim or masculine presenting individuals. Jim wonders if there are other social identities, such as disability, that are contributing to Connor's perceived unwillingness to engage or perform job responsibilities.

In addition to the difficulties she has been having with Connor, Tonia mentions that RAs have come to her reporting negative interactions that they have had with him. Some of these interactions include racist comments about Black individuals and affirmative action, criticisms about survivors of sexual assault, negative remarks about people with disabilities, and comments expressing disgust for poor and working class individuals. As a member of each of the communities Connor verbalizes distaste for, Tonia fears that holding him accountable may make her appear irrational, angry, and incompetent as a supervisor.

Although she wants to address Connor's behavior, she worries about the impact it will have on her, the RAs she supervises and the numerous students she serves. Addressing Connor's behavior can out RAs who shared concerns confidentially and create mistrust, further marginalize/isolate Connor, and open Tonia up to be harmed. Tonia wants to remain engaged by supporting everyone's growth and learning, minimize potential harm to residents, and maintain her positive reputation as a professional in her department and field.

QUESTIONS TO CONSIDER

1. With harm already occurring across positions of power because of varying dominant identities, what might be the most effective way to address/repair hurt without further marginalizing involved parties and creating a dynamic of mistrust?
2. It is discovered that Connor has a connection to a couple of the identity groups he voices disdain for, meaning that he may be dealing with his own internalized oppression. How might you as a supervisor provide support to his educating and unlearning processes?
3. Do you hold an employee accountable (via job action) for differing but harmful views that don't align with the department's values? If so, what steps should be taken to hold them accountable? If not, how should their behavior be properly addressed if it continues?

REFERENCES

Arbinger Institute. (2015). *The anatomy of peace: Resolving the heart of conflict.* Oakland, CA: Berrett Koehler Publishers.

Bolman, L. G., & Deal, T. E. (2017). *Reframing organizations: Artistry, choice, and leadership* (6th ed.). San Francisco, CA: Jossey-Bass.

Bridges, W. (2009). *Managing transitions: Making the most of change* (3rd ed.). Philadelphia, PA: Da Capo Press.

Buckingham, M., & Coffman, C. (1999). *First break all the rules: What the world's greatest managers do differently*. New York, NY: Simon & Schuster.

Darling, J. (2011). *Restorative justice in higher education: A compilation of formats and best practices*. Retrieved from www.skidmore.edu/campusrj/documents/Darling-2011-campus-programs.pdf

The Editors. (2003, Summer). *Peace: How realistic is it? Tricycle*. Retrieved from https://tricycle.org/magazine/peace-how-realistic-it/

Edmondson, A. C. (2012). *Teaming: How organizations learn, innovate, and compete in the knowledge economy*. San Francisco, CA: Jossey-Bass.

Eisler, R. (2002). *The power of partnership: Seven relationships that will change your life*. Novato, CA: New World Library.

Gibson, C. B., & McDaniel, D. M. (2010). Moving beyond conventional wisdom: Advancements in cross-cultural theories of leadership, conflict, and teams. *Perspectives of Psychological Science, 5*(4), 450–462.

Hemphill, P., & BLM Healing Justice Working Group. (date unknown). Tools for addressing chapter conflict. *Black Lives Matter*. Retrieved from https://blacklivesmatter.com/resource/chapter-conflict-resolution-toolkit/

Keehner, J. (2007). Effective supervision: The many roles, responsibilities, and opportunities. In R. L. Ackerman (Ed.), *The mid-level manager in student affairs* (pp. 103–126). Washington, DC: National Association of Student Personnel Administrators.

Lancaster, L., & Stillman, D. (2002). *When Generations Collide: Who They Are. Why They Clash. How to Solve the Generational Puzzle at Work*. New York: Collins Business.

LeaderShape. (2016). *Faculty manual*. Champaign, IL: LeaderShape, Inc.

Manning, K., & Coleman-Boatwright, P. (1991). Student affairs initiatives toward a multicultural university. *Journal of College Student Development, 32*, 367–374.

Mmeje, K., Newman, C. B., Kramer II, D. A., & Pearson, M. A. (2009). The changing landscape of higher education: Developmental approaches to engaging emerging populations. In S. R. Harper & S. J. Quaye (Eds.), *Student engagement in higher education: Theoretical perspectives and practical approaches for diverse populations* (pp. 295–312). New York, NY: Routledge.

Pope, R. L., Reynolds, A. L., & Mueller, J. A. (2014). *Creating multicultural change on campus*. San Francisco, CA: John Wiley & Sons.

Rosenberg, M. (2015). *Nonviolent communication: A language of life-changing tools for healthy relationships.* Encinitas, CA: Puddle Dancer Press.

Scott, K. (2017). *Radical candor: How to be a kick-ass boss without losing your humanity.* New York, NY: St. Martin's Press.

Sharoni, S. (2017). Conflict resolution: Feminist perspectives. *International Studies.* doi:10.1093/acrefore/9780190846626.013.130

Shonk, K. (2014). *How to resolve cultural conflict: Overcoming cultural barriers at the negotiation table.* Retrieved from www.pon.harvard.edu/daily/conflict-resolution/a-cross-cultural-negotiation-example-how-to-overcome-cultural-barriers/

Smith, K. K., & Berg, D. N. (1997). *Paradoxes of group life: Understanding conflict, paralysis, and movement in group dynamics.* San Francisco, CA: Jossey-Bass.

Taylor, S. L. (2003). Conflict resolution. In S. R. Komives, D. B. Woodard Jr., & Associates (Eds.), *Student services: A handbook for the Profession* (4th ed., pp. 525–538). San Francisco, CA: Jossey-Bass.

Thomas, K. W., & Kilman, R. H. (1974). *Thomas-Kilman conflict mode instrument.* Tuxedo, NY: XICOM.

Ury, W., Brett, J. M., & Goldberg, S. B. (1993). *Getting disputes resolved: Designing systems to cut the costs of conflict.* Cambridge, MA: Harvard University Press.

Watson, N. T., Rogers, K. S., Watson, K. L., & Liau-Hing, Y. C. (2019). Integrating social justice-based conflict resolution into higher education settings: Faculty, staff, and student professional development through mediation training. *Conflict Resolution Quarterly, 36,* 251–262. https://doi.org/10.1002/crq.21233

Watt, S. (2007). Difficult dialogues, privilege and social justice: Uses of the privileged identity exploration (PIE) model in student affairs practice. *College Student Affairs Journal, 26,* 114–126.

Wilgus, J. K., & Holmes, R. C. (2009). Facilitated dialogue: An overview and introduction for student conduct professionals. In J. M. Schrage & N. G. Giacomini (Eds.), *Reframing campus conflict: Student conduct practice through a social justice lens* (pp. 112–125). Sterling, VA: Stylus Publishing.

Zehr, H. (2002). *The little book of restorative justice.* Intercourse, PA: Good Books.

Part III

Action at the Organizational Level

Chapter Nine

Sustaining Identity-Consciousness

Part of what makes supervision hard to define and do effectively is the broad range of knowledge and skills it requires. In 2015, ACPA and NASPA identified and published ten core competencies for student affairs professionals. These competencies include: 1) personal and ethical foundations; 2) values, philosophy, and history; 3) assessment, evaluation, and research; 4) law, policy, and governance; 5) organizational and human resources; 6) leadership; 7) social justice and inclusion; 8) student learning and development; 9) technology; and 10) advising and supporting (ACPA & NASPA, 2015). Although supervision is officially categorized and described more fully under the competency of organizational and human resources, effective supervision encompasses many of these competencies. Unfortunately, most of us do not receive instruction on how to supervise, instead learning primarily from our own supervisors who likely did not have any training themselves (Holmes, 2014). As supervisors, we play an important role in setting the tone and creating inclusive work spaces where individuals are valued and diversity is embraced (Stock-Ward & Javorek, 2003). Consequently, supervisory skill-building and training are critical to effectively create more just organizations and processes (Perillo, 2011).

As the landscape of student affairs and higher education continues to evolve and change, there is an increasing expectation for student affairs administrators to develop specific skills to address social justice topics and the diverse needs of faculty, staff, and students on their campuses (Dixon, 2001; Harper & Quaye, 2015; Howard-Hamilton, Cuyjet, & Cooper, 2016). We believe that awareness alone is not enough—instead, what is required is sustained identity-consciousness in our supervisory practices at the individual, supervisory, and organizational levels. This means that along with increasing awareness of our own biases and identity-based dynamics in our interpersonal work relationships, we must also support our supervisees as they bump up against oppressive institutional structures.

It is also important that we pay attention to practices, reactions, language, and priorities to identify gaps, inconsistencies, and barriers to creating inclusive environments (Bailey & Hamilton, 2015). In order to continue developing an identity-conscious lens across individual, interpersonal, and institutional levels, we must engage one of its foundational tenets—critical consciousness.

Freire's (1970) concept of *conscientizacao*—deeper consciousness or critical consciousness—is foundational to our conceptualization of identity-conscious supervision. Challenging us to "intervene in reality in order to change it" (Freire, 1970, p. 4), critical consciousness involves 1) coming to an understanding of one's social identities and their role in perpetuating oppression and 2) acquiring knowledge of historical and contemporary manifestations of systemic oppression (Quaye et al., 2018). Critical consciousness requires a process of developing an awareness of one's social identities and the societal conditions that create and sustain oppressive dynamics between social identity groups (hooks, 2010; Zúñiga, Nagda, Chesler, & Cytron-Walker, 2007).

Critical consciousness-raising is essential to sustaining our identity-conscious supervisory practices. By broadening our critical consciousness as supervisors, we can more effectively utilize an identity-conscious lens to support supervisees at the individual, interpersonal, and structural levels. In the following sections, we will share strategies for sustaining identity-consciousness enhancing our ability to engage in more just supervisory practices.

SUSTAINING CONSCIOUSNESS—INDIVIDUAL

Supervisory practices that inspire and make room for self-reflection—"a critical aspect of meaning-making" (Ardoin, 2014, p. 129)—should be an essential element when working to deepen consciousness at the individual level, both for the supervisor and the supervisee. As supervisors, we can utilize self-reflection to explore the ways in which our personal and social identities contribute to our understanding of supervision and supervisory dynamics.

Core Values

As we work to develop consciousness at the individual level, we can begin the process by deconstructing our core values and beliefs. This process is critical because when we neglect to take the time to explore our value system we tend to assume that what is normal for us is also commonplace for others (Pope, Reynolds, & Mueller, 2019). Our familial, cultural, and societal backgrounds profoundly affect our values and worldview and we are often not aware of the extent of this influence until we take a step back to examine ourselves. For example, I (Robert) was raised in a family, where both of my parents were small business owners. Their role modeling taught me an ethos that "if you don't work, you don't eat," which continues to influence the ways in which I make meaning of time, work hours, and productivity. Even though my work in higher education is privileged by the consistency of a salaried paycheck, I still work in ways that replicate my parents' values around hard work to earn that next paycheck. While student affairs work is very rarely 9–5, the result of my socialization normalized unhealthy levels of work for me, thus decreasing my ability to have work-life balance and role model it for my staff.

Internalization

Another critical aspect of self-reflection is examining the role of dominance in our socialization and its influence on our behaviors in the workplace. Due to historical context, systems of oppression often normalize dominant groups' ways of being in the world. People from both dominant and subordinated groups take in messages that uphold and reinforce dominant group superiority and subordinated group inferiority (Harro, 2018). When people holding dominant group identities absorb this process of socialization, they experience "internalized superiority/dominance" (Goodman, 2011). At times individuals are conscious of internalized dominance, but more often it manifests as "unconscious, internalized values and attitudes that maintain domination, even when people do not support or display overt discrimination or prejudice" (hooks, 1989, p. 13). For people holding subordinated group identities, "internalized oppression" or "internalized inferiority" undermines their self-esteem, sense of empowerment, and intragroup solidarity (Goodman, 2011). These internal manifestations show up in behavior and decision making.

Rewards and Punishments

From an early age and throughout life, messaging about social identities provides implicit and explicit rules of how these identities should be performed in society, originating from interpersonal interactions, social institutions, media, laws, and cultural norms. When a person performs social identity roles as expected, they are "rewarded"; however, failure to perform according to the cultural norms will likely result in "punishment" (Harro, 2018). For example, staff who speak in ways that align with their cultural backgrounds (i.e., swear words, non-English accent, slang) are perceived as inarticulate, unprofessional, or lacking executive presence as compared to staff who speak more in alignment with "proper" English standards in the United States. Language use rewarded and punished in this way can result in discriminatory hiring and promotion practices across levels within student affairs, even unconsciously. While difficult, it is important that supervisors work to bring the unconscious manifestations of internalized dominance and oppression into their consciousness to engage more deeply in reflective practice at the individual level and interrupt the system.

Growing up in a Black family, I (Robert) learned that I needed to "work twice as hard to get half as much"—a common adage among People of Color and individuals coming from immigrant and working-class backgrounds. Throughout my career, I have consistently tried to go above and beyond to avoid being perceived stereotypically as lazy. This has often resulted in stretching myself too thin, placing a strain on my mental and emotional health. At the same time, as a cisgender man I also learned that my voice had value and should be asserted when I have a strong opinion. The result prompted me to speak over colleagues, particularly women and nonbinary colleagues, in meetings asserting my perspectives regardless of their silencing impact. Both of these internalizations created dissonance in relation to my values and prompted me to engage in self-reflection to elevate my identity-consciousness around race, ability, and gender.

Critical Self-Reflection

These internalized behaviors can become normalized within organizations given the frequency in which they are exhibited. In describing the components of critical self-reflection, Brookfield (1987) includes identifying and challenging assumptions, becoming aware of how context shapes what is considered normal and natural ways of thinking and living and imagining and exploring alternative ways of thinking and living (pp. 7–8). Brookfield encourages educators to try to awaken, prompt, nurture and encourage this process of self-reflection without making people feel threatened or patronized. Each of these components of critical self-reflection provides a foundation for deepening reflective practice at the individual level. In addition to the dynamics shared in this section related to time, productivity, and voice, we can also benefit from reflecting on our personal relationship to competition, individualism, objectivity, conflict, either/or thinking, and paternalism as additional patterns of thought and behavior rooted in dominant ways of being that ground our professional values systems (Jones & Okun, 2001). It is essential that we reflect on our values and behaviors to make the unconscious conscious and explore their impact on self and others.

SUSTAINING CONSCIOUSNESS—INTERPERSONAL

Institutions use various management mechanisms to maintain conformity within the culture and punish actions of employees who act in contrast to the culture. For instance, staff who wear clothing or shoes that fall outside the rigid boundaries of typical business or business casual attire are perceived as unprofessional. The ripple of this dynamic, beyond the impact on an individual, is that it becomes an additional barrier for People of Color, women, gender nonconforming, people with disabilities, working class, and LGBTQIA professionals to professionally advance in the field. In order to disrupt these barriers, it is important to track patterns of exclusion and inequity at the interpersonal level.

Tracking Group Dynamics

While attending the Social Justice Training Institute, we learned the critical skill of *panning* or *tracking* with an "inclusion lens"—the ability to recognize differential experiences and treatment by group membership (Obear, 2012). Tracking dynamics at the interpersonal level prompts us to pause and pay attention to the ways in which social identity undergirds patterns of practice and behavior. Supervisors interested in tracking interpersonal dynamics at the group level can utilize the following questions to reflect on the supervisory relationship and team dynamics (Obear, 2013):

- What differences are present on the team? Which group memberships? How many staff do you have from various social identity groups?
- Who talks during meetings? Who initiates topics?
- Whose ideas are discussed in depth? Whose ideas do not receive much discussion and/or are discounted?
- Who interrupts others? Who gets interrupted?
- Who is sitting with whom or talking in groups after the meeting?
- How do decisions get made? Who holds power and influence?
- Who brings up issues of equity and inclusion?
- How does your team/supervisee respond when issues of equity and inclusion are raised?

As we continue to practice the skill of panning, it becomes more natural for us and creates opportunities for us to connect with others in exploring

161

dynamics. Through reflection and dialogue, it also helps us interrupt the judgments and stories we create around these patterns.

Strategies for Engaging

Hare and LeBoutillier (2014) encourage developing the skills of noticing (thoughts, information), nurturing (emotion, personal connections) and naming (meaning making) the related social issues at play in each dynamic of difference. For example, supervisors can track the political and social construct of disability/ableism with their supervisees. Throughout my career, I (Robert) have supervised and been a colleague to staff who navigate chronic illness. The skill of *noticing* prompted me to explore reflective questions related to my own lack of awareness around ability and who raises concerns related to ableism within my work with students or in the workplace environment. As I explored these questions as an able-bodied person, I found that my awareness was limited in noticing ableist patterns of practice and often absent in naming these dynamics. Once I noticed these dynamics, I realized that I needed to increase my own consciousness of ableist practices in my behaviors, assumptions, and supervision practices.

The skill of *nurturing* prompts us to ask ourselves, "What is my level of comfort?" in exploring issues related to ability/disability. As part of these reflections, processing can also extend to the exploration of emotion. What emotions are surfacing for us and others as conversations unfold? What dynamics are we *panning* and *tracking* within our supervisory relationships or team engagement? As we notice interpersonal dynamics that are not inclusive, it is useful to ponder whether it is an isolated incident or a possible pattern of practice (Obear, 2013). One of the most pervasive emotions I (Robert) have tracked in my work with staff with disabilities is the pursuit and utilization of workplace accommodations. While necessary, there are a range of emotions for the individual pursuing an accommodation that are important to support and additional emotions that surface from other staff with less knowledge or belief that a particular accommodation is needed. It is critical to focus on staff seeking the accommodation when processing these emotions personally and collectively. Occasionally, staff will share openly with others but often accommodations are confidential, which creates curiosities and skepticism among staff that are important to track and challenge. Within our practice of nurturing, we can follow up to check in on the emotional impact of disclosure (or lack thereof), offering affirmation and support.

The final step of *naming* tends to be the most challenging but is critical in order to address underlying concerns and dynamics. In this process, supervisors commit to listening deeply and actively to multiple voices and competing views, thinking critically about their own identities, beliefs, values and positionality, participating authentically and intentionally in difficult dialogues, and being open to personal development (Watt, 2015b). In my own experience, I have found it useful to name what I do and do not know with staff and colleagues. At times, we are able to engage each other to increase my learning and other times I sought out knowledge from campus partners, literature, and personal reflection. Engaging other staff provides the greatest challenge given the necessity to maintain confidentiality. Often the questions and critiques are rooted in personal needs of staff. It is helpful to explore the needs of other staff as an independent dynamic worth supporting and developing solutions for. As supervisors, we can apply dialogue frameworks shared in Chapter 6 throughout the process of "naming."

SUSTAINING CONSCIOUSNESS—STRUCTURAL

In order to sustain an identity-conscious supervisory practice, we need to understand prejudice, power, and oppression (defined in Chapter 1), exploring how systems work together to create barriers to access and success in higher education. Oppression exploits, devalues, and deprives people privileges at the personal, interpersonal, institutional, and cultural levels (Blumenfeld, 2010) that are conferred without question to those with power (Barker, 2003; Young, 2018). Systems of racism, white supremacy, and settler colonialism intersect with structures of classism, ableism, genderism, heterosexism, and nationalism to create situations of increasing jeopardy for minoritized professionals and reinforced power for dominant groups (Quaye et al., 2018). When we ignore these dynamics, "we become unwitting accomplices to frustration, discrimination, and even failure" (Pope et al., 2019, p. 55). Many campus community members are rightfully demanding a deconstruction of these structural inequities (discussed in Chapter 8) and are taking steps to name the restrictive nature of dominant cultural norms in higher education.

Historical Implications

Facing increasing campus uprisings fueled by a continued history of inequality and the reemergence of nationalistic movements in the United States, ACPA developed the *Strategic Imperative for Racial Justice and Decolonization* (SIRJD) as a possibility framework to address structural inequities in higher education and student affairs (Quaye et al., 2018). The imperative outlines several principles for action undergirded by the consistent context of history. The framework challenges us to not only develop an awareness of our role in reproducing racism and colonization but also identifies the need to take actions that shift how institutions create and exacerbate racism and colonization. We can utilize the SIRJD Syllabus as a tool to increase identity-consciousness at the structural and institutional levels. Most notably, the syllabus includes resources on the history of higher education that can enhance consciousness of the colonial and white supremacist power structures that undergird higher education practices. Increasing consciousness of history is a necessary step in starting the process of sustaining identity-consciousness at the structural and institutional levels.

Cultural Manifestations

Supervisors can start the process of sustaining structural identity-consciousness by exploring the very culture of student affairs work. We are socialized in a culture, specifically a work culture that praises and celebrates individual achievements. We are evaluated based upon our individual effectiveness (individual goals and accountabilities) and acknowledged for our individual efforts (employees of the year awards). This fits with our cultural narrative of the white male myth of individualism and emotional distance (Elliott, 2008) and breeds a sense that individuals have more value than the team.

The culture also normalizes workplace behaviors such as competition, assertiveness, and arrogance, which directly informs how supervision is performed. In particular, these workplace cultural norms rooted in whiteness and masculinity create dynamics where we need to be right and be viewed as right, even when we are wrong. However, these behaviors are really only accepted when used by white men: "when women challenge directly—which they must do to be successful—they get penalized for being 'abrasive'" (Scott, 2017, p. 156). Differentially appropriate workplace behaviors undergirds a system of written and unwritten rules that further penalizes women, gender-fluid and trans colleagues, colleagues of color, and colleagues from working-class backgrounds. As they attempt to navigate a workplace culture, they see the behaviors that have been normalized, but are criticized or penalized for using them. They likely search for acceptable behaviors but struggle to find clear direction. This is a frustrating and dehumanizing experience, and it serves to separate, further clarifying that the individual achievement is what matters most. When supervision is informed by this culture and way of being, it upholds structural inequities.

164

Means of Production

Colleges and universities seem increasingly concerned with productivity and the output of good "products." While there are some good reasons for that which we cannot fully explore in the context of this book, this notion can run counter to the "process" that learning entails (Alvim & Barnhart, 2017). For our purposes, what is important to note is that when product or the full pursuit of productivity alone takes precedence over process and people, the consequences draw notable parallels to coloniality, white supremacy, and dehumanization. The value of product over people surfaces as a pervasive pattern as supervisors seek to support staff experiencing emotional fatigue and stress in response to national incidents (Squire & Nicolazzo, 2019). We can deepen our consciousness of the ways in which our departments operate, upholding business as usual in these contentious times.

It feels like yesterday that I (Robert) was sitting in my office watching the video release of the murder of Eric Garner. As I watched the video alone in my office, another colleague came and stood at my door. It took us two seconds to realize we had just taken in the same violent imagery. Over the course of the next hour, we sat and held space for each other to process, mourn, and feel the impact of the assault on each of our Black bodies. After sitting together, we regained our composure, walked into our center, and held this same space with our students as they processed the racialized violence they experienced throughout their lives and on our campus. I wish I could say this workday was different than most, but it was not. It was endemic of a much larger pattern and practice required of our work in multicultural affairs.

Sadly, the experience we shared that day continued repeatedly as our nation wrestled with the reality of police violence, anti-Blackness, and white supremacy. Many of my colleagues across the country share similar memories and are often left facing the pressure to "get back to work." In these moments, student affairs supervisors must intentionally seek to increase their consciousness of these and other structures that limit the capacity for individuals to be more fully human as they engage at the institutional level. Supervisors interested in deepening consciousness at the structural level can utilize the following questions to reflect on their supervisory practices (Quaye et al., 2018):

- What is the history of my campus and how has it benefited from systems of oppression and colonization?
- What do I need to learn to begin to promote social justice, racial justice, and decolonization in my supervisory practice?

165

- How can I facilitate opportunities for supervisees and colleagues to develop critical consciousness on issues related to justice and equity?
- How are the interests and power of dominant groups reinforced by the management policies and practices I develop and uphold?
- What responsibilities do I hold to remove barriers that prevent minoritized members of my team from exercising their own voices in defense of their agency?
- What possibilities lie ahead if my supervisee(s) and I know each other as fully human? What future can we imagine together? How might that focus on possibility benefit students?

MOVING TO ACTION

As an identity-conscious supervisor, it is not enough to know what the problem is or to understand what needs to happen. Action is required to move beyond consistent inaction in management and instead identify, engage with, and combat the barriers that exist whether they be personal, interpersonal, or structural (Pope et al., 2019). Love (2018) theorizes a liberatory consciousness, which enables humans to be aware of how oppression manifests in their world. A liberatory consciousness requires action that advocates for systems change on behalf of and in concert with others who are continually underrepresented and underserved. In order for that to happen, it is essential that we challenge our dichotomous thinking, decolonize our mindset, and embrace both/and perspectives (Quaye et al., 2018, Watt, 2015b).

Student affairs leaders and supervisors need to be mindful and aware of power dynamics, minimizing them whenever possible. As supervisors seeking to sustain identity-conscious practices, applying a liberatory consciousness moves away from a scarcity and perfectionist mindset, regularly inviting new voices to the table and expanding decision-making to include more perspectives. As we move to action, there is also a need to align our time and resources—including budget allocations—with our espoused priorities. In other words, we need to recognize that if something is not getting our time or resources, it is not actually a priority.

While more senior leaders may have a broader range of influence, supervisors at all levels are encouraged to consider their spheres of influence and leadership. We should construct practices that reflect an understanding of systemic oppression applying an identity-conscious lens. As an example, supervisors and leaders can consider the division of labor among staff, particularly staff of color, and establish compensation structures that reflect actual workload, including consideration of emotional labor and tokenization. As supervisors, we should also set clear, consistent expectations with teams and expect that our supervisees will do the same with theirs (Career Press, 1993). This includes setting expectations that all staff are engaging in inclusive practices, holding staff accountable for having a high level of identity-consciousness (Pope et al., 2019). When concerns surface that supervisees or supervisors are not engaging in inclusive practices, then they should be acted on quickly to ensure accountability is maintained as a priority (Farris, 2018). Staff accountability for oppressive or biased behaviors and attitudes is essential, no matter how good they are at other parts of their job.

Supervisors and leaders in student affairs should actively create hiring practices that minimize implicit bias and invite diverse candidates to apply. Additionally, it is important to pay close attention to hiring and attrition trends, noticing and acting when there are patterns of minoritized professionals leaving an office or division frequently, or when minoritized professionals are consistently not identified as hirable candidates for open positions (Farris, 2018).

For example, I (Robert) served on a search committee where we interviewed a candidate who identified as a disabled man of color. Throughout the interview, the candidate used casual, pejorative language. As the phone interview progressed, I noticed colleagues shut down and disconnect. As we approached the committee meeting to discuss his candidacy, I anticipated my own triggered response to their reflections. The first person to speak was a white cisgender woman, who said, "I really struggled with this candidate's interview. It gave me pause. Not because they weren't qualified, but because of how they engaged. I found myself disengaging and then questioned why I disengaged." The comment took us all aback and caused us to pause. The comment serves as a helpful roadmap for how supervisors can address their own biases, deepen consciousness, and invite in reflection to shift inequitable decision making. My colleague's ability to name the bias allowed our committee to have an amazing conversation about ways we were holding similar biases that reinforced notions around "fit" and campus culture (Reece, Tran, DeVore, & Porcaro, 2018). As we processed further, we realized and named that the candidate was the only Person of Color that we phone interviewed, of eight candidates, prompting even further conversation on why that might be. Developing the skills to notice, nurture, and name allows us to move from consciousness to action.

CONCLUSION

Supervision is nearly universal in the field of student affairs. Staff members from an entry-level academic advisor to the vice president of student affairs all have someone to whom they report. Moreover, many student affairs professionals also have the responsibility to supervise others in committee and project-based work. It is important that we, as student affairs supervisors, adopt and replicate positive and intentional strategies for building critical consciousness in order to improve organizational health and better prepare practitioners for a future that will undoubtedly be rife with difference (Watt, 2015a). Shifting the approach to an identity-conscious practice requires focused skill development to deepen awareness at the individual, group, and systems level. Patton and Bondi (2015) describe this work as ongoing, requiring continual reflection, and perseverance. It involves "moving beyond words towards actions that disrupt oppressive structures and understand one's positionality in oppression" (p. 489). Student affairs supervisors are well positioned to call attention to issues but should understand how their day-to-day actions, behaviors, and attitudes resist or perpetuate inequity. How we build consciousness as an organization is inextricably linked to what we are teaching our students. Ultimately, this shift in consciousness has the power to increase the potential that our institutions prepare students to be good citizens in an ever-changing society.

Case Study
Maggie Chen-Hernandez, Sharon Chia Claros and Jonglim Han

Angela (she/her), an APIDA cisgender woman working at a Spirit University, a predominately white public institution in the Midwest. She struggles to navigate a culture of whiteness in predominantly white spaces, where APIDA experiences and voices are often overlooked and stifled as a consequence of being regarded as the "model minority." During a search committee meeting for the Director of Student Activities, an executive-level administrative position, resumes of several applicants are being reviewed. Serving on the selection committee, Angela comments to her supervisor and chair of the selection committee, John (he/him), an African American, cisgender, male administrator, that the experiences listed in Candidate A's resume do not align with the desired qualifications in the position description. John responds, "We are moving Candidate A forward because they are a *diverse* candidate." Angela then comments, "Well, Candidate B is also diverse. They've indicated that they're APIDA." John quickly responds, "You know what I mean." Angela is perplexed and asks, "No, what do you mean?" John explains, "We need an African American candidate for the pool."

The exchange with John leaves Angela with the impression that she should "stay in her lane," and that APIDAs are not seen as People of Color. This experience further reinforces Angela's growing fear that her voice and experiences as an APIDA woman are not valued. Most recently, John rejected her request to serve as her unit's representative for the university's newly created Diversity & Inclusion workgroup. Based on the power differential between their positions, Angela does not feel comfortable bringing this concern up to John.

As a Midwesterner, John grew up in a community where there was minimal representation outside of a Black/white binary. Additionally, Angela is the first APIDA staff member he has worked closely with and supervised. He appreciates Angela's contributions to their unit and during their biweekly one-on-ones. Their interactions lead him to believe that Angela enjoys working in their unit since she has expressed that she loves her work and position in the unit.

A few weeks pass after the selection committee interaction, and to John's utter surprise, Angela sends an e-mail to inform him that she is actively seeking employment elsewhere.

KEY QUESTIONS

1. What role might John's socialization play in his interaction with Angela and consciousness of APIDA communities?

2. What dynamics are you panning in this case study? As John, how could you name these dynamics in a conversation with Angela following her e-mail?

3. What institutional and cultural dynamics might be undergirding how race is being viewed and contextualized at Spirit University?

REFERENCES

ACPA & NASPA. (2015). *Professional competency areas for student affairs practitioners*. Retrieved from www.naspa.org/images/uploads/main/ACPA_NASPA_Professional_Competencies_FINAL.pdf

Alvim, H. G., & Barnhart, A. (2017). Mindfulness as a pedagogy of supervision: Reclaiming learning in supervised practices in student affairs. *Journal of Research, Assessment, and Practice in Higher Education, 2*(1), 27–40.

Ardoin, S. (2014). *The strategic guide to shaping your student affairs career*. Sterling, VA: Stylus Publishing.

Bailey, K. W., & Hamilton, J. (2015). Supervisory style. In M. J. Amey & L. M. Reesor (Eds.), *Beginning your journey: A guide for new professionals in student affairs* (4th ed., pp. 67–94). Washington, DC: NASPA.

Barker, R. L. (2003). *The social work dictionary* (5th ed.). Baltimore, MD: NASW Press.

Blumenfield, W. J. (2010). How comprehensive is multicultural education? A case for LGBT inclusion. *Journal of Multiculturalism in Education, 5*(2), 1–20.

Brookfield, S. (1987). *Developing critical thinkers: Challenging adults to explore alternative ways of thinking and acting*. San Francisco, CA: Jossey-Bass.

Career Press. (1993). *The supervisor's handbook* (2nd ed.). New York, NY: Author.

Dixon, B. (2001). Student affairs in an increasingly multicultural world. In R. B. Winston, D. G. Creamer, & T. K. Miller (Eds.), *The professional student affairs administrator: Educator, leader, and manager* (pp. 65–80). New York, NY: Brunner-Routledge.

Elliott, C. M. (2008). *Raising change: Fathering as a feminist experience* (Doctoral dissertation). Retrieved from ProQuest.

Farris, V. E. (2018). *"I wish they would. . . ": The role of white student affairs professionals can play in disrupting systemic racism in the supervision of people of color in higher education* (Unpublished doctoral dissertation), University of Pennsylvania, Philadelphia.

Freire, P. (1970). *Pedagogy of the oppressed*. New York, NY: Continuum.

Goodman, D. J. (2011). *Promoting diversity and social justice: Educating people from privileged groups*. New York, NY: Routledge.

Hare, S. Z., & LeBoutillier, M. (2014). *Let the beauty we love be what we do: Stories of living divided no more*. Pawleys Island, SD: Prose Press.

Harper, S. R., & Quaye, S. J. (2015). Making engagement equitable for students in U.S. higer education. In S. J. Quaye, & S. R. Harper (Eds.), *Student engagement in higher education: Theoretical perspectives and practical approaches for diverse populations* (2nd ed.) (pp. 1–14). New York, NY: Routledge.

Harro, B. (2018). The cycle of socialization. In M. Adams, W. J. Blumenfeld, D. C. Catalano, K. DeJong, H. W. Hackman, . . . X. Zúñiga (Eds.), *Readings for diversity and social justice* (4th ed., pp. 27–33). New York, NY: Routledge.

Holmes, A. C. (2014). *Experiences of supervision skill development among new professionals in student affairs* (Unpublished doctoral dissertation). Iowa State University, Ames.

hooks, b. (1989). *Talking back*. Boston: South End Press.

hooks, b. (2010). *Teaching critical thinking: Practical wisdom*. New York, NY: Routledge.

Howard-Hamilton, M. F., Cuyjet, M. J., & Cooper, D. L. (2016). Understanding multiculturalism and multicultural competence among college students. In M. J. Cuyjet, C. Linder, M. F. Howard-Hamilton, & D. L. Cooper (Eds.), *Multiculturalism on campus: Theory, models, and practices for understanding diversity and creating inclusion* (pp. 11–21). Sterling, VA: Stylus.

Jones, K., & Okun, T. (2001). The characteristics of white supremacy culture. In *Dismantling racism: A workbook for social change groups*. Retrieved from www.showingupforracialjustice.org/white-supremacy-culture-characteristics.html

Love, B. J. (2018). Developing a liberatory consciousness. In M. Adams, W. J. Blumenfeld, D. C. Catalano, K. DeJong, H. W. Hackman, . . . X. Zúñiga (Eds.), *Readings for diversity and social justice* (4th ed., pp. 610–615). New York, NY: Routledge.

Obear, K. (2012). Reflections on our practice as social justice educators: How far we've come, how far we need to go. *Journal of Critical Thought & Praxis*, *1*(1), 30–51.

Obear, K. (2013). Panning group dynamics with an inclusion lens. *Building Inclusive Organizations*. Workshop handout available by request from kathy@drkathyobear.com

Patton, L. D., & Bondi, S. (2015). Nice White men or social justice allies? Using critical race theory to examine how White male faculty and administrators engage in ally work. *Race Ethnicity and Education*, *18*, 488–514.

Perillo, P. A. (2011). Scholar practitioners model inclusive, learning-oriented supervision. In P. M. Magolda & M. B. Baxter Magolda (Eds.), *Contested issues in student affairs: Diverse perspectives and respectful dialogue* (pp. 427–432). Sterling, VA: Stylus Publishing.

Pope, R. L., Reynolds, A. L., & Mueller, J. A. (2019). *Multicultural competence in student affairs: Advancing social justice and inclusion* (2nd ed.). San Francisco, CA: Jossey-Bass.

Quaye, S. J., Aho, R. E., Jacob, M. B., Dominique, A. D., Guido, F. M., Lange, A. C., . . . Stewart, D. L. (2018). *A bold vision forward: A framework for the strategic imperative for racial justice and decolonization.* Retrieved from www.myacpa.org/sites/default/files/SIRJD_GuidingDoc_0.pdf

Reece, B. J., Tran, V. T., DeVore, E. N., & Porcaro, G. (2018). From fit to belonging: New dialogues on the student affairs job search. In B. J. Reece, V. T. Tran, E. N. DeVore, & G. Porcaro (Eds.), *Debunking the myth of job fit in higher education and student affairs* (pp. 1–26). Sterling, VA: Stylus Publishing.

Scott, K. (2017). *Radical candor: How to be a kick-ass boss without losing your humanity.* New York, NY: St. Martin's Press.

Squire, D., & Nicolazzo, Z. (2019). Love my naps, but stay woke: The case against self-care. *About Campus, 24*(2), 4–11.

Stock-Ward, S. R., & Javorek, M. E. (2003). Applying theory to practice: Supervision in student affairs. *NASPA Journal, 40*(3), 77–92.

Watt, S. K. (2015a). Multicultural initiatives as a practice of freedom. In S. K. Watt (Ed.), *Designing transformative multicultural initiatives: Theoretical foundations, practical applications, and facilitator considerations* (pp. 11–22). Sterling, VA: Stylus Publishing.

Watt, S. K. (2015b). Authentic, action-oriented, framing for environmental shifts (AAFES) method. In S. K. Watt (Ed.), *Designing transformative multicultural initiatives: Theoretical foundations, practical applications, and facilitator considerations* (pp. 23–39). Sterling, VA: Stylus Publishing.

Young, I. M. (2018). Five faces of oppression. In M. Adams, W. J. Blumenfeld, R. Castañeda, H. W. Hackman, M. L. Peters, & X. Zúñiga (Eds.), *Readings for diversity and social justice: An anthology on racism, antisemitism, sexism, heterosexism, ableism and classism* (pp. 49–58). New York, NY: Routledge.

Zúñiga, X., Nagda, B., Chesler, M., & Cytron-Walker, A. (2007). Educational goals of intergroup dialogues. In *Intergroup dialogue in higher education: Meaningful learning about social justice* (pp. 9–18). ASHE-ERIC report series. San Francisco, CA: Jossey-Bass.

Chapter Ten

Influencing Institutional Change

When we commit to identity-conscious supervision, we also need to be committed to shifting the culture of supervision in our workplace. Justice-centered supervision within an oppressive, unjust work environment will have little effect on the culture, although it could be transformative for the supervisor/supervisee relationship and work experience. The colonized, supremacist mental model is built into the code of the organization in formal, informal, and "organic" ways (Paperson, 2017). This mental model is demonstrated in how we hire, evaluate, and support professionals.

Without a system change approach, the impact of identity-conscious supervision is limited to individuals and not sustainable within an organization. Individual change is not enough to influence a systemic change. While we want individuals transformed in their practice, we also need organizations transformed in their practice as well. An important element of the Identity-Conscious Supervision model is the commitment to influence or change the organizational culture toward justice. This needs to be an organizational and personal goal for all supervisors and supervisees committed to social change.

This starts with us first reimagining a more just organization in terms of supervision. We can quite easily reflect on our actions in the supervision experience and understand how our actions can evolve and change to create conditions for a just workplace culture in our area. A just workplace culture includes identity-conscious supervision, equity, universal human design, and justice and inclusion built into the ethos of the workplace. But it is harder to imagine how we can influence this institutional change across a department, division, or the college/university. Our individual efforts to make change won't matter, and our identity-conscious supervision practice will have limited impact outside of our team if the institutional system does not change as well.

Once we have the conceptualization of what could be possible, the next step is to connect with our colleagues, engage them in dialogue, and build alliances across the institution. This could look like a series of conversations, trainings, or development of shared commitments. The goal of this effort is to build capacity within the alliance, to develop the "choir" if you will. All of us need the training, practice, and support of this process. Kotter (2007), discussing his model for the transformational change process, talks about the importance of building a "powerful guiding coalition" to lead the change effort (p. 4). Most great shifts in our culture have been started by gatherings of the willing. This alliance or coalition serves to bring others, especially supervisors, into this process, it develops a community of support, and it builds a collective to address resistance to change.

We also need to consider that identity-consciousness is a paradigm, and that this paradigm is different than the current paradigm in operation at most, if not all, institutions of higher education. A paradigm is a mindset out of which a system arises, including the structures, rules, delays, goals, and parameters (Meadows, 2008). This identity-conscious paradigm will lead to new ways of organizing and being in higher education.

COMPONENTS OF THE CULTURE

Like most organizations, the culture of higher education has been slow to change, despite the efforts to increase the diversity of the student population, expand pathways for access, and increase the diversity of faculty and staff (Pope, Reynolds, & Mueller, 2014). In spite of our efforts to change, the system is resilient and resistant to change. Defined and created during a time when college was for white men only, the organizing structure in higher education and the relevant processes, intentionally or not, reflect the needs of white men. The shifting of the structure and processes, if it has happened at all, has been slow and still surprisingly contentious. The continued violence against women, trans, gender-fluid, differently abled, working class backgrounds, and People of Color in higher education demonstrates the systemic resistance within higher education.

Further, higher education reflects society at large. Higher education is a capitalist enterprise, aligned to make money—the not-for-profit status indicates what it will do with the money it makes, not how much it makes. In a talk in 2018, Rupa Marya illustrated how capitalism is supported by "systems of supremacy and domination," cheap labor, and invisible labor. She went on to say that the outcomes of capitalism are the exploitation of resources (including workers) and trauma. These same structures and outcomes exist in institutions of higher education, and they persist in spite of shifting personnel, shifting social norms, evolving mission statements and work for equity and inclusion. Frank (2013) did a study on why professionals leave the field of higher education and found that new professionals leave because of a feeling of exploitation—overworked and underpaid, with few growth or promotional opportunities.

As employees, we are part of this institutional socialization network. As we bring new professionals to our campus, we ask them to accept (or they are forced to accept) the culture that already exists at the institution. We implicitly expect this. Even if we are clear about the ways the culture is unjust, we are participating in this indoctrination of new professionals through the onboarding process. Unless examined and rebuilt, the structure and processes reflect these same dominant norms, and perpetuate marginalization and microaggressions (Perez, 2016). Policy and procedure manuals often reflect these dominant ideologies and ways of thinking and being, often creating exclusive working environments and reinforce values and conditions of exploitation. Many institutions have unwritten practices as well that further support dominant ideologies in the workplace.

At a former institution I (Craig) was at, there was a formal and very structured room reservation process. But, if you knew who to talk to and had a good relationship with that person, you could bypass that system and get a reservation immediately. I used this unwritten process to accomplish our team's and department's objectives, but I also never told any of my supervisees or colleagues about the existence of this unwritten process. This unwritten process maintained dominance within the organization, with certain people allowed to participate, and I became a keeper of that dominance through my participation.

There is a challenge in approaching systems change work: we still need to get the work done. Students need to be served, classes need to be taught, budgets balanced, rooms cleaned, programs planned, machines fixed, food cooked, etc. The trick is learning to hold both at the same time—developing the need for change, collaboratively mapping the path, and seeing ways to advance along that path while taking care of the immediate work. Often this effort falls to marginalized groups, and we need to make sure that all team members help hold the daily work and the systems change work. Even with an identity-conscious supervision perspective, supervisors will need to communicate the goals and expectations for the work needed and the way that the work is done and support them along the way.

IDENTITY-CONSCIOUSNESS AS A PARADIGM

Practicing with an identity-consciousness mindset is a new paradigm, and it has the potential to radically change the system. Not only is it a challenge to the dominant norms, but it also allows us to bring a systems-aware approach to our work so that we can effectively interrupt how the system of oppression shows up in the higher education workplace. This is part of what is radical: formalizing this awareness—while it has been clear to employees, especially when they are being treated in ways that marginalize them, it is rarely acknowledged by supervisors, human resources, leadership, or an organization.

Another radical element is being explicit about an identity-conscious supervision approach. This becomes an invitation for others to use this supervision approach. It also helps others understand actions—when people don't understand the frame behind behaviors and decisions, they revert to the dominant frame for understanding. "Institutional neglect of racism and injustice is the exercise of power, the kind of power that refuses to notice and refuses to speak". It is lack of acknowledgment and identification of how it exists in the system that allows oppression and injustice to continue.

Awareness of the frame in our supervision style increases clarity and awareness. Being explicit also enlists others into an accountability cycle (feedback loops). Our work to supervise and work from an identity-conscious framework is uncharted enough both for the organization, for us, and for our supervisors and supervisees. As we work to build a new model based upon this identity-conscious paradigm, we will bump up against the current oppressive model, revert to automatic, old ways of being, and even make mistakes. Having others in our accountability teams will help us continue to do the work necessary to create these changes.

This identity-conscious framework also radically brings love and care into how we work alongside and care for the people we work with. We suspect that most of us bring a loving care to our work with students, but that loving care doesn't also feed our work and being with our colleagues. We want us both to become system thinkers and system feelers (Mackey & Sisodia, 2014) that, while we are working to shift the system, we are also working to shift our being with each other toward loving care.

The system won't create this consciousness or this model automatically. We have to be intentional. We have to be courageous. We have to become the leaders and supervisors we wish we had (Sinek, 2014). Good leaders lead both systems and people with love and care.

Last, any change efforts will be faced with resistance, especially paradigm-shifting change efforts. And the "higher the leverage point, the more the system will resist changing it" (Meadows, 2008, p. 165). Collectively engaging areas of resistance is essential to success (Pope et al., 2014). On one level, "Remarkable visions and genuine insight are always met with resistance" (Godin, 2008, p. 129). As we have shared, identity-consciousness is a big enough change effort that it will challenge people's sense of comfort and order.

On another level, systems are self-preserving (Meadows, 2008) and forces are in place to keep the status quo system in operation. We employees are still invested in the current system, even if we are not quite clear how. We show up in collusion and internalized privilege and oppression. We need to work through our internal resistance as well as the organizational resistance. We also want to reframe resistance. In our experience, resistance is a strong indication that we are doing needed work in the right area. Facing resistance reminds us we are right where we need to be.

We need to make these changes in how we supervise and how we are supervised. We need to show our colleagues there is a new way, and we need to encourage and support them moving to that new way.

A PRIMER ON SYSTEMS

Before we can embark on any kind of systems or workplace culture change, we need to understand what systems are and how they operate. While it is helpful to discuss systems here, this is not intended to be a full systems overview or to provide you with a complete understanding of higher education systems or even the myriad of ways different institutions operate. Our intention, however, is to provide a framework for understanding the complexity of systems and help you appreciate how complexity and systems may show up on a particular campus.

Donella Meadows (2008) describes a system as a "set of things interconnected in such a way that they produce their own patterns of behavior over time" (p. 2). This is a wonderfully simple way to describe what can be incredibly complex. As we look at what makes a system, there are a number of different things to consider. There are the elements of the system, which are the individual parts that make up the system. These elements can be physical (the people, the buildings, green space, etc.) or intangible (school spirit, the sense of campus, sense of pride, etc.). Next, there are the interconnections between those elements, how they relate, and work in concert with each other (or not). The interconnections connect the revenue collection, the budgeting process and resource allocations, and the actual expense of money. The interplay of applicants, admission requirements, the process by which admission and the faculty determine who to admit, and how well these students succeed at the institution are also interconnections. These interconnections are also at the individual level, mapping how the people interact with each other and in what contexts. Last, there are the forces that drive the system. These are often outside forces, like the economy, or federal and state regulations.

Internal forces also drive the system like values, institutional culture, and the perception of educational mission, either written or unwritten. All of these need to be functioning for the system to be "alive," and yet each part is also resilient enough to adapt to change without collapsing the system (Meadows, 2008). Systems will respond toward preservation and adapt to keep functioning.

Institutions of higher education, like all organizations, are designed and organized in such a way that they produce their own way of behaving and being (Meadows, 2008). There are distinct cultures at colleges and universities compared, and each institution of higher education has a unique manifestation of that higher education culture. Bailey and Hamilton (2015) also echo these ideas. Organizational culture shows up in the patterns of shared values, beliefs, assumptions, and symbols.

These patterns are driven by several elements, including:

- the purpose of higher education
- the vision of the institution
- where the college or university is located and the regional needs
- the people who work there
- the politics of the state, region, and institution
- who the institution envisions will enroll as students (stated and unstated).

These influences lead to particular behaviors and interrelationships. Every element of an organization (a system) is interrelated (Hersey, Blanchard, & Johnson, 1996). Budgets are a great example: who influences budgets, resource allocation and access all shapes how processes form and sustain as well as what partnerships are needed for a program or project to be successful. People at higher levels of an organization have few guidelines on how they can access and use money; people lower in the hierarchy have many. Faculty and academic departments rarely have discretionary money available to them for things like cocurricular programming, or food for events, and so they need to partner with other departments (usually student affairs departments) if they wish to continue in these ways. This creates a narrowing of priorities and a zero-sum approach to the larger mission-driven activities of an institution. It is also why diversity, equity, and inclusion programs and services end up under-resourced or cut altogether.

These patterns persist over time as well (Meadows, 2008). The system of an institution is resilient enough to accommodate a continual influx of ever-changing students, new faculty, staff, and administrators and still maintain its sense of institutional culture or identity. This institutional identity persists over generations, and while an institution's identity may evolve somewhat to reflect the current values and needs, the institutional identity, as a product of the system, is baked in. At each of our institutions, if you compare the comments from faculty, staff, and students on the climate surveys over decades, there is consistent feedback. We suspect this is similar at other institutions as well. It is a mistake to underestimate the systemic roots of institutional identity, thinking it only exists in the current moment in time or because of the current people and their contributions.

"Changing the elements usually has the least effect on the system" (Meadows, 2008, p. 16). Changing all of the members of a basketball team doesn't alter that you have a basketball team—the number of wins and losses might change, but the purpose doesn't—they will still behave like a basketball team. Changing the membership on the university's advisory committee or in a particular department also doesn't alter the performance of the behavior of the committee or the department either. Nor does just increasing the numbers of underrepresented managers, supervisors, or team members alter the behavior and experience toward equity and inclusion.

There are systems within systems too (Meadows, 2008). Faculty have an institutional culture, and so do student affairs teams, administrative staff, custodial staff, buildings and grounds, etc. Each of these subsystems has its own variant on the institutional culture, each with its own structure, patterns of behavior, hierarchy, and forces. These subsystems interrelate as well, sometimes in partnership with each other and sometimes in conflict. Oppression is pervasive and resilient. We may even belong to multiple subsystems at the same time, creating overlaps in our individual system network. This complexity of nested systems within institutions of higher education creates barriers for understanding and communication between people within different subsystems, especially if you just stay within your system.

For example, imagine the temperature in the classroom. The people in the classrooms the most (faculty and students) want control over the temperature in the classroom when they are in it. A comfortable temperature depends on a number of factors, including time of day, time of year, height of the building, as well as individual factors. Professor L may like the room warmer; Professor P may want it colder, and students may want it at a third temperature. At most institutions, the thermostats are locked down by facilities, and to make a change, you have to request for someone to come adjust it. This system is built with little control and a lot of frustration as these nested systems collide. If an organization hasn't invested the time to understand faculty needs, student needs, and facilities' needs related to the HVAC system, and design a structure and process around meeting all of those needs, conflict will fester. Similarly, if an institution hasn't invested the time and energy to understand the needs of students, faculty, and staff around equity and inclusion, the efforts to address it won't likely be effective and could perpetuate conflicts.

The system is complex enough that one or two vantage points are not enough to understand it all. Understanding can come from focus groups, surveys, internal review, or other data collection methods. It needs to be done collectively and in partnership so that a group has a shared sense of the mapped system. This process should occur cyclically and over time as well. Any assessment will be a snapshot in time, and it will be important to document the dynamism of the system in the assessment.

MAPPING THE WORKPLACE CULTURE

"Before you disturb the system in any way, watch how it behaves" (Meadows, 2008, p. 170). We are quick to identify a problem and even quicker to offer a solution. It is important to slow down and pay attention to data, observations, and behavior over time so that we know what problem we are observing and why it is happening (or what it is the result of). We also need to document it so that we can develop an accurate assessment—we are prone to remembering moments in time rather than moments over time. It is easier to remember the one time that you came to the meeting late rather than understand and remember the pattern of attendance for everyone on the team.

A first step for changing the workplace culture is thorough assessment of the environment or a mapping of the system. This assessment should be broadly considered and approached from multiple angles, perspectives, and experiences. Our assessment should be reviewed by as many people in as many different systems as possible. This allows us to document elements of the system that we aren't aware of. As we discussed earlier, if we don't have a sense of the mindset behind the structures, our map will be incomplete or inaccurate.

As Meadows (2008) describes, we need to understand what the elements, the interrelationships, and the purpose of the system are. We also need to understand our position within the system from which we are mapping— the President, an administrator, a faculty member, a mid-manager, an administrative assistant, a custodian, or a student. Each of these perspectives could be different. And while it is a good idea to map from multiple lenses, it is difficult to do them all. Knowing which ones to focus on and why is important. We also need to understand which of our group level identities we are working from as well and consider how to bring in more experiences from those with different identities. The meaning of teamwork varies across cultures and communities, "and, in turn, impl(ies) poten-tial differences in team norms and team-member behaviors" (Gibson & McDaniel, 2010, pp. 451–452). Including perspectives and experiences from multiple levels paints a more comprehensive narrative of the institu-tion. For example, at one of our institutions, the overall numbers by race and gender looked promising; however, when we looked at data by level, we found that the president's cabinet all shared predominantly privileged identities, mid-level managers and entry level personnel are comprised of predominantly marginalized identities. It is crucial that have more com-plete understandings so we can work to cocreate the new structures, processes, and interrelationships so that we have a shared understanding and shared meaning of teamwork, norms, and behaviors in the workplace.

We also need to pay attention to the system and its behaviors over time. The history gives us lots of information. What's happening and how did we get here? What is working and what isn't? (Meadows, 2008). We also need to understand how oppression manifests within the system. Our institutions and their workplace cultures "create and sustain injustice" (Bell, 2016, p. 5), and it is important that we both shine a light on those oppressive systems and work to change them. Our assessments need to include mapping of the dominant norms and rules as well as the experience of various peoples on campus.

Further, managers who can interpret and make use of culture have a better chance of influencing their organizations (Bolman & Deal, 2013). Managers utilizing organizing principles as a strategy to develop coalitions will move culture change initiatives strategically forward. But that is only part of what is needed as well. Jay Forrester, one of the preeminent systems thinkers, points out that while people embedded in a system who have done this mapping "know intuitively where to find leverage points (places to influence change in a system's behavior), more often than not they push the change in the *wrong direction*" (Meadows, 2008, p. 145, emphasis included). An example of this are initiatives to increase hiring more professionals from marginalized identities. Adding candidates of color is an important element in this system change initiative, but if the hiring supervisor doesn't address the implicit bias of those involved in the search process, or if an institution has inequitable hiring processes, little change will happen. Mapping needs to include understanding the system, where the leverage points are, and what are the consequences of engaging the leverage points in different directions.

We also add that many managers and supervisors lack the positional power or aren't empowered to make these kinds of changes. The inter-section of positional power and identity politics profoundly impacts the mapping process. It is worth ensuring multiple identities and voices are represented. Influencing change in these cases involves educating those that do have that power, which may or may not be possible, or worth one's time. Many leadership hierarchies are built with communication in a one-way flow, from the top to bottom. These barriers are often more about a need for control by those in leadership position, and it contributes to a felt sense of marginalization.

Even if a person has the kind of influence to create change and knows the effective way to intervene, shifting workplace or organizational culture often takes several years (six to ten years or so) to take effect (Mmeje, Newman, Kramer II, & Pearson, 2009). "New social orders are established gradually" (hooks, 2000, p. 161). It will take our deep and intentional investment over time. This time period typically extends beyond the career tenure of many faculty and professionals at one organization. Supervisors must learn how to develop patience in pushing for broad organizational changes while still utilizing their own agency to shift culture within their spheres of influence.

CHALLENGING THE CULTURE

One meaningful way to address systemic oppression is by addressing when conformity of rules or process is required, and when conformity to rules or process isn't. Some functions require conformity (i.e., finance, food preparation, federal mandates) because of safety, regulation, accreditation, or limited resources require it. But other areas, especially in our role as educators, allow for multiple ways of meeting an established outcome. Sometimes supervision is conflated with conformity of practice, and it can lead to oppressive working conditions if conformity is expected in areas where it is not needed or required. Engaging a team member or colleague, finding out who they are, and what support they need to continue to grow is a lovingly imperfect process that takes place over time—nothing in that is about rules. We get into difficulty when we, or our colleagues and team members, treat everything we do by following the rules.

We know that systems don't change because we will them to, or because we intend to do good. Systems change work requires intention, understanding how the system works, the power to intervene, implementing the change in effective ways, and having the patience to wait for the results. Donella Meadows (1997) calls this "modeling the system" so that you can understand where the levers are and how to shift them. Hersey et al. (1996) agree that diagnosing the environment is the most important step in any change effort.

Identity-conscious supervision has the potential to be a higher-order change. Hersey et al. (1996) discuss the models for first-order and

182

second-order change, which was developed by Watzlawick, Weakland, and Fisch (1974). First-order change are changes incorporated into the existing paradigm or ways of being at the organization level (adaptation) or at the industry level (evolution). Second-order changes are changes that shift or change the paradigm at the organization level (metamorphosis) or the industry level (revolution). Pope (1995) developed a new model for multicultural interventions that was based on Watzlawick, Weakland, and Fisch's model but written to address the target of change at the individual, group, and system level.

First-order change at the individual level is changes in awareness, at the group level is changes in membership, and at the institution is changes in programming education. Second-order changes at the individual level is a shift in paradigm, at the group level, a shift in the organizational structure (reorganization), and at the institutional is a shift in the system (Pope, 1995). Our mapping and systems change work should keep this in mind. Our commitment to improve supervision practices and working relationships and center them in identity-conscious ways needs to include transforming the workplace culture at the second-order change level.

INFLUENCING INSTITUTIONAL CHANGE

Pope, Reynolds, and Mueller (2019) remind us that "paradigm shifts are essential for student affairs practitioners to create equitable, just, and inclusive campus environments" (p. 94). Identity-conscious supervision is one of those paradigm shifts necessary to carry that "equitable, just, and inclusive campus environments" into the staff and faculty environments.

Without this paradigm shift to launch this change effort forward, the supervisor/supervisee relationship can easily fall into a system that enforces conformity, completion of tangible performance outcomes, and one-way power direction rather than a relationship-centered system built on high trust and a sense of empowerment. While there is no one best way to lead (Hersey et al., 1996), supervising from a high-trust, relationship-centered model creates a stronger likelihood of high morale, high value, and high-performance workplace cultures. In Bolman and Deal's framework (2017), it is shifting from the structural paradigm toward the human resources paradigm.

Engaging the team from a place of care and from a place of performance is vital to the success of an identity-conscious approach as well as the success of the organization. As long as supervisors have no confidence or trust in the employees and lead using power and fear, employees will continue to feel unvalued, uncared for, and unsafe.

183

But changing is hard and engaging the team from a place of care and performance is also crucial to helping individuals move through the change process. People cling to the familiar when their frames of reference are disoriented by change (Deutschman, 2005). And as long as people are holding on to the current model (and feel that their paycheck is threatened by them moving to the new model), they will never change. And that will be like swimming upstream.

It takes bold, courageous, connected leaders to lead through fear and lead into the change that is needed. It also takes belief—belief in what we do and how we are changing the world through education. Belief overcomes fear (Godin, 2008), and it makes space for hope and possibility—something that people want to be a part of. It starts with us, and through our deep self-work.

In addition, we need to develop and clarify a new purpose for our system, as Meadows (2008) describes it, built around the creation of a community built for social justice, as Bell describes (2016). We need to shift the "values, traditions, beliefs, rites, myths, and rituals" (Mmeje et al., 2009, p. 304) to support this new purpose as well.

After we have mapped the system and cocreated the shared vision for the new identity-conscious paradigm, we are ready to develop the strategic path to get there. Pope et al. (2019) offer a number of models and frameworks for developing that strategic path for multicultural organizational change (Pope, 1993; Grieger, 1996; Watt, 2015) and successfully moving organizations forward.

Without the guidance of a strategic effort or plan, this social justice change efforts is likely to be "uncoordinated, uneven, and unsuccessful" (Pope et al., 2019, p. 121). But even if our institution is not there yet, it is important that we start, and lead and influence where we can. While the goal may be the institution, it is important to start where we are and build capacity to support the larger change effort.

COALITION BUILDING AND PARTNERSHIP

As we consider new paradigms that have the power to bring about second-order change at our institutions, we need to be mindful of making changes *with* rather than changes *to*. Second-order change shifts or changes the paradigm at the organization level. As hooks (2000) reminds us, "Struggles for power (the right to dominate and control others) perpetually undermine feminist movement" (p. 91) and other social justice movements. These struggles will undermine our efforts to transform the culture through identity-conscious practice. Even when we explicitly work in equitable and inclusive partnership, power is still such a tempting and destructive element in our system. Understanding that power allocation is a trap that will undermine or destroy these change efforts allows us to plan for it and use our strategic resources to manage that trap.

One of the key ways to do this is to build coalitions. An important part of the change process is developing partnerships with other people and other departments and cocreating the new ways of working together. Boggs and Boggs (1974) suggest it starts with the mutual reorganization and rebuilding of the entire society designed for the benefit of all people. We also need to name how power is at play in our current system, as well as our hopes for how power will be used in the transformed system. hooks (2000) reminds us that we have to recognize and acknowledge that we can't have equitable power within the current system. Before we can work to reconstruct, we have to reconcile both how power is used and what our relationship to power is.

CONCLUSION

It is essential that our identity-conscious practice hold institutional change as one of the goals. We know the harm and pain that this system has caused and is causing; we know how institutions of higher education replicate systems of oppression and perpetuate harm, even in spite of good people attempting to make good change. We know too that the structure of supervisor/supervisee relationships is also held up by these same systems. Individual change is not enough; identity-conscious supervision practice is not enough if the work and focus is left at the team/department/division level. That identity-conscious practice is important, but if we don't intend to change the system, all we have done is develop a good practice within an unjust system.

We want all practitioners to develop the skills necessary to initiate and influence systems change at our institutions. We need to observe, understand, and identity the components of the system so that we can next map it out. These processes allow us to challenge the status quo and work with others to shape a vision for a new kind of institution. Once we have a more holistic understanding of the system and where we want to go, we can begin to adjust effective levers to facilitate positive change.

We can't do this work alone. We need to work in partnership and in coalitions. It is ineffective to tackle a system on our own; that will lead to quick burn out. This lone approach also replicates the dominant white, male, American cultural norms—that of the rugged individualist who can save the world. We need to continue to challenge ourselves to be in community, work toward partnership, build powerful coalitions, and together create a vision for our new, just relationships and organizations.

Case Study
Amy Miele and Kevin Pitt

You are a Director of Student Conduct at a small private institution. You supervise one full-time conduct coordinator, one graduate assistant, and an administrative assistant. Your office gets roughly 700 cases per year, which are adjudicated by you and your staff. While you and your staff have discretion to adjudicate all cases as you see fit, leadership has strong concerns about drug use on campus. Due to safety concerns, the Vice President of Student Affairs is insistent that all students found responsible for any type of illegal drug possession, marijuana or otherwise, are suspended for at least one year. In contrast, they feel that underage drinking should be handled educationally and without punitive sanctions.

Your staff members approach you about feeling like this particular institutional practice is disproportionality affecting Students of Color. Staff go on to explain that while the practice was intended to curb dangerous drug use on campus, they aren't seeing the cases they expected. During their conduct meetings, the vast majority of students say they were smoking a minimal amount of marijuana to relieve stress due to the high academic pressure. There often are not any other illegal drugs present or any additional policy violations involved.

When you look into the data, you see that more Students of Color are being cited and found responsible for drug possession than white students. When you dig deeper into the data, you see that the drug possession is almost always small quantities of marijuana for personal use. You start to realize that this particular policy and practice may not be producing the intended results.

A few weeks later, your conduct coordinator tells you that suspending students for minimal marijuana use is resulting in unintended consequences. They recently met with a student who was homeless and living out of their car during their period of suspension, since university housing was their only place to live. They explain that your graduate assistant met with a prominent Black student leader on campus who ultimately got suspended for consuming half of a marijuana brownie.

Your staff no longer feels it's appropriate to suspend every student found responsible for drug possession. They ask you to address this issue with senior level administrators and to fight to change the practice moving forward.

Behind the scenes, you know that senior leadership is not typically open to change. When you've tried to suggest small changes in the past, they've been very resistant. You get the sense that you are labeled as the "troublemaker" and don't want to stir the pot any further, especially given their passion to end drug use on campus.

As you are deciding on the best course of action to take, you get a phone call from the Vice President of Student Affairs, telling you to go to their office immediately. When you arrive, they explain that a leader in the student government association went to the president about the drug policy on campus. Given the small campus size, the student government heard stories of Students of Color being suspended for small quantities of marijuana. They are upset that the institution is suspending students for low-level drug offenses as opposed to trying to find and sanction the drug dealers on campus.

As you begin to share the information you and your staff have collected to the Vice President of Student Affairs, they quickly cut you off. They say they're not interested in hearing your opinion on the matter and instead need you to back up the institution's decisions. They give you a speech about being a team player, knowing when to speak up, and knowing when to listen to leadership. They explicitly state that you need to understand the difference in order to survive at this institution.

The Vice President of Student Affairs then tells you to meet with the student government association representative and explain the purpose of the drug policy to them—keeping the campus safe.

KEY QUESTIONS

1. How do you determine your next step, and what is it? What are all the options to influence institutional change in this scenario?
2. How do you be a conduit for culture change while addressing the immediate situation while maintaining your job and/or reputation?
3. What role do your values and identity play in your decision-making process?

REFERENCES

Bailey, K. W., & Hamilton, J. (2015). Supervisory style. In M. J. Amey & L. M. Reesor (Eds.), *Beginning your journey: A guide for new professionals in student affairs* (4th ed., pp. 67–94). Washington, DC: NASPA.

Bell, L. A. (2016). Theoretical foundations for social justice education. In M. Adams & L. A. Bell (Eds.), *Teaching for diversity and social justice*. New York, NY: Routledge.

Boggs, G. L., & Boggs, J. (1974). *Revolution and evolution in the twentieth century*. New York, NY: Monthly Review Press.

Bolman, L. G., & Deal, T. E. (2013). *Reframing organizations: Artistry, choice, and leadership* (5th ed.). San Francisco, CA: Jossey-Bass.

Bolman, L. G., & Deal, T. E. (2017). *Reframing organizations: Artistry, choice, and leadership* (6th ed.). San Francisco, CA: Jossey-Bass.

Chang, J. (2016). *We gon' be alright: Notes on race and desegregation*. New York, NY: Picador.

Deutschman, A. (2005, May). Change or die. *Fast Company*, p. 94. Retrieved from www.fastcompany.com/52717/change-or-die

Frank, T. E. (2013). *Why do they leave? Departure from the student affairs profession* (Doctoral dissertation). VTechWorks. Retrieved from http://hdl.handle.net/10919/19306

Gibson, C. B., & McDaniel, D. M. (2010). Moving beyond conventional wisdom: Advancements in cross-cultural theories of leadership, conflict, and teams. *Perspectives of Psychological Science, 5*(4), 450–462.

Godin, S. (2008). *Tribes: We need you to lead us*. New York, NY: Penguin.

Grieger, I. (1996). A multicultural organizational development checklist for student affairs. *Journal of College Student Development, 37*, 561–573.

Hersey, P., Blanchard, K. H., & Johnson, D. E. (1996). *Management of organizational behavior* (7th ed.). Upper Saddle River, NJ: Prentice Hall.

hooks, b. (2000). *Feminist theory: From margin to center*. Cambridge, MA: South End Press Classics.

Kotter, J. P. (2007). Leading change: Why transformation efforts fail. *Harvard Business Review*. Retrieved from https://hbr.org/2007/01/leading-change-why-transformation-efforts-fail

Mackey, J., & Sisodia, R. (2014). *Conscious capitalism: Liberating the heroic spirit of business*. Boston, MA: Harvard Business Review Press.

Marya, R. (2018). *Decolonizing healthcare: Addressing social stressors in medicine*. Retrieved from https://bioneers.org/decolonizing-healthcare-addressing-social-stressors-in-medicine-ztvz1812/

Meadows, D. (1997, Winter). Places to intervene in a system (in increasing order of effectiveness). *Whole Earth*, 78–84.

Meadows, D. (2008). *Thinking in systems: A primer*. River Junction, VT: Chelsea Green Publishing.

Mmeje, K., Newman, C. B., Kramer II, D. A., & Pearson, M. A. (2009). The changing landscape of higher education: Developmental approaches to engaging emerging populations. In S. R. Harper & S. J. Quaye (Eds.), *Student engagement in higher education: Theoretical perspectives and practical approaches for diverse populations* (pp. 295–312). New York, NY: Routledge.

Nichols, K. N., & Baumgartner, L. M. (2016). Midlevel managers' supervisory learning journeys. *College Student Affairs Journal, 34*(2), 61–74.

Paperson, La. (2017). *A third university is possible*. Minneapolis, MN: University of Minnesota Press. https://doi.org/10.5749/9781452958460

Perez, R. J. (2016). A conceptual model of professional socialization within student affairs graduate preparation programs. *Journal for the Study of Postsecondary and Tertiary Education, 1,* 35–52. Retrieved from www.jspte.org/Volume1/JSPTEv1p035-052Perez2057.pdf

Pope, R. L. (1993). Multicultural-organization development in student affairs: An introduction. *Journal of College Student Development, 34,* 201–205.

Pope, R. L. (1995). Multicultural-organization development: Implications and applications in student affairs. In J. Fried (Ed.), *Shifting paradigms in student affairs: Culture, context, teaching and learning* (pp. 233–250). Washington, DC: American College Personnel Association.

Pope, R. L., Reynolds, A. L., & Mueller, J. A. (2014). *Creating multicultural change on campus*. San Francisco, CA: John Wiley & Sons.

Pope, R. L., Reynolds, A. L., & Mueller, J. A. (2019). *Multicultural competence in student affairs*. San Francisco, CA: Jossey-Bass.

Sinek, S. (2014). *Leaders eat last: Why some teams pull together and others don't*. New York, NY: Penguin.

Watt, S. K. (2015). Authentic, action-oriented, framing for environmental shifts (AAFES) method. In S. K. Watt (Ed.), *Designing transformative multicultural initiatives: Theoretical foundations, practical applications, and facilitator considerations* (pp. 23–39). Sterling, VA: Stylus Publishing.

Watzlawick, P., Weakland, J. H., & Fisch, R. (1974). *Change: Principles of problem formation and problem resolution*. New York, NY: WW Norton & Company.

Chapter Eleven

Conclusion

As we reflect on our journeys toward identity-conscious supervision and writing this book, a couple of ideas remain poignant for us. First, each of us had several painful stories around our supervision experiences. These were distressing experiences that significantly impacted us during our professional formation and shaped our understanding of supervision. These experiences happened with our formal supervisors and happened in meetings, town halls, lunchtime, and celebrations. These narratives extended beyond campus type, region, identity, and position. We had good experiences being supervised and supervising others too, and we learned from them, but our reflection is that the painful experiences had a more lasting effect than the positive ones.

We were also struck by the commonalities we found between our stories. We (Robert, Shruti, and Craig) have different backgrounds, many different identities, and different career paths in student affairs in higher education. Yet we found ourselves connecting, relating in across our experiences, and sharing stories from fellow colleagues across the field. We realized that there was a universality to our experiences. It was comforting to know that we weren't alone in our experiences, and we were deeply troubled by this as well. It is problematic that these painful experiences happened consistently, over time and across our field. This indicated to us that there is a problem in the system.

Last, the energy we found in connecting across our shared experiences inspired us to create something innovative. We wanted to shape the supervision world we want to be in. Our experiences brought us together to talk about a vision for a better way to supervise; one that made space and honored our identities, our gifts and strengths, and empowered our full selves to be a part of our profession. That vision conversation led us to present our ideas at annual conventions and conferences. The voices of participants at those sessions, particularly their stories, feelings, and emotions helped us hone our ideas. We are proud of our vision and of this contribution to the profession. We feel that this is a positive step toward a more just and equitable professional experience in student affairs and higher education. We hope you feel inspired to apply these tools to your practice after reading this book.

REVISITING THE MODEL

We want to revisit the model in its entirety. As we do so, we are reminded of insight from Jeff Chang (2016): "Inequity and injustice are not abstract things. They impact real people and real lives" (p. 3). This model is more than a new way for us to consider our professional practice. It can serve as a structure for us to interrupt inequity and injustice at multiple levels.

Relationships remain at the center of identity-conscious supervision. Our own experiences in our identity-conscious practice have reinforced this to us, and we know centering relationships highlights our work toward justice. Supervisors who develop and operate with a strong sense of self and build trust and vulnerability into the supervisory relationship take one step toward dismantling oppressive supervision patterns built on dominant norms.

We need to continue our work in transforming the experience of a supervisee and invest in the development of the supervision practice with an identity-conscious lens. Changing the supervisory relationship is not abstract for us. Our colleagues and incoming professionals deserve to have different experiences than many of us. We hope for compelling and profound learning that comes from deeper connection that generates working in partnership for change. To achieve this new standard, all of us need to continue to foster our identity exploration, engage with conflict, and balance the expectations in our positions and supervisory relationships.

Finally, we want to reiterate the need for us to intentionally create communities that bring identity-consciousness to the organizational level to influence our institutional cultures toward equity and justice. Institutional change and identity-consciousness are interdependent with the components from the individual (Chapters 2–5) and supervision levels (Chapters 6–8). As many examples in the book demonstrate, we cannot influence institutional change without also fostering change in our relationships, practice, and community. Continuing our reflective practice, managing power dynamics, and showing up courageously in our identity-conscious supervision sustains our commitment.

Identity-conscious supervision practice and the simultaneous impact on institutional transformative work require sustained commitment. Taylor (2016) reminds us of this: "organizing is long-term and often tedious work that entails creating infrastructure in institutions, finding points of vulner-ability and leverage in the situation you want to transform" (p. 4). This work is necessary for student affairs to build environments where individ-uals in the margins thrive and to disrupt the repetitive cycle of dominant norms. It will take all of us working consistently side by side.

We are mindful that this model is a good start toward creating more just institutions, and that people often want and need a list of action items to help them start this work. While there are several concrete action steps contained within each chapter in the book, we have resisted reducing them to a check list of actions or tools to take. The primary reason for this is that we want to focus attention on the being rather than the doing. We want individuals to reflect on their behaviors, attitudes, and skills before they start marking off items toward identity-conscious supervision. We all need to consider how to incorporate an identity-conscious supervision approach into our professional practice, and we hope that it begins to change profes-sional socialization in student affairs and higher education. We know that if we focus on the process of becoming, the doing will naturally follow.

At the risk of counteracting our own hopes, we also know there are some good places to start or revisit. As we began reflecting on our own supervision practice, we recognized our own areas for growth in identity-conscious supervision practice, and these were some of the places where we started.

1. Start doing your own work—It is essential that we deepen our understanding of ourselves, our identities, and our relationships to them. We age, learn new things, and work at new places in new positions. Our perspective and knowledge evolve, and our "knowing of self" must also evolve. Once we learn something or deepen an understanding, we need to put it into practice in our lives. And this is where courage is helpful—courage helps us act when we feel vulnerable. We must reflect, practice, and reflect again.

2. Discuss openly—As we are engaging in our self-work, it is important to find community. Find professionals who are working on their identity-conscious practice and talk about the experiences. We learn that we are not alone in the struggles. Discussing openly is also important so that people around us understand our intentions. When we show up differently because we are practicing our identity-conscious supervision, it can be confusing if people don't understand what we are doing. Our default in our current model will lead to distrust of our intentions and our behavior. Courage can help us here too, as we share about our efforts for our imperfect practice.

3. Learn from others—It is important to listen to others' experiences with identity-conscious supervision practice and fully take in their learning. It is important to also listen to the people that we supervise to be partners with them in this practice. They will have good guidance and feedback for us. Both will help inform our future practice.

4. Practice, practice, practice—Along the way, we will learn about the ways that identity-conscious supervision practice matters in our life and the lives of those we supervise. Remember those moments so that we remember why we are doing this work when it is difficult. And like other professional development opportunities, we should set goals for ourselves, regularly evaluate ourselves, and identify the places where we want to grow and improve.

SUMMARY

We believe in the power of naming who we are and in having someone hold us to that. Developing this model provided each of us with an opportunity to practice this idea. Making sense of our identities through reflection and community allowed opportunity for grounding and wholeness. We don't do this enough with each other. We also believe in the power of lifelong learning because we recognize that our work around identity-conscious supervision practice will never be done. There are systems of oppression in operation that will try and tell us that centering identity-consciousness will never work. As we unlearn and relearn in community, we can be resilient in finding new ways to deepen our understanding of systems, refine our identity-conscious practice, and engage more consistently in alignment with our values. We hope this model brings innovation, resilience, and hope to those who supervise and are supervised.

REFERENCES

Chang, J. (2016). *We gon' be alright: Notes on race and resegregation.* New York, NY: Picador.

Taylor, A. (2016, March). Against activism. *The Baffler*, p. 30. Retrieved from https://thebaffler.com/salvos/against-activism

Appendix

IDENTITY-CONSCIOUS SUPERVISION

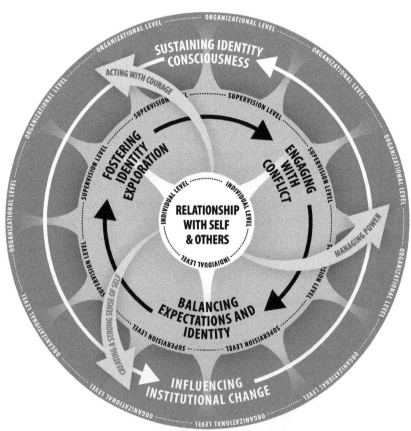

Figure A.1: Identity-Conscious Supervision
Source: (Brown, Desai, & Elliott, 2020)

Author Bios

Robert Brown (he, him, his) serves as the Director of Social Justice Education at Northwestern University in Evanston, Illinois, where he leads several curricular and cocurricular social justice education initiatives. Prior to joining Northwestern, Rob held professional roles in Residence Life and Multicultural Affairs at Washington University in St. Louis and the University of Wisconsin–Madison. He identifies as Black, Christian, able-bodied, cisgender, heterosexual, male, middleclass, U.S. citizen, and in his lower 30s.

Robert has presented and facilitated regionally and nationally on topics related to social justice education, racial justice, inclusive pedagogy, identity-conscious supervision, assessment and evaluation, college men and masculinities, and civic engagement. He is an alumnus of the Social Justice Training Institute (SJTI), a past faculty and intern with SJTI, and Lead Facilitator with LeaderShape, and he has held leadership roles in NASPA and ACPA. Robert holds a B.S. in Finance and Community Service Studies from DePaul University, an M.A. in Student Affairs Administration from Michigan State University, and he is currently pursuing his Ph.D. in Higher Education Leadership at Colorado State University. Robert's research interests explore topics related to equity and inclusion in higher education, faculty development and critical pedagogy, and identity-conscious supervision and management.

He is a member of Alpha Phi Alpha Fraternity, Inc. and enjoys traveling, golfing, binge watching TV shows, cooking, watching sports, and spending time with his wife, Ashley, and friends around Chicago! Rob works diligently to bring his professional experiences, research interests, and passion for social justice to life through his work as a social justice educator, always seeking to create space for community building, healing, and liberation.

Dr. Shruti Desai (she, her, hers) serves as Associate Director/Chief of Staff at the Gephardt Institute for Civic and Community Engagement at Washington University in St. Louis, where she leads a team focusing on student engagement, assessment, strategic planning, and storytelling. Prior to that she served as the Assistant Vice President at McKendree University in Lebanon, Illinois, where she oversaw Title IX, Counseling Services, and Residential Life. Shruti held professional roles in Residence Life at Washington University in St. Louis, the University of Kansas, and Texas Tech University. She identifies as abled, cisgender, middleclass, queer, female, Indian/South Asian, and close to 40.

Shruti's research examines resilience in women of color in Senior Student Affairs Officer roles. Shruti has worked to lead systemic change for LGBT and individuals of color for students and professional staff. Shruti presents regionally and nationally on identity-conscious supervision, creating supportive cultures for marginalized identities, building a culture of assessment, and resilience. She is an alumnus of the Social Justice Training Institute (SJTI) as well as a past faculty and intern with SJTI. Her passion lies around getting beyond the false binary of race in America, examining identity as intersections of power and privilege and data as storytelling.

Shruti has received numerous awards, including NASPA's Asian Pacific Islander Knowledge Community mid-level professional of the year as well as the James R. Holobaugh award for outstanding service to the LGBT community and Advisor of the Year. Shruti was recently accepted to the NASPA Supporting, Expanding, and Recruiting Volunteer Excellence (SERVE) academy. Shruti holds a B.A. in Psychology from Mercer University, an M.Ed. in College Student Affairs Administration from the University of Georgia, and an Ed.D. in Higher Education Leadership from Maryville University. Shruti lives in St. Louis with her incredible wife and their zoo of two dogs and a cat!

Dr. Craig Elliott (he, him, his) is a father, a partner, a feminist anti-racist, and a revolutionary at heart. He is married to Nicole (over 22 years) and is father to Jackson and Thomas. He has worked in student affairs for over 25 years and currently serves as the Assistant Vice President of Enrollment and Student Services and Assistant Professor at Samuel Merritt University in Oakland, California. He identifies as white, cisgender, male, heterosexual, upper-middleclass, Buddhist, able-bodied, U.S. citizen, and in his early 50s.

Craig has presented numerous programs at the local and national level on equity, inclusion, social justice, and leadership, and has served in a variety of leadership capacities in ACPA, NASPA, and NCORE. Notably, Craig is currently serving as President of ACPA-College Student Educators International. He is a Social Justice Training Institute alumnus, serves on the faculty with Student SJTI, is a Co-Lead facilitator for the LeaderShape Institute, and is on the board of World Trust.

Craig's research interests explore white supremacy and internalized dominance, feminism and masculinity, the intersection of transformative learning and social justice, and institutional change. Craig is part of the editorial collective for Rad Dad, a zine on feminist and social justice parenting, which has published three anthologies. He has contributed chapters on feminism and fathering, coauthored articles on institutional barriers to inclusion and equity and transformative learning, and coedited three anthologies on feminist parenting.

Craig also serves in his local community in scouting and soccer. He loves soccer, music, time with his family, and really good, strong coffee.

Contributor Bios

Michelle L. Boettcher (she, her, hers) teaches research, law, and ethics in the Higher Education and Student Affairs programs at Clemson University. Her research focuses on senses of belonging and community in the context of higher education particularly the experiences of first-generation college (FGC) students. She identifies as a white woman, a member of the LGBTQ+ community, and FGC. Her research focuses on community and senses of belonging in higher education. Prior to Clemson she worked as Assistant Dean of Students and Director of Judicial Affairs at Iowa State University and in residence life programs at multiple institutions.

Maggie Chen-Hernandez (she, her, hers) has been a student affairs practitioner in multicultural affairs for over three decades, tirelessly working on sustained efforts that positively impact the academic and socioemotional experiences of minoritized student communities at PWIs. Growing up in the Midwest as the child of Taiwanese immigrants, Maggie has worked to build a unified APIDA community by advocating for the creation of Asian American studies programs, empowering student leaders to create the Midwest Asian American Student Union (MAASU) and serving on statewide Asian American advisory committees. Maggie currently works to advance social justice learning opportunities at Michigan State University's Mosaic Multicultural Unity Center.

Sharon Chia Claros is a mid-level professional at Michigan State University committed to diversity, equity, and inclusion. She is a woman (she, her, hers) of color and serves in MSU's Asian, Pacific Islander, Desi-American/Asian Faculty and Staff Association, a part of the faculty and staff Coalition of Racial and Ethnic Minorities.

Rhina Duquela is currently the Dean of the W.E.B. DuBois College House at the University of Pennsylvania. She identifies as a cisgender, straight,

Latinx, Christian woman and uses she/her/hers pronouns. She was born in the Dominican Republic and raised in the Bronx, New York. She earned her B.S. in Secondary English Education and her M.S. in Higher Education and Student Affairs Administration from SUNY Buffalo State. She has worked in Residence Life, Student Conduct, and Academic Affairs. Rhina is now pursuing her doctorate in Higher Education at the University of Pennsylvania.

Dr. Antonio Duran (he/him/his) is an Assistant Professor in the Administration of Higher Education program at Auburn University. Stemming from his own experiences as a queer Latino man, Antonio is passionate about improving the systems and structures influencing queer and transgender people of color (QTPOC) on college campuses. Namely, his research employs intersectional frameworks to complicate the study of college student development as it relates to QTPOC populations. Additionally, Antonio is interested in how spaces designed to support marginalized communities on campus (re) produce systemic oppression for those with multiple marginalized identities.

Meghan Reyonne Griggs (she/her/hers) is a Ph.D. student in the Higher Education Leadership and Policy Studies program at the University of Houston, where she serves as a research assistant in the Provost's Office. As a scholar-activist, Meghan's scholarship centers on Black women empowerment, and she is currently studying how Women of Color experience incivility on college campuses. Meghan previously served as an Assistant Director of Undergraduate Admissions at Rensselaer Polytechnic Institute and an Executive Intern and Program Analyst working directly with the President of Lonestar College–Tomball. She holds a B.A. in Mass Communications and an M.A. in Organizational Communication.

Jonglim Han is a mid-level professional at Michigan State University committed to diversity, equity, and inclusion. She is a woman (she, her, hers) of color and serves in MSU's Asian, Pacific Islander, Desi-American/Asian Faculty and Staff Association, a part of the faculty and staff Coalition of Racial and Ethnic Minorities.

Reyes J. Luna (he, him, his) is an openly gay, Latino man with over 26 years of higher education experience working at five different institutions ranging from small private, state system universities, to large research 1 universities. Reyes is currently serving as the Director of Residence Life within University Housing Services at California State Polytechnic University, Pomona (Cal Poly Pomona). During his 18 years at Cal Poly Pomona, he has served in multiple roles within Student Affairs (Interim Executive Director of University Housing Services, Director of Judicial Affairs, Interim Pride Center Coordinator, Senior Coordinator and Area Coordinator for

Residence Life) and Academic Affairs (Lecturer in Ethnic and Women's Studies and Liberal Studies).

Tynesha McCullers, M.Ed. (she/her/hers), is a strong-willed higher education professional at the University of Maryland. At UMD, Tynesha supervises RAs, facilitates dialogues and affinity spaces, lectures on power and oppression, advises trips and councils, and mentors students. Resident Life, the Office of Diversity & Inclusion, Leadership & Community Service-Learning, Fraternity & Sorority Life, and the Incentive Awards Program are where Tynesha's work happens. Tynesha holds a B.S. in Human Development & Family Studies and an M.Ed. in Higher Education & Interdisciplinary Studies. As an educator, Tynesha values social identity, social justice and liberation work, leadership, and advocacy.

Amy Miele (she/her/hers) is the Assistant Director of Student Affairs Compliance and Title IX Investigator at Rutgers University, New Brunswick. She identifies as a white, heterosexual, cisgender woman, who is temporarily able-bodied. She is also about 5'1" tall and looks younger than her age, which frequently impacts how others perceive her. Amy has roughly eight years of experience as a student affairs professional and supervisor. She holds an M.A. in Criminal Justice from Rowan University and is a current Ph.D. student in Higher Education at Rutgers University. Outside of work, Amy enjoys taking family walks with her husband, Jeff, and dog, Nico.

Gustavo A. Molinar, M.A. (he/him/his/él) is a Resident Director at the University of California, Riverside. Originally from Houston, Texas, holds his B.A. from The University of Texas at Austin and his M.A. from The Ohio State University. Informed by his identities as a queer, Latino man, Gustavo is dedicated to contributing positively to the experiences of students who are first-generation and people of color. He has worked professionally in residence life, student wellness, and multicultural affairs. In his spare time, Gustavo enjoys running, photography, and traveling.

Dr. Braelin Pantel (she/her/hers) is the Associate Vice President for Student Engagement & Wellness/Dean of Students at Metropolitan State University of Denver. In this capacity, she provides leadership and supervision for 13 student affairs functional units. Braelin is a mom and identifies as a straight, white, Jewish, cisgender woman. Braelin holds a B.S. in Psychology, an M.A. in Higher Education Administration, and a Ph.D. in Higher Education and Student Affairs Leadership from the University of Northern Colorado. Braelin's research interests relate to the experiences of college students of size and body size as a social identity. Currently, Braelin benefits from thin privilege.

Viraj Patel (she/her/hers) is the Dean of Harnwell College House at the University of Pennsylvania, where she is also pursuing a Doctor of Education in Higher Education. She is an experienced community organizer, social justice advocate, facilitator, and administrator. Prior to this role, Viraj has worked at campuses in Residential Education, Graduate Student Services, Off Campus Student Affairs, and Multicultural Affairs and has experience working with nonprofit organizations. In her spare time, Viraj enjoys spending time with her family, reading, running, discovering new recipes to try out in the kitchen, and traveling.

Kevin Pitt is currently the Director of Student Conduct at Rutgers University, where he oversees the adjudication of the Code of Student Conduct and Code of Academic Integrity violations and assists with the adjudication of Title IX for Rutgers University's three New Brunswick campuses. Previously Kevin has served as the Deputy Director of the Office of Student Conduct at the University of Pennsylvania and has served as the Assistant Director in the Office of Student Conduct at the University of Maryland, College Park. Kevin is currently a Ph.D. student in Higher Education at Rutgers, New Brunswick.

Brandi Scott serves as the Associate Dean of Equity and Student Achievement at Metropolitan State University of Denver. Brandi identifies as a white, lesbian, cisgender woman with a disability. Brandi was a first-generation college student and is passionate about creating access to and equitable services for students from underrepresented backgrounds. Brandi supervises eight professional staff and seven programs/centers. Brandi is currently working on her Doctor of Higher Education Leadership with a focus on understanding systems of racial injustice and inequities in higher education.

Kathy Sisneros identifies as a brown, cisgender lesbian using she/her pronouns from northern New Mexico, which she still considers "home." I am a first-generation college student who grew up working class. I am the first on both sides of my family to earn a doctorate and am now firmly middleclass with a working-class mindset. I serve as an Assistant Vice President for Student Affairs at Colorado State University, overseeing the Student Diversity Programs and Services units. Additionally, I oversee institutional efforts supporting undocumented students; transgender, nonbinary students; free speech and the first amendment for students; and other diversity, inclusive, and equity efforts.

Index

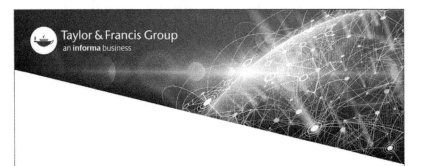

CPSIA information can be obtained
at www.ICGtesting.com
Printed in the USA
LVHW080453050123
736521LV00013B/473